D0056123

HUNGRY NATIONS

THE PERIMETER OF THE HUNGRY NATIONS

They are hungry for food, they are hungry for stability, they are hungry for international prestige, for education, for health, housing, culture.
They are hungry for the twentieth century.
But where are the resources to relieve this hunger?

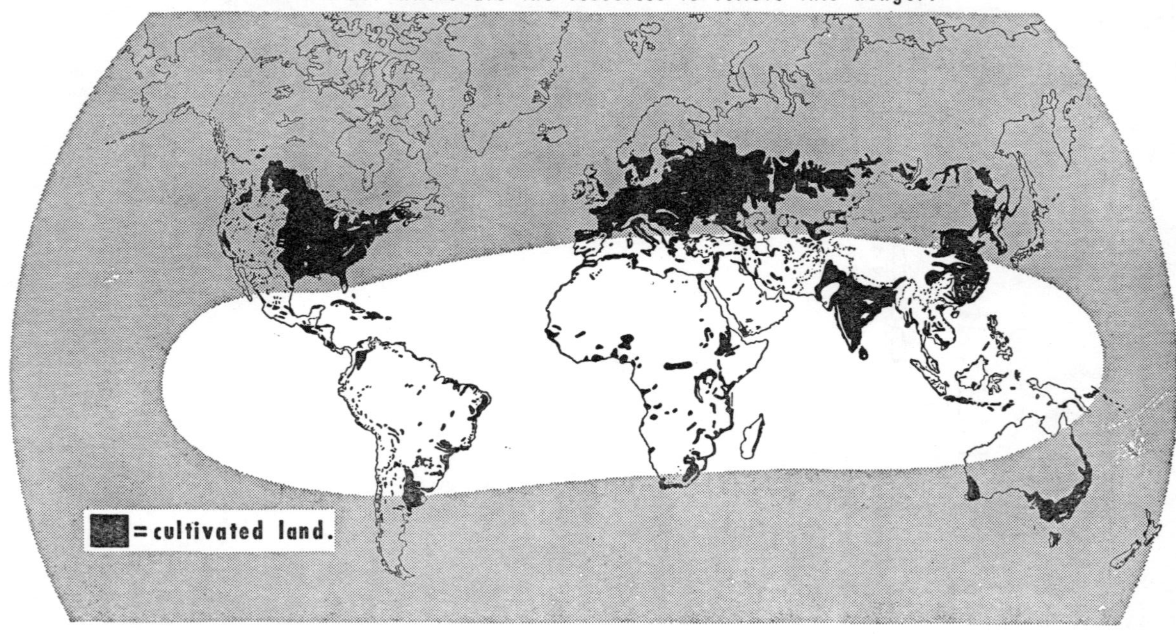

HUNGRY NATIONS

BY WILLIAM AND PAUL PADDOCK

LITTLE, BROWN AND COMPANY • BOSTON • TORONTO

LIBRARY OF CONGRESS CATALOG CARD NO. 64-21481

Third Printing

The authors wish to acknowledge with thanks permission to quote the following copyrighted material:

An excerpt from A TREE GROWS IN BROOKLYN by Betty Smith, Copyright, 1943, by Betty Smith, by permission of Harper & Row, Publishers.

A stanza from "The Coffee Song," by permission of Redd Evans and Valiant Music Company, 1619 Broadway, New York, N. Y.

A stanza from "Merry Minuet," © 1958 Sunbeam Music Corp., used by permission only. All rights reserved. Words and Music by Sheldon Harnick.

Published simultaneously in Canada
by Little, Brown & Company (Canada) Limited

PRINTED IN THE UNITED STATES OF AMERICA

Preface

THE TWO authors, brothers, tried writing this in the editorial "we." It proved stilted, so the honest "I" is used in the personal portions.

This may confuse when the illustrations jump from Honduras to Afghanistan to the Sahara to the Petén in the same time periods. But so what? Read them as they come. "I" can mean either of us.

As for background, one of us is a plant pathologist and agronomist with a decade of work in Central America plus intensive traveling throughout Latin America and the Near East. The other is a retired Foreign Service Officer of the State Department with twenty years of posts in a dozen impoverished countries, including Russia and Communist China, plus one prosperous country, Canada, plus the United Nations, which has its ins and outs of prosperity. For each of us there has been a procession of hapless, despondent nations along our separate traveling paths.

I feel sorry for these waifs of the modern world. I am dismayed to see the heartbreaking efforts to develop these countries go to naught. Despite mountains of hard work and oceans of sweat and the struggle of intelligent citizenry and dedicated leaders, despite the parallel work of sincere foreign aid personnel and heaps of money, still the development fails to happen.

The fault lies not with the humans nor with lack of money. The fault lies deep within the development projects themselves. Even before the first shovel is turned, even before the appropriated money reaches the palm trees or the arid sands, the wrong decisions have been made, the decisions to develop the wrong things.

That is why I have written this book—which is not about foreign economic aid, although the pesky phrase keeps cropping up. Rather, it is about how these sovereign yet nevertheless forlorn nations can carry forward their own development based on their own resources. The foreign aid is nice to have, but the citizens must themselves pull their nation upward by pulling at their own bootstraps. This they can do even though their resources are indeed limited. This they can do if they make the right decisions, if they proceed with the right kind of development projects.

I hope the most serious readers of these chapters will be the leaders of the newly emerging, underdeveloped countries, such as the officials who sit in on all those interminable project committee meetings, and the ones who go out into the back country to persuade a valley to adopt a new technique, and the newspapermen, and the professors, and the intellectuals of divers backgrounds. Thus, if you are acquainted with such a person, this would indeed be an advantageous book to send him.

Contents

PART IV

HUNGRY NATIONS

Prologue

A CLUE TO the inward nature of a people is their traditional daily greeting, such as the Spaniards' religious "May you go with God!" and the cheerful "Good day!" of prosperous Europeans. I leave it to the psychologists to explain the Americans' morbid worry about aches and pains with their "How are you?"

The most sophisticated greeting I have heard is that of the Woloffs, dominant tribe in Senegal and Gambia, "Do you have peace?"

The Chinese, those ultrarealists, have learned through the harsh centuries to come straight to the point and say, "Have you eaten?"

All else is subordinate, including love, health, peace, liberty, religion. Only after a meal can man make use of the mind that sets him above the animals.

And so now I greet you quite seriously:

"Have you eaten?"

There is a lad here,
which hath five barley loaves,
and two small fishes:
but what are they
among so many?

John 6:9

Part I

1

Big Ideas, Big Hopes—but Little Resources Lead to Hungry Nations

THERE WAS once a country that had everything.

It had enough food, enough clothing, enough shelter. The old king had ruled for fifty years. The princes and the peasants and priests and merchants were relaxed in their traditional rounds. No one worried much about ambition and such frills. Feast days came and went. The river rose and fell forty feet each spring and some years it would rise forty-one feet and everything would get soggy, but what will be will be.

True, this country had its portion of ailments. Babies often died early. When a tooth hurt the only thing to do was to pull it out. There would be an occasional bad monsoon, an occasional plague of locusts, an occasional invasion by someone or other. The Siamese came once or twice every century and acted badly, and two hundred years ago they even grabbed away the wondrous Emerald Buddha. The French came and stayed awhile but did not interfere with things much. The Japanese came, apparently because they had no place else to go that season.

The religion of the country glossed over these troubles as the natural unpleasantnesses to be found along the road of life. So no one became excited over them. In fact, no one seemed to get excited over anything except the next festival or a new love dalliance or why-my-grandson-didn't-give-me-full-respect-at-the-temple-yesterday.

The people never understood why outsiders called this country the "eternal paradise."

The name of the country is Laos, and today the country that had everything has nothing. With the same resources and the same number of people, suddenly there is not enough food or enough clothing or enough shelter. Even though the Lord Buddha in his infinite munificence is now providing quantities of all these through a mechanism called "foreign aid and military assistance," and even though the quantities are beyond the wildest dreams of a few years ago, still they are not enough to satisfy this new, ever greater coveting of the people.

Laos makes a tidy example for study because it does not have all those complexities, like overpopulation and hunger, that befuddle the students of Guatemala or Pakistan or the Ivory Coast or Morocco. You see, Laos has not one thing that interests international commerce, not even one thing. Nothing in Laos, neither animal nor vegetable nor mineral, is needed by any part of the outside world – or at least nothing is worth the cost of transport. Driblets of this or that, such as the beautiful silk, do appear on export statistics, but these are of little consequence in the national life.

The one exception, I am reluctant to add, is the opium which the Meo tribesmen raise and smuggle out to Bangkok, making them the most comfortably fixed group in the country. At least, this was so until the Americans retreated from that hinterland area and left the rugged, pro-West Meos to be taken over by the communists – except insofar as they turned guerrillas.

Today, Laos is a sovereign nation, votes in the United Nations and has embassies here and there. How does it pay for its international obligations when it has no international trade generated out of resources, to mention only one of a number of pertinent points?

When I arrived there in 1954 as part of the newly opened American Embassy, the French were withdrawing from Indochina upon the conclusion of that disastrous colonial war; the mischievous "Control" mission of Indians, Poles and passive Canadians, as set up at the war's end, was already busily paving the way for communist expansion; and the populace was still drifting along in their "eternal paradise." Desires had not yet come alive for transistor radios, celluloid baby rattles and Hong Kong T-shirts emblazoned with a bucking cowboy. Economic aid had not yet begun. It soon did.

To cope with the communist invaders from Viet Minh and China a Laotian army was created. Such a national army was quite unheard of within the traditions and, more important, within the economy of the country. To pay for the army the American Government sent in money. This was called economic aid and military assistance. Within a couple of years the stuff wrecked the traditional routines of contentment. The natural resources remained as elusive as ever, but the new aid money (a half-billion dollars in a decade[1]) took the place of resources. It was as absolute a gain as all that sudden oil which is now gushing up within the boundaries of Kuwait and Libya.

With this boom-money suddenly at hand, items from abroad were craved, which meant, at least in the circles that count, that they had become necessities. Around the world this sort of craving is often called "rising expectations."

With ease, entrepreneurs emerged to facilitate the spending.

As every schoolboy, but not every adult, knows, each import must be paid for by an export. And Laos has no exports because it has no developed, marketable resources.

And so each imported item was paid for from the American treasury, because there was no foreign exchange created by foreign trade – that is, it was not paid for out of native resources. Every pocket mirror and matching comb, every Volkswagen, every bolt of cloth from Japan was, and is, paid for via Washington. This also includes the other newfangled "necessities," such as clinics, paved roads and embassies abroad.

The administrators of the foreign aid projects in Laos – and there is quite a variety of these projects – hope this activity will change the nation's economy to such an extent that exports will some day balance imports and then foreign aid no longer will be needed.

Unfortunately, the majority of these foreign aid projects are directed not at resource development but at superficial things like public health, schools and roads for automobiles. Worse, instead of curtailing the rising wants of the citizens, the foreign advisers buttress and encourage the new craving for quick, temporary things.

In no way do I mean this oversimplified description as a criticism of American policy or Laotian astuteness. As long as Laos remains noncommunist, the United States gets its money's worth out of the half-billion dollars.

The headlines of the world's press blame this new kind of life in Laos on the Cold War. Yet the Cold War is only a catalyst that has caused a number of stagnant elements, already present, to rise to the surface and burst into action.

The same situation is found in any number of other countries around the globe where the people also want all sorts of everything. However, it is not easy, except in Laos, to isolate exactly what has caused this sudden surge of wants. Certainly one should not put all the blame on foreign aid. For one thing, in contrast to Laos, the foreign aid money is usually only a small item in the overall economy. And the desire for modern new things was there, below the political surface, long before the aid began.

Students of this subject say these expanding desires grow out of the movies, the picture magazines, the local press, the odd but fascinating possessions of foreign residents and tourists, plus, in a few cases, the sight of the gay goings-on of high society in the capital city.

A Mexican professor has remarked that the luscious picture of a strawberry shortcake in a *Saturday Evening Post* left behind in a bus station can create more avid coveting and discontent among the hungry than all the political agitators put together, and yet most Mexicans have never seen a strawberry and do not know what it tastes like.

A new and active channel for creating ideas and, therefore, wants is the transistor radio. In contrast to the old single radio set tied to an electric generator at the village plaza or local teahouse, every hut in even the most remote valley, it seems, now has its own transistor tuned in constantly on the highly assorted thought waves of highly assorted countries.

Perhaps the greatest force currently pushing this wave of surging desires is the Americans abroad, the tens of thousands of businessmen, tourists, government officials and representatives of all those private institutions. The fabric of most noncommunist countries is by now thoroughly impregnated with Americans.

The typical American, you must remember, is a firm believer in action, at least when it comes to other people's affairs. Nothing is beyond reach if only you get cracking. Thus, his constant advice to all foreigners within earshot is to knuckle down, work hard, and you too will achieve the boss's daughter and live in a fine house overflowing with modernities.

This philosophy, this point of view that each nation can achieve an American middle class standard of living, seems to govern most development planning. Oddly, Russia's limited foreign aid projects are designed ostensibly toward the same goal.

The main thing, so says our American, is to get the show on the road, and if everyone works hard success will surely come.

But will it?

Thoughtful observers have already noted that in America big success now comes via a thorough knowledge of complex tax laws, plus the guts to strike out on one's own as an entrepreneur willing to outfox the competition – not bad qualities, incidentally, for a nation to instill in its young.

Observers have also noted that Americans, when all is said and done, are not really very hard workers after all, compared to such as the Chinese and Indian peasants, who labor from dawn to dusk, hungry, weakened with parasites, and with no decent place to rest at night.

Yet so often I have seen Americans create euphoria among foreign listeners, dazzling them with the vision that their hopes and desires, their rising expectations, are not only valid but also attainable within just a few years. They insist that if only the populace gets moving and works hard, the various problems will then, somehow, fall into place and success be achieved almost right away.

Regardless of how today's populations around the world have acquired their desires and ambitions, whether out of the movies or from the urgings of careless politicians or overenthusiastic advisers, our mid-twentieth century has been well labeled "The Age of Rising Expectations." The expectations sprout upward, like hothouse plants unaffected by the cold facts of life, whether in Laos, India, Chad, or wherever.

I protest these expectations as hopelessly beyond the nation's potential. I emphasize, alas and alack, that these nations are not going to achieve their exalted aspirations, no matter how brilliant and honest their leaders may be, no matter how hard the people may work and how much they sacrifice, no matter how wisely the foreign aid money is spent. In every country where I have lived or visited my observation is that these expectations, sometimes expressed as five-year or seven-year plans, have outstripped the capacity of local resources to produce.

At some particular point each nation, both the leaders and the people, must come to realize this. The realities of life, as ordained by a harsh and stern God, will eventually catch up with them. We can only hope the realization comes within the framework of peaceful adjustment and not via internal bloody revolution or external grabbings at the possessions of neighbors.

Mexico is a country to keep in mind. It already has had its social revolution, its so-called land reform, its development projects. Its capital city now glitters with great skyscrapers, fine university buildings and busy factory plants. Yet most of the country's population continues to be hungry – probably as hungry, for the majority, as in the days of Porfirio Díaz before the Great Revolution began in 1910. And so its writers and reflective thinkers are beginning to wonder why this should be. Octavio Paz, Mexican poet and diplomat, writes:

> The truth is that the resources of our nation as a whole are insufficient to finance our development or even to create what the experts call an "economic infrastructure," the only solid basis for real progress. We lack capital, and the rhythm of internal capitalization and reinvestment is still too slow. Thus our essential problem, according to the experts, is to obtain the resources vital to our growth. But where, and how? [2]

In these chapters I explain the basic factors that, whether you like them or not, must restrict the ambitions of a citizenry to their available resources, a term that embraces all that fragile, probably temporary delight known as foreign aid and military assistance.

As a counterbalance, I propose a set of guidelines for mustering the maximum return from the limited reserves of the foreign aid recipients. Doing this should provide a surplus which, at least by comparison with what they now have, ought to generate a modicum of prosperity. These guidelines can function, however, only when a country calms down from its carefree "expecting" and faces up to reality – and obviously, that is easier said than done.

Specifically, the countries I have in mind are the dozens of smaller ones, like Laos, each struggling within its own national framework of troubles. It is the larger ones, like Brazil, Mexico, India and Communist China, that get the headlines with their king-size problems and mammoth plans to overcome them. Thus, when the outsider thinks of the subject of development plans in general and foreign aid in particular, he automatically thinks of their massive imponderables. He forgets about Laos, Upper Volta, Somalia, Syria, Jamaica, Cambodia, Rwanda, Bolivia, each tightly confined within rigid boundaries which contain a woefully short range of resources. Note that the new sand-covered sovereign nation of Mauritania has a single iron mine as its only important asset.

Nevertheless, the principles I expound apply to the large countries as well.

These countries, both small and large, are desperately in need of proper advice and guidance as they strive to gain that elusive prosperity and to acquire a dignified, respected position in the international community. More than any other factor, this is why they grasp so eagerly, and often so blindly, at the foreign aid projects and technicians offered to them; certainly it is not mere greediness for the free money.

Yet the tragedy of foreign aid is that the countries which give aid are today already too far advanced technically and intellectually beyond those who receive it. In many instances it is now impossible for the two groups of officials or private citizens even to understand each other. They truly live in separate worlds.

Several generations ago the United States–Western European bloc orbited off into a planetary sphere separate from that of the backward countries. By now, the economist or engineer trained in an American university is often unable to give effective help in, for example, Nicaragua or the Sudan. Indeed, when he does give advice, it may lead to disastrous effects.

Language of the space age is not amiss here.

American economists worth their salt are today deep in the discussion of what will be the effect of the technological fallout of our exploding, brand-new space industry. Something like $30,000,000,000 to $40,000,000,000 is estimated for United States expenditures on space projects before 1970.[3] This is merely the figure used at the moment this sentence is in the typewriter. Who knows what will be the revised figure by the time this page is published? Even as stated, there is a $10,000,000,000 variable, a figure large enough, I dare say, to cover the entire budgets of the majority of the aid-receiving nations during the same period! Yet seven years ago the American space industry had hardly even been born.

I note the allocations of three American companies for expansion facilities for 1963; not their operating budgets but merely the allocation for expansion. Procter and Gamble scheduled $50,000,000, General Electric $120,000,000 and General Motors $1,200,000,000. These three figures of only three companies totaled $80,000,000 *more* than the total combined budgets of Bolivia, Costa Rica, Dahomey, Dominican Republic, Ecuador, Guatemala, Haiti, Honduras, Ivory Coast, Malagasy Republic, Mauritania, Nicaragua, Nigeria, Panama, Paraguay, El Salvador, Senegal, Upper Volta and Uruguay.

So our American economist goes by jet out from this level of professional activity. A dozen hours later he is in Nairobi on an aid mission. Maybe he talks glibly of the Kenya GNP (and who can determine that complex statistic out of the many imponderables of a primitive society?). He may also talk of the muddle arising from using a herd of cows as a status symbol – instead, I suppose, of a proper automobile that Detroit likes to obsolesce each year.

Our American is definitely out of place in these discussions. Actually, it may be quite dangerous for the Kenyans even to sit at the same planning table with him. He is a Tiffany salesman reduced to Woolworth's beads. He is Picasso showing a housewife how to paint. He is a Pentagon general groping to understand a guerrilla fighter.

The local officials would be better off in many cases, perhaps in most cases, to close their ears to the alien adviser and to follow their own native common sense.

Unfortunately, the officials of the undeveloped countries do not have confidence in their own judgment. They are mesmerized by the achievements of the orbiting West. They listen supinely to anyone from that celestial world. They comprehend the visiting oracle's pronouncements no more than did the Greeks at Delphi, yet like those ancients they eagerly rush forth blindly to obey.

2

How Big Are Your Resources?

THEY USED to call them "backward countries," but the sensitive toes of nationalists squirmed and so the phrase was changed to "undeveloped countries." The toes still squirmed and so everyone, at least everyone in Washington's bureaucracy, was ordered to use "underdeveloped countries." This was still too brutal. One now hears of "less well developed," "emerging," "less privileged," "have-not," "catch-up," "low-income," "needy," "poorest third," "recipient," "expectant," "restless." How gentle, O Webster, can one get with sensitivities?

Let us now step on toes.

The poverty of these nations puts them today at the back end of the parade of civilization. They trail behind in the dust. Wherever the parade goes they tag along. They are backward.

What has any one of the backward countries done to advance civilization in the past several decades? Offhand, I can't think of anything, neither invention nor idea. Of some three hundred and fifty recipients of Nobel awards through the years, only five have been nationals of backward countries – one in literature from India, one in physics from India, one in literature from Chile, and two in physics (prize shared) from China. Thirteen others came from Argentina, Greece, Spain, Yugoslavia, Portugal, Poland and Hungary, and these may or may not be classified as backward, depending on one's standards. Certainly

Argentina before Perón's economic chaos should not be so ranked.

The raw products of the backward countries are, of course, necessary, but, like all material things, are they truly vital? Unless the products were cut off too sharply, civilization, I am confident, would adapt itself to their loss and go on its way. Even without the oil. At least, I hate to think that mankind's welfare is so tenuous that it would collapse if rampaging Arabs should block off the black viscosity.

Of course, parade is not a good figure of speech. It connotes a fixed order of march. Actually, today's leaders could become tomorrow's trailers. However, I speak here of today's backward countries, not yesterday's or tomorrow's.

And the parade is rapidly losing cohesiveness. Today's leaders are racing farther and farther ahead of the straggling, gasping plodders.

Fortunately, an easy definition of "backward country" is at hand at the present time: one that receives foreign economic aid is backward; one that does not is not.

I realize that economists and politicians and student shouters can hastily bring forward other definitions, but this one will do for us.

Thus, India is backward but not Japan; Chile but not New Zealand; Mexico but not Luxembourg. And the same goes for the communist satellites versus aid-giving Russia. Having once lived in Russia, I know I am stretching a point in saying that Russia is herself not a backward country. However, the common consent of public opinion throughout the world puts her up at the front of the parade alongside the United States. So let us leave her there for a while and later on review her economic right to such a forward position.

Why are some countries backward today and others not?

Why do some countries have higher standards of living than other countries?

The cause of backwardness is a lack of resources. The stock of resources in a backward country, in proportion to the size of the population, is not sufficient to generate a *surplus.* The citizens cannot accumulate the capital which they must have to develop their country. The nation falls behind in the onward sweep of civilization. It becomes backward until sometime, if ever, something happens that increases productivity and thus enables the people to acquire the means for starting their country forward on the road of progress.

Occasionally, minerals or oil are found that for a few decades bring in enough money for buying food from abroad. Sometimes, oftentimes, extra resources are acquired as a result of successful wars, by cattle raiding so to speak — Russia's occupation of Eastern Europe and Manchuria is a clear-cut example. Sometimes a turn of economic events allows a poor agricultural region to produce a suddenly new and prosperous crop that will carry the economic load for an entire nation, as bananas are nearly doing today in Ecuador. Or a new international situation may allow a nation to develop special financial routines to help pay for food imports, such as the no-income-tax joys of the Bahamas.

A more exact term than "backward" is "hungry."

Hereafter, I shall refer to these "undeveloped," "less well developed," "poorest third," "emerging" nations simply as *hungry.*

They are hungry for food, they are hungry for stability, they are hungry for international prestige, for education, for health, housing, culture. They are hungry for the twentieth century.

I suppose the opposite of a hungry nation is a *comfortable* nation living in an environment capable of supporting its modern desires.

I begin with resources.

A nation's resources can, in practice, be almost anything, down to the gold fillings in the teeth of Nazi victims.

Panama has a canal. Lebanon has the only ski runs in the Near East. Brazil has coffee, which may or may not be an asset depending on how sophisticated an economic analysis you want to employ.

A resource is, for want of a better definition, anything tangible or intangible that can increase the well-being of a nation.

The clearest, although not the most accurate, measurement of a country's resources is the level of its exports. This is because each item exported has been created from the surplus production derived out of the resources of the nation. The more exports, the greater a country's well-being.

This is the generalization that is the basis of the economic thinking of both the hungry countries and such powerhouses as Britain and Japan. So, disregarding what the ivory tower theorists may say in American economics classes, I repeat: The more exports, the more imports that can be paid for by those exports, and so the more well-being.

Unfortunately, impatient leaders juggling tariffs, subsidies, tax rebates and so on forget the converse of this rule: each beautiful new import must be paid for by an export.

Once I had to make a forced landing on a grass strip near Escuintla, Guatemala, when rain clouds and too many volcanoes round about made it unwise to go farther. The airstrip was next to a nearly deserted plantation, and I spent the time until the clouds cleared wandering about it. I came upon a fairly new paper mill with much of the equipment labeled "Fisher Governor, Marshalltown, Iowa" – my home town! Eventually, I found the caretaker and asked, "Whatever made the owners of this plantation think they could operate a paper plant out here in the middle of nowhere? Why did they buy this machinery?"

"Why not?" he said. "Five years ago we sold citronella oil on the world market at a dollar twenty-five a pound. We could buy anything! Now the market has collapsed and we can't even buy gaskets for your Marshalltown valves."

World War II cut the West off from the citronella production centers of the Far East, and certain Latin American farmers stepped into the vacuum and had themselves a fine boom. The boom continued for several years after the war until Java and Formosa finally overcame political turmoil and began again to produce citronella cheaper than anyone else. The Guatemalan farmers were forced out; they could not export their product profitably to the international market.

The wisdom of buying the paper mill is not at issue here. I merely want to illustrate that citronella exports paid for the machinery, so that they "could buy anything."

Even though foreign aid subsidies may at times pick up the tab for excess imports, as in the extreme case of Laos, or a fortunate loan may postpone the unhappy day of stringency, nevertheless this basic fact of economic life in a hungry country still governs: the amount of imports is controlled by the amount of the nation's surplus resources available for export, and a nation with limited resources automatically is going to have limited imports of tractors, road machinery, pretty automobiles and, I add, newsprint for angry anticapitalistic writers.

And how great are your resources, my Egyptian or Korean or Trinidadian or Senegalese? How much are you importing per capita? What part of your imports do you pay for out of your own surplus production, namely, exports? What part is given you for free out of the resources of another country, namely, foreign aid?

Aid on the scale that is now provided – and still more on the scale contemplated in the calculations of capital needs to cope with increasing populations – is already beyond the capacity of the recipient countries to repay. Antonin Busch has shown that the principal borrowers from the International Bank and the Export-Import Bank have on the whole failed to increase their exports and that "no export increase occurred in the Latin American countries if petroleum from Venezuela were excluded." [1]

A national resource can be intangible, such as the noble character of the people, their history of peaceful government, their brotherly love without class tensions, and other virtues extolled by orators. On examination, these splendid virtues, when they do exist, do so because they are supported and nurtured by a surplus of tangible, very tangible, physical resources.

There are three types of tangible resources, and only three: the air, the land, the water. If these terms sound childish, you are too far removed, in comfortable living, from the basics of human life.

The form in which these three are found – their proportion and their arrangement – will determine the prosperity of a nation. All the happy daydreaming of happy nationalists and all the desperate planning of dedicated leaders will not change this fact.

The Lord, unfortunately, has not divided these three equally. No two nations, no two provinces have the same combination of land, water and air resources. Consequently, no two nations, even among the rich ones, have the same wealth, nor the same level of prosperity.

The mere fact that a country is blessed with favorable proportions of these resources does not insure its prosperity. They must be properly used, and at the right economic moment, for full development. Liberia since its birth has wallowed in the miseries of nothingness. Now iron is found and, depending on the wisdom of its leaders, the sky is the limit for the next half-century.

Oil, as everyone knows, spouts up in the darnedest places. It also demonstrates a good point to remember about resources, including the nutrients in your agricultural soil. Once they are out of the ground they are gone forever and ever, and never no never will they ever be back again. Such expendable assets must be used wisely to produce the capital required to develop other, less easily available facets of the nation's resources.

Agricultural products are thoroughly bound within the God-fixed arrangement of land, air and water. And the same liability of expendableness is present. It is easy to recognize an oil deposit or an iron mountain as expendable. Too few citizens realize that agricultural richness is similarly a resource that is equally susceptible to exhaustion – the nutrients in the soil, the water table underneath, the forest cover above. Until the nation's citizens are educated to such realization, their future will be indeed dubious.

Let us now discuss basic agriculture in terms that apply equally to Iowa, Ceylon, Kazakhstan and the sands of Mali.

Agriculture, if it is going to be of any good to anyone, must combine successfully and in the right time sequence several quite disparate factors. One is land with enough of the right texture to allow roots to penetrate it and with the correct combination of minerals to feed those roots. Another is enough rainfall at least to wet those roots now and then. Another is enough warm sunshine to get the seeds sprouted and the blades out of the ground. Another is topography; man has proven he can be a farmer while standing on one foot clinging to an overhanging rock, but there is a limit to acrobatics.

All this is evident, but few understand how little land there is in this not very large world of ours that combines these factors correctly.

Nowhere do these factors combine themselves so favorably as in the Middle Western states. We who have grown up there forget the uniqueness of this area. A square mile of Iowa farmland transported to almost any spot in Latin America, Africa or Asia would be so astounding that the people would make pilgrimage to it as to a shrine. This, I do assure you, is no exaggeration. Khrushchev himself has been such a pilgrim.

To say the obvious, a desert may have fine soil, but it has no rain; the Arctic has moisture but not the right temperature; mountains are too up and down. And so it goes. For this reason only 7.7 per cent of the land surface of the planet Earth is cultivated.[2]

Regarding the one factor of rainfall only 9 per cent of the area of Australia has adequate precipitation for agriculture. Africa has 25 per cent, Asia 29 per cent. On the other hand, 79 per cent of Europe has adequate rainfall.[3]

The United States and Canada have 22.7 per cent of all the world's cultivated land. Latin America, in contrast, with just as many people to feed, has only 6.5 per cent.[4] This is no one's fault. This is merely how the Lord bounced the ball.

Man, as a matter of fact, has done an extraordinarily effective job of trying to make the most out of what he has. Through his aeons of survival, he has done a good trial and error job of finding out what will grow best in each particular corner of our staggeringly diversified globe. By now – and this is an important point — most of the odd plants from the far-off countries have been tried out in all the other far-off countries.

Rather, they have been tried by nonscientists. A plant may have failed miserably in the hands of even an experienced farmer, but an agricultural scientist may come along tomorrow and adapt it successfully for that farmer and all his neighbors. This is, of course, the great hope for modern agricultural expansion, and much will be said of this in later chapters.

Our thesis here, and one that is so casually ignored by economic planners, is that by this time man has already learned through his trial and error routines where agriculture is possible and where it is not. If an area of a country is empty of farmers, cattlemen, rubber bleeders and mistletoe pluckers, then there is a very tangible reason why that valley is empty. The soil perhaps is thin, or the rainfall deficient, or the sunshine erratic or the topography awful.

When land is not in cultivation the reason is that man can farm other land more profitably, even at the marginal subsistence level. This does not mean the land cannot be farmed. Any piece of ground can be farmed if one puts enough capital into it. One could, for example, raise the finest tomatoes in the world on top of the Matterhorn. All one has to do is to build a greenhouse there, get a helicopter to fly in the manure and the coal for the heating plant, import a trained agriculturist and let him go to work. But could these tomatoes, even though the tastiest, lushest in the world, be sold for a price to cover the cost of production?

The rice terraces of Bontoc in the Philippines are a more truthful, although equally unreal, illustration. Before the war I visited that area in company with a local official. He had asked me to bring from Manila a supply of lemon drops and cigarettes. With these as gifts he financed a lively evening of dancing and singing. My point is that the surplus of good things here was so meager, so close to nothingness, that a bag of candy and some cigarettes were enough to set off a party. Yet few people in the world work so hard, both physically and intelligently, as these farmers of Bontoc. The terraces and irrigation channels that through the centuries they have built on the almost perpendicular hillsides are engineering marvels. The retaining walls were constructed only by an unimaginable number of hours of the roughest physical labor. Soil has had to be carried to the terraces in sacks slung over the farmers' backs, and the farmers can reach some of them only by hand-over-hand rope climbing. These terraces, expressed differently, are capital created out of centuries of hard work. The capital is as valid a resource as the canals and dikes of the Netherlands or the transportation network of the United States. Nevertheless, despite this hard work, intelligently applied, the people of Bontoc regarded a bag of lemon drops as a great luxury. Their overall resources were not enough to give them a higher standard of modern living.

The gremlin that mixes up the otherwise lucid thinking of economic planners, nationalist leaders and big and little entrepreneurs is the memory of the Western Hemisphere and Australasia lying virginal and eager before the immigrant Europeans.

Those days, dash it all, are now long gone. So get them out of your minds and face reality. Today, if a piece of land is sparsely settled there is a reason for it, believe me, and the reason is not because people are too lazy or soft to pioneer. The land is empty because it does not have enough resources to support a population.

"The requirements of nature for food production are so rigid that thus far man has been able to use only a small proportion of the earth's land surface and has been defeated in most of his attempts to extend his boundaries." [5]

"Less than 5 per cent of the soils of the tropics measure up to the popular conception of potential fertility." [6]

I here present illustrations of what is meant by the dire pronouncement that man "has been defeated in most of his attempts to extend his [agricultural] boundaries."

I start with the Petén because it is so very, very empty.

Once it was the center of the great Mayan civilization. Yet today it has nothing. Can it again rise to prosperity?

This jungle province covers one-third of Guatemala. As in so many hungry nations with similar wild areas, the citizens of Guatemala of all levels and classes, not just a few government planners, firmly believe the Petén is their Land of the Future, their shining Shangri-La of tomorrow, the oncoming bread basket that will fill the stomachs and banish poverty. Also, typically, 99 per cent of the Guatemalans have never been to this area, let alone tried to grow anything there.

In 1953 I became director of the Iowa State College–Guatemala Tropical Research Center in Antigua, searching primarily for new corn varieties. In 1956-1957 I was an agronomist with the American aid mission in that country. During those years I flew over much of the Petén and went by dugout canoe and horse through part of it. Oilmen and loggers have tramped this area more than I, but I claim special knowledge of the Petén for having tried to grow corn both in the center of it and on its fringes.

It was this experience as a corn grower that led to my studies of other empty areas of the world and my dictum: if a piece of land anywhere on this globe of ours is today sparsely settled there is a reason for it. The reason: even hungry people can feed themselves better somewhere else.

The Petén, mostly jungle with some savannas, covers fifteen thousand square miles of the Yucatán Peninsula. On my first visit I chartered a DC-3 to fly me to Tikal, site of the ruins of the greatest city of the Mayan civilization, outranking both Chichén Itzá and Copán, which are better known to the outside world. During World War II a landing strip had been hacked out of the jungle at Tikal. My plane rolled to the end of the bumpy strip, I jumped out, and the plane roared off, leaving me alone, exceedingly alone, with my duffel bag. In Guatemala City I had been told this area was completely uninhabited. The crown of the jungle here rears up a hundred feet and the silence is appalling. There were no signs of the ruins. I had with me a map, sketched on a cocktail napkin by a friend while we sat on the floor at a party. I had little faith in its scratchings as I perched on my duffel bag trying to orient myself. Fifteen feet away three wild turkeys watched me.

I chose a direction and entered the jungle. Within only a few feet I stumbled on a small campfire burning brightly. "Uninhabited" is, of course, only a figure of speech. People of one kind or another live, even though thinly, in the most deserted areas. I never did see the person or persons connected with this campfire. Probably it was left by a lone chicle hunter making a rough living by tapping, over a route of dozens of miles, the sapodilla plum trees whose latex gives the gum chewers of the world their wads.

I interpolate: when you sit in on committee meetings and people say that such and such an area is waiting to be developed, remember the *chicleros* who have crisscrossed the Petén for the last half-century, plus the oilmen and the loggers, and still that fabled richness remains to be discovered. Why? Because there is no richness there.

I eventually did find the ruins, great, stately, tree-covered pyramids which today a corps of archaeologists is unearthing. Also, today a reasonably comfortable hotel is there for the occasional tourist.

On another trip into the Petén I intentionally tried to find a completely uninhabited area. I was traveling with a former college professor of mine who was searching for the indigenous food plants of the Maya. Again we flew in, and then went by dugout canoe down the Pasión and Usumacinta rivers. This area, I was assured in Guatemala City, was truly uninhabited.

If this was a population vacuum, give me Times Square. This was the first week of March, a short time before Holy Week, and Guatemalans by custom eat dried fish during Lent if they can afford it. Along these "deserted" rivers we saw dozens of groups of people fishing and drying their catch. Later, when I was flying back to the capital, this dried fish was stacked around me, floor to ceiling. Delightful flight!

If this Petén were the rich agricultural area people elsewhere believe it to be, these fishermen would long since have become farmers. Their dried fish income was as brief as a Christmas tree vendor's. To say that they and the *chicleros* are not agriculturally oriented is to beg the issue.

Respected archaeologists estimate that the Mayan population was in the millions. Adjusting to the Petén area the figures that Sylvanus G. Morley worked out for all the Mayan empire, the Guatemalans conclude that the population for that district must have been between 6,000,000 and 26,000,000.[7] Today there are 15,000 in all the Petén,[8] including the principal town Flores, border guards, military posts and a couple of lumber camps. It is indeed one of the least populated areas in the Western Hemisphere. Why?

The Mayan civilization, despite new archaeological discoveries, is still hidden by mysterious perplexities. Many details of its everyday life are now known, but not *how* great cities could exist in these ferocious forests, *why* each area was suddenly abandoned and new cities were created whole and fully functioning hundreds of miles away, *why* the civilization was already wasted away and rapidly vanishing even before the Spanish *conquistadores* arrived, *why* the Mayas' primitive descendants have inherited none of their forebears' ability to control their jungle environment.

But one thing is clear to me as an agriculturist. Despite what the archaeologists say, the Petén could never have had these millions of inhabitants, and I doubt it ever will in the future unless research develops some totally new product for the area to produce. The Guatemalan dreamers should look at the Petén through the eyes of an agriculturist rather than those of an archaeologist. Let us not argue how many grass shacks the Mayas inhabited around a temple at one time nor how many hands were needed to build a pyramid.

When talking about "undeveloped" land, one should remember that generally it is remote and none of the planners, most probably, have ever been there. No one knows much about the place.

As for the Petén, Charles S. Simmons has made the only authoritative survey of its soils. He did this about 1950 and the results have been ignored ever since. He found that less than 14 per cent of the Petén is suitable for agricultural development, or an area equal to only 1918 square miles. Even this is broken up into small bits of usable land, each of which would require its own major capital improvements to eliminate drainage problems, soil acidity and so on.[9]

Archaeologist Morley wrote that it took 12.4 acres to support one Mayan.[10] Combining this figure with Simmon's survey and bypassing Morley's disregard for what land is cultivable and what is not, my arithmetic indicates this would have meant only 98,969 people in the Petén in Mayan times.

Tackling the population guessing from another angle, we have today the commonly accepted and well-substantiated figure that it takes a minimum of two pounds of corn a day to support the average Guatemalan. It must have been similarly true in Mayan times.

Because of weeds, insects and soil exhaustion, the Mayan, as does his counterpart today, must have farmed only about a third of his land at one time, leaving two-thirds lying fallow in a sort of crop rotation system.

Using only one-third of the land that Simmons says can be farmed, we find the Petén might have supported a population of 375,000. Even this is probably a generous estimate.

So we have one figure of 99,000 and another of 375,000. It is anybody's guess where the true statistic lies.

Officials in Guatemala never mention such low figures when talking up plans about developing the Petén. Instead, their thinking is derived from Morley's conclusions of 6,000,000 to 26,000,000. And so they toss about figures of speech that the nation has nothing to worry about because the Petén will absorb all their uninhibited birth rate (49.5 per thousand per year,[11] one of the highest in the world), and soon the wealth of the future farmers of Petén will flow in a beautiful stream to the shops and bureaucracies of Guatemala's capital.

There are several flaws in this picture, but the most glaring is that wild horses cannot today drag your Guatemalan, regardless of the state of his poverty and starvation, to the Petén to live. He looks upon the area as a crawling mass of poisonous snakes, poisonous spiders and poisonous red-eyed bugs. Also, it is awfully hot.

Thus, there is the human element. This could change, of course, if the government cleared the land, killed off those poisonous things, provided housing, movies and cold beer and guaranteed an annual return from the land.

I mention the human element first, but in fact it is the least important. The trouble with the Petén is not the lack of pioneers but the conditions that caused Simmons to say that less than 14 per cent of the area is suitable for agriculture, and that even this area is a scattering of bits and pieces each requiring expensive capital improvements.

Having tried to grow corn there, I know government planners must come up with some special crop desired outside the Petén, such as citronella, dragon blood resin, iguana tail meat or maybe something like coffee, but *not* coffee of which the world's cup is already overflowing. Otherwise, the government money put into the Petén will surely be wasted. Otherwise, the new settlers imported there will subsist on what they themselves raise; their standard of living will merely equal the plight of hundreds of similar lost villages in the rest of the country.

Those Mayan cities?

My unarchaeological supposition is they were primarily religious centers. They could not have been active cities surrounded by multitudes farming in the shadows of the pyramids. I hazard that farming was carried out on plots scattered over a radius of perhaps a hundred miles and food brought to the temples in the form of a Mayan tithe for the support of the priests.

The Mayan had no miracle food. He ate the same things the Central American Indian does today – corn, beans, peppers. He had the same fight with the brutal jungle and the same fight with voracious weeds and insects. And it is a hard fight.

This is why most Guatemalans today live crowded together in the highlands and why most Bolivians live in the *altiplano*. Agriculture in the highlands is productive; in the jungle, by comparison, it is not. The Aztec and Inca civilizations were also located in the highlands.

One can only wonder at the military pressures that must have forced the Mayans to settle as refugees in the difficult lowland tropical jungles and marvel that this gifted race survived to create their civilization there. It must have been a terribly rough ordeal. Of all the world's civilizations it must have been physically the most difficult to develop.

But could they ever have numbered in the Petén more than a few hundred thousand? This I doubt.

The most controversial, the most frustrating, the most maddening single American foreign aid project probably has been the Helmand River development in the southwest part of Afghanistan. The files in Washington and Kabul are full of the charges and countercharges about why and how and who and which caused the troubles.

The Helmand is often and not quite correctly called the first American aid program, but apparently it was the first in Eurasia.

I was stationed in Kabul in the embassy just after the war when the Helmand affair was first reactivated (Japanese engineers under contract to the Afghans had done some work earlier). The Afghan Government had ended the war with a sizable bank account of accumulated cash. It decided to use this money on certain development projects and hired an American engineering firm to carry them out. American Government money was not then involved. The largest of the projects was a couple of dams in the headwaters of the Helmand for irrigation works

The ancient city of Kandahar, traditionally founded by Alexander the Great, was made the headquarters of the project, but the region to be developed was in an adjacent area of mostly empty scrub and desert. I once became completely lost there on a jeep trip, as I would find my way blocked by a gully or the washed-out remnant of some old irrigation work and would have to turn off into a new direction. After eight hours of this, when I was down to my last couple of cans of gas, evening came and I luckily spotted the light of a hunter's hut and thus acquired a guide back to the main trail.

The Helmand is six hundred miles long and empties into a huge swamp-lake on the Iranian border. I traveled by carry-all into the Seistan region on the Afghan side of this swamp-lake.

The trip was not connected with the plans then being drawn up in Kabul; my objective was to learn what all the shouting was about between the Iranian and Afghan governments concerning the sudden decrease in the flow of waters into this mutually owned swamp-lake (the reason, everyone finally agreed, was merely another bad drought).

I was told I was the first European-American ever to have visited this section of several hundred square miles.

For centuries, perhaps for more than a thousand years, this had been a prosperous area. Then Tamerlane came roaring in toward the end of the fourteenth century and spitefully destroyed the irrigation system. The Seistan has remained a nearly uninhabited desert ever since. Only a string of desolate villages, huddled along the banks of the Helmand, live on.

Yet, as I drove along the one trail, always in sight were ruins of old walled towns and villas abandoned over six hundred years ago. The French archaeological group in Kabul had given me gunny sacks to fill with any shards I might find. There were so many ruins alongside the trail I soon filled the sacks and, in fact, became bored with such easy archaeological pickings. The only persons I saw during one day was a group of men, obviously bandits, who suddenly appeared in a low spot in the road; surprised to find a non-Afghan in the carryall they meekly asked if I would give a lift to one of their men.

With these ruins as evidence of former agricultural prosperity, surely a reconstruction of the old irrigation systems, such as planned for the Helmand River, could revive the area. Here was no Petén jungle to fight. Just bring in the water and the desert will exude milk and honey the same as in the glorious past.

Today, fifteen years and $85,000,000 later (or is it $100,000,000 by now?), it is obvious the Helmand project is not that simple. In the rehashing of all that has gone sour with this affair it is natural to criticize, based on hindsight, who did what wrong and what fouled up what. How did all that salt get on the land? How did that water table shell become so impervious? Adequate surveys were not made at the beginning. Afghan officials blew hot and cold in their support. The engineering company made a clutch of mistakes. American aid officials, when they took over the project, also blew hot and cold and made their own errors. Pull out of the file cabinets whatever set of details you are interested in.

The real truth, however, the basic, rock-hard truth, must be deeper than such human failings. This was empty desert land. There were reasons why it was empty. There were reasons why agriculture had vanished. The local people had tried over and over again to farm and failed. They had brought in water and yet this had not been the answer. Building modern dams and concrete-lined irrigation ditches is also, it now appears, not the answer.

Considering the vast sums spent on this Helmand project, it is likely that agriculture of a sort will be forthcoming. But can the produce ever repay this initial huge cost of development?

It is important to emphasize that the Afghan Government has spent great sums of its own money here; by no means is this merely an aid-financed project. When the cash reserves it had accumulated during the war were exhausted, it borrowed money from the Export-Import Bank. During most of the 1950's probably 20 per cent of its entire budget went into the Helmand development.

If a portion of these sums had been spent on improving the already existing agriculture surrounding the city of Kandahar, the results today might well be flourishing and the bazaars redolent with economically sound income.

A new colonization plan, an example which the aid people hold up as a model for all undeveloped countries, is just getting under way in the Alto Beni Valley of Bolivia.

Here, two hundred miles from the capital, La Paz, the government is settling two thousand families. It is planned that in ten years these families will have raised their annual income from $90 a year to $1200 (thirteenfold!). The government (via loans from the United States) is spending $1000 per family to move people from the cold highlands and settle them in the hot Alto Beni jungle, plus an unknown, open-end sum to construct a highway across unbelievably difficult terrain.[12]

Although coffee and cacao will be grown, the primary products will be winter vegetables to compete with those presently flown into the capital from Peru for the diplomatic corps and the equivalent Bolivian elite of La Paz. This would seem a limited, rather fickle market on which to establish a complex development project. Of such is not the heart's blood of a nation's future economic stability.

The Bolivian Government is aggressively pushing other colonization projects as a sign of its "quickening pace of progress." In fact, "in two more generations," says its Minister of Agriculture, "Bolivia will be a tropical country." [13]

I pray the Alto Beni project will succeed and the two thousand families achieve a comfortable life. But I caution that the glowing publicity is all too premature and that planners of other countries should inspect the Alto Beni news releases, as the years proceed, not through the rosy glasses of hope but by the black and white statistics of actual achievement.

The planners in the halls of Guatemala City and Kabul also talk briskly of developing the Petén and the Helmand Valley into places for prosperous cattle ranching.

So let us discuss how to raise cattle where today there are no cattle. What I mean is, let us discuss if there are no cattle in an area today there must be a reason for it.

How do you raise cattle in an area that has already proven itself by empirical practice to be no good for them in the first place?

To illustrate this cattle subject, I move to Nicaragua.

The filing cabinets of Managua also have their happy plans for developing the undeveloped.

For instance, one target district is the Caribbean coastal strip where the geography is roughly similar to that of the Petén. The population there today is just as thin in number and as emaciated in body and as discouraged in mind as its counterpart in the Petén. And yet, I again emphasize, centuries of trial and error and great physical effort have already gone into seeking how to make a good economic living there. The formula, unfortunately, has yet to be found. The resources have yet to be found.

Another Nicaraguan target area, however, is a different kettle of geographical fish. This area, known as the Macantaca, is open, rolling country well away from the humid, rank coastland. The planners plan to make this a big cattle district.

I happened to be in Managua and was invited along for the ride when a couple of local businessmen flew a big-time Texan cattleman there on an inspection trip. The proposed deal was to initiate large-scale ranching, produce a cheap grade of beef and fly it to the United States. Specifically, the Texan and the local businessmen were to go into partnership with the Somoza family (which rules the nation as a satrapy). A hundred thousand Somoza-owned acres were to be turned over to the Texan for ranching if he came in on the project.

Need I add that this true son of the Lone Star already had itching ants in his pants at the prospect of a hundred thousand acres of anything, be it scrub, bush, or shifting sand.

As it turned out, the land was beautiful. The terrain had a slight roll and the scattered, parklike grouping of trees formed a fine open prairie. It must have been the same sort of sight that welcomed the first covered wagons as they broke through the rough forests of Arkansas and the swamps of Louisiana to reach the great open reaches of Texas. Here was no dry, blank plains country. It was true prairie.

And the forage grass was wonderful, not quite knee-high. Occasionally there was a pleasant pond of water. This was indeed Arcadia.

Why, then, were the few scattered cattle so dismally scrawny?

The Texan said they were the runtiest, awfulest cows he had ever seen. He said the trouble must be that the cattle were the wrong breed.

I pointed out that probably every known kind of cow had already been brought into this area at some time in order to get a herd started, beginning with the first Spanish *hidalgos.* I emphasized that these remnants of the fifty-seven varieties were evidence that something was basically wrong with the land itself or the local climate.

By coincidence – at least, I suppose it was coincidence – the Texan had arrived shortly after the beginning of the rainy season. We now all took a long, thoughtful look at the beautiful countryside.

I give you the cycle of the seasons throughout most of the tropics and subtropics, just as the Lord on high, for reasons known only to Himself, created them.

First, cast from your mind the illusion of twelve months of unending rain, or unending heat, or unending, palm-fringed paradise. It just isn't so.

Second, forget about the tropical deluges. At least a third of the land in Latin America, most of which falls within the tropics and subtropics, is classified as arid. India is more dry than wet, and so is Africa.

The cycle of the seasons, with variations round and about the various topographies, is strictly rainy and dry. The rainy season lasts generally five and a half months and the dry six and a half, plus or minus a month or so depending on your location.

The key to the cycle is this: in the rainy season *all* the rain comes, in the dry it just gets dustier and dustier and dustier. The economy of the tropics revolves around this basic, unalterable fact of life.

Here is how this cycle of two seasons affects, to give a clear-cut example, the cattle of the Macantaca area of Nicaragua.

The dry season is *really* dry. Streams dry up. There is no water for farming, no water for livestock and no grass. It is a bad time. By the end of the dry season the cattle are rattle-boned and barely survive until the rains come. A certain percentage die.

But the rains do come. The grass springs to life. The streams run full spate. Life revives for man and his beasts and his lands.

The grass is now excellent for feeding.

And our Texan arrives to look over his prospective cattle barony.

This Eden lasts, alas, for only a few weeks. The grasslands then become saturated, and where the drainage is poor often turn into swamps. It is not unusual to see cattle standing in a beautiful savanna in grass as "high as an elephant's eye," yet also standing in water three or four inches deep. As one friend said, "These tropical savannas would be great for cattle if the geneticists would only breed a web-footed cow. If they can't do that, then we will have to invent mud shoes for the beasties."

This succulent grass becomes, in a few weeks, rank and extremely coarse. It ceases to be good for cattle feed. Although it will keep them alive, it makes poor silage for use in the dry season.

Here, then, is the cycle of the seasons, and this is why the cattle we saw were so runty and this is why our Texan had second thoughts and went back to God's country and this is why the Macantaca area through all these centuries has never developed a viable economy. Many and many a man from the first *conquistador* has tried to make a go of this land. The dry and the rainy seasons and the bad drainage of the soil have defeated them every time.

I warn: think twice before spending money, time, sweat and tears on empty land. There is a reason, believe me, why that land is empty today. Spend the money instead on improving the agricultural areas that are already producing, but only at quarter-speed.

All the nations surrounding the Amazon Basin have their plans for its development. The Amazon, that gargantuan Petén, is basically a vast rain forest. Agronomists have already demonstrated that of all the soils of the world, that of a rain forest is perhaps the poorest nutritionally. The huge trees keep alive merely from the sun, from the excessive rainfall and from their self-made compost piles of leaves, which guard the soil's attenuated supply of nutrients. Clear away the trees and no useful crop will grow for more than a couple of years on the quickly exhausted soil – at least, research has not yet found a crop that will. Of course, I admit the amount of research on this problem has not yet amounted to a tinker's dam.

The Amazon Valley had settlers fifty years before Massachusetts was colonized. Yet it still cannot feed itself. Every year beans are shipped into the Amazon Valley from southern Brazil, although most people are in agreement that beans can be raised in the Amazon Valley. The question is, with how much difficulty? Obviously, it is cheaper to ship them in than to raise them.

> The adjective most often used to describe the interior of British Guiana is "vast." "Vast," too, are the natural resources; these are invariably "untapped." The impression created is that forests have simply to be cut down for a wealthy new state to grow. In fact, a good deal of the untapped interior rests on infertile white sand, and the problem of reafforestation has yet to be solved . . . The Rupununi [area of British Guiana] is not a land so much for the pioneer as for the romantic.[14]

Yet the wishful, airy statements of persons without agricultural training continue to delude both the officials of these countries of the Amazon Basin and also the public abroad. Typical, perhaps, is the following quotation from an interview with a geographer. As a geographer his eminence is unquestioned; as an agriculturist he appears gullible.

> QUESTION: Could the [Amazon] basin support more [population]?
>
> ANSWER: From the point of view of climate and soil, if you had Chinese in there, you could have millions of them. If they lived on the flood plain and used the alluvial soils for rice paddies cultivated by hand, there is nothing in the physical character of the land that wouldn't support them. But the Portuguese have not used the flood plain. All Portuguese agriculture, including our Ford plantations that

were in there in the '20's – all of these are in the hill country, back from the river, where the soil is miserably poor. At the present time, there are Japanese settlers raising pepper and jute, but again on miserable soil.

Q: Why is that?

A: It's absolutely against their tradition – Brazilian tradition – to use flat land. This is a curious thing.

Q: Are insects the cause?

A: No. The hilly lands I am talking about are not high enough to be free of insects. The cause is elusive. It's tradition. When a Brazilian farmer has a choice between flat land and sloping land, he always selects the slope.

Q: How much land would there be in these Amazon plains?

A: There would be enough to support another major nation on the flood plain of the Amazon. It remains almost entirely unused and empty. The river floods this flood plain during the rainy season, so you have to go in there and control the water.[15]

The cause of the Amazon's emptiness is not, unfortunately, elusive "tradition." If only the solution were that easy! A large proportion of Brazilians are today living as wretchedly as any group of Chinese. They would be happy to cultivate rice paddies in the Amazon flood plain by hand if this type of agriculture were feasible. The reason they do not is bad soil.

Khrushchev inaugurated with fanfare his "virgin lands" program in the arid steppes of Kazakhstan in 1954. In that year alone a hundred million acres of marginal lands there and in Siberia were converted to grain production.[16] Hitherto, the area, at least in Kazakhstan, had been utilized through the centuries as grazing lands for nomad horses and sheep.

The first couple of years production blossomed because the rainfall happened to be good, and then it lagged because the rainfall was not so good.

In 1960 Khrushchev decided to make a showpiece out of Kazakhstan's portion of the project. Tikhon Sokolov, one of the Communist Party's most successful agricultural production agents, was put in charge, and no expense was spared to make the showpiece a success. The latest reports from Russia, however, indicate that the whole agricultural program has foundered. Production in the Virgin Lands territory has declined for the past four years. Mr. Sokolov's showpiece in northern Kazakhstan is a flop, and Mr. Sokolov himself is out on his ear. He promised 11 million tons of grain in 1962 but the actual production was only 5.2 million tons. Farm machinery is going to pot, the milk yield has dropped, and grain production is so far off that thousands of animals have died for lack of fodder.[17]

If land is not in production, the simple willing it into an agricultural paradise is not enough!

In Lima I met up with a group of agriculturists from the University of North Carolina. They had just visited the "vast" areas on the eastern slopes of the Andes and were full of enthusiasm for the plans under way to increase the production of the area. "All that is necessary is to roll up the Peruvian sleeves, get to work, clear the jungle and plant it to an improved grass," one of them said. I asked if the area was heavily grazed now. "No, there are too few people there and not enough cattle." I asked how long this place had been grazed. "Not more than four or five years, maybe only three."

I am sure it *was* producing wonderful forage when they saw it. But half a dozen years from now? People have tried utilizing this area before and failed. Why are there so few people there now? There is a reason. The reason is not because the Peruvians failed in the past to roll up their sleeves and work.

I repeat my point in case you missed it.

A country's standard of living, its prosperity, its degree of backwardness, its hungriness, is tied irrevocably to its resources. A country is poor and hungry for the same reasons that a poor man is hungry. The poor man is hungry because he has no capital in the bank and a poor nation is hungry because it has no resources in its ground. A rich man is rich because his bank account is full and a rich nation is rich because its resources are bountiful.

Only through the proper development of its resources will a nation ever have an acceptable standard of living. In most hungry nations of the world, the only resource that can be developed economically is agriculture. Hence, my emphasis on agricultural development throughout this book.

For a nation to progress, her resources must produce more than her people can use. It is this *surplus* which will determine the prosperity of the nation. It is this excess which will buy the prosperity. Yet this future prosperity will probably be rather moderate because the resources, unfortunately, are moderate – whether agricultural lands, minerals, natural harbors or whatever.

A country must direct what reserves it has into making its resources produce this surplus.

Industrialization? That is frosting on the cake.

The empty, virgin lands? Leave them to the birds.

3

How Rich Are the Rich in Your Circle?

THOSE RICH FAMILIES in the undeveloped, backward countries out there where all that talk is going on about too much money in too few hands – are they truly as rich as all that?

The "fourteen families" of El Salvador, the "sixty" of Ecuador, the "thousand" of Iran, or whatever the number that has been popularized.

President Kennedy and his New Frontiersmen were vociferous about how Alliance for Progress money would curtail through social reform the power of the old-line families in Latin America, how the Alliance was to be a "self-help" program to help the *poor* people, in contrast to previous plans that, or so it was claimed, did little more than help the rich rich get richer, and how levelized living would now blossom for one and all.

Officials of the Johnson administration continue this as the official American policy.

Itinerant journalists and emotional travelers keep on bemoaning the existence of the rich out there in the impoverished nations of the world.

Yet how rich are these rich, really?

There are, of course, groups that the press rushes to play up as having unlimited funds while on their gay rounds in New York and the Riviera. In our generation they are represented by the oil sheikhs of the Near East, the São Paulo inflation playboys and . . . but there does not seem to be a third group.

Earlier generations included the Indian maharajahs, the sugar barons of Cuba, the cotton kings of Peru, the cattle lords of the Argentine and that shrewd group of Jews from Baghdad who made good in Shanghai. Generally, their days of glory lasted for a single generation or less, as, presumably, will also be true of the sheikhs and São Paulans.

And there is the dictator, or similar gang of politicians, temporarily in power – although "temporary" can mean twenty years. They often do hijack great wealth, but they prudently stash away their loot in the sympathetic, no-questions-asked bank vaults of Switzerland. This does, of course, further impoverish the nation, but that is not the point at issue here. These are not the ones under critical, emotional, socialistic fire.

No, the target is the old-line families who in popular imagination succeed by hook or by crook in maintaining a level of excessive wealth generation after generation.

The key word is "wealth." Yet who can define that elusive phantom? That which is dollars to one person is pennies to the next. The big-time money to the rent-hounded free-lance writer and to the salaried Washington official is not so much-a-much to the wheeler-dealer.

My own observation from living in many of these countries is that, *by American standards* objectively applied, the old families are really rather short on wealth. The power, yes, and the social prestige and the close ties of interlocking kinships, but not necessarily the hard money. It is for this reason I consider that Alliance for Progress officials and native socialists are following a false spoor in their efforts to flush out this so-called "concentration of wealth" and thereby alleviate the troubles holding back the countries from economic development.

A family I know well in one of the hungrier nations, whose name I intentionally omit, is a good case in point.

One son had been the personal aide of the former prime minister. A second son is now the private secretary of the current prime minister, the political opponent of the former one. Thus this family is firmly entrenched in the two major political parties. The youngest son is out of politics, but he told me the family is going to train him to be a communist, just in case.

He said it as a joke, but it would be in line with the clan's opportunistic history of exerting great influence within the circle of each government through many generations.

This family is recognized as one of the wealthiest in the nation. Yet the wife of the oldest son asked me for advice about where to send their boy to school in the United States. They already had one boy at Lawrenceville School and she said they simply could not afford the tuition fee for two children there; where could I suggest a cheaper school for him?

This is, I hazard, a typical example in almost any one of the poor countries of a family with great prestige, very real power politically and believed locally to be filthy rich; but it could not afford the extra $1000 a year that the Lawrenceville level of tuition required above that of the school where the second boy was sent.

The standard of living of Honduras is on a par with most of the hungry nations around the world. Thus, the following is pertinent. An official of the Central Bank told me that in the area of Tegucigalpa, the capital, there are only six or eight persons who have an annual income as high as $25,000. Considering what poor land and resources Honduras has and the small amount of cash circulating, it would, in fact, be surprising if the nation had a larger number of "rich" people. By American standards, need it be said, a $25,000 annual income is certainly not in the upper upper class.

The misconception of wealth in these hungry countries arises from various factors. Usually it is just a case of comparative values. Where most of the population live in grinding poverty, the few who do not stand out like lighthouses.

Another cause lies with the foreigners residing in these nations. They are fully alert to the prestige and power of these few families and they see the obvious evidence of supposed wealth in the big houses and the elegant life often lived in them.

Generally, it is easy to impress these foreigners, whether businessmen or diplomats. Their own backgrounds in industrialized America and even in Europe normally lack the servants and settled solidity of good living found at the level about which we are talking. Yet upstairs maids do not here mean big money in the bank.

Also relevant is the custom in these countries for a person to put his savings into land and into a fine house in the capital. Through generations of unsettled politics and coups d'etat this has been the safest investment. Hence there is the tendency to have a more elaborate home than would be owned in the United States by a family with comparable cash income.

I remember how impressed I was by the magnificent turn-of-the-century houses lining the Paseo de la Reforma in Mexico City when I first arrived there in 1932 (now office buildings have replaced them). All the wealth and glitter of the fabled luxury of the Porfirio Díaz era were epitomized here, when the great families had their *haciendas* in the hinterlands running full blast and the women wore only Paris dresses and the sons had English governesses and every few years the whole tribe went to Cannes for the season, or so it is said today.

But when I returned to the United States it was a shock to note that the houses lining Summit Avenue in St. Paul, Minnesota, built during the same generation, were just as large and lavish as those on the Reforma, and actually were about the same in number. The implication was that the stories of great wealth of those landed families of the Díaz regime were, apparently, exaggerated. Their real wealth, their cash in hand, must have been about the same as that of the burghers of this prosperous but not particularly distinguished city of St. Paul. Maybe the principal difference is that it is more romantic for an income to come from a twenty-thousand-acre *hacienda* in Jalisco than from a wholesale hardware company down on Third Street.

Also implied here is that the wealth and resources feeding into Mexico City in 1910 were, it appears, about equal to those of the trading area around St. Paul.

The term "family" is, of course, a helter-skelter kind of word. In the United States many have pointed out that increased security of living, both physical and financial, has been a major cause in the breakdown of the old tradition of a family supporting and protecting its several generations up to and including widowed cousins twice removed.

Such security does not yet exist in these hungry nations. Therefore, the large cohesive family of maiden aunts and the helpful cousin who is governor of a province is still a potent, viable unit. Collectively, such a family numbering (if it can, in fact, be numbered) a hundred souls may have considerable capital. However, as in a stock company, the money is divided. With each generation of highly procreative children the original source of the wealth becomes more diffused. The prestige of the name remains with the core of the family and the latent political power, but the cash has become lean.

In the capital city of nearly every one of these nations the middle-grade embassy employee who receives $12,000 a year, including assorted allowances, moves in the highest income circles. That is what makes the diplomatic life such a heady experience for the couple fresh from Nebraska or South Carolina. They usually envy the fifty-year-old mansion and the staff of servants and the accumulated evidences of wealth of Mr. Local Big Name around the corner, in contrast to their own cramped apartment which was the only vacant quarters they could find. Yet, likely as not, their neighbor would be ecstatically happy if he could count on $12,000 a year – with the extra built-in dividend that he would not have to share it with his brothers, cousins, grandparents-in-law, and so on. In fact, even deducting the American income tax rather than his own nominal tax would not change his views.

A West African friend from a family just as influential in today's new national government as it was in the old colonial days said to me, "Here we always have the crushing burden of relatives and hangers-on who keep most of us poor and drag us into debt. It is not that salaries are inadequate. It is that the African tradition of hospitality and mutual help has become a curse to the industrious."

Afghanistan has its coterie of powerful families, old in lineage and stable in landed property, although the lack of surnames makes it difficult for the outsider to catch on as to who belongs to which grandfather. For a week I once spent each evening with a distinguished, wonderfully cultured gentleman as he traced out for me, with graphs and genealogical lines, the family of which he was the accepted head. In the end I could only throw up my hands in front of all the confusion of blood lines, but it was obvious he had a key family member in just about everything going on in the country and also that he was related in varying degrees of consanguinity to almost everyone of influence including the royal house. And it was also apparent to me that he was probably pretty well strapped for funds, although we did not discuss that sordid, uncultured subject. His properties, extensive as they were in acreage, could not possibly bring in the income needed for all his family and in-law responsibilities. After all, Afghanistan is nearly all up-and-down mountains and stony, arid fields. It is a rough country in which to get a profit of a hundred dollars.

In Java in 1939 I was the youngest and lowest American officer in Batavia (Djakarta today). My annual salary was $2750 plus an allowance to cover rent. This was more than double what any of the men my age were receiving in the business houses and government offices of the city. Recently I met a Dutch friend from those days, a member of a family with old colonial roots. He said one of his clearest memories was his shock at learning of my fantastically high salary as a junior officer. He suddenly realized that if the American Government could pay such salaries, then all those stories he had heard of the country's stupendous wealth were really true after all.

Where the rich are not so rich, how very poor the rest must be.

If almost any minor American city can equal in number and affluence the few families who rate as local nabobs, what about the barefoot ones?

Ask any housewife with servants in a hungry country what her major problem is. Her answer most likely will be the stealing of food.

I once had a little weekend house in an old colonial village in the highlands of Central America. There had been silver mines there, but these had long since played out. Yet a couple of hundred souls still continued to live on somehow. To the outsider like me the charm and atmosphere of the old streets gave the feeling that here was the truly peaceful, idyllic life. It was idyllic for my weekends only because I brought my food with me and could relax on my balcony without having to worry about my next meal. Not so with the villagers. I paid my caretaker, who had the inappropriate name of Feliciano (Happiness), the going, acceptable wage. After a while he came to me and said, "I am sorry, I cannot keep my family alive on what you are paying me. You must pay me in food." Thereafter, although I continued to pay Feliciano the same wage, he walked down off the mountain to my home every Thursday to carry back to his family from my garden the produce that he needed.

A bureaucratic refinement of the American Government is the cost of living allowance. This grants to the American official living outside the United States a special allowance, in addition to his salary, to make up the gap between the higher cost of living at his foreign post and the lower cost prevailing in Washington, D.C. If the latter is higher, the official does not receive the allowance.

The procedure operates automatically through a complicated set of prices which the normal American family must pay in this foreign city in comparison to the cost of the same items in Washington. The long list includes medical care, laundry, a can of peaches, a pound of beef, a pair of socks, a shirt, a movie ticket, and so forth. The system is quite scientific and on the whole works effectively.

What is surprising is how many cities there are in the hungry countries that are considerably more expensive for an American to live in than Washington. Yet by American standards there is certainly nothing cheap about our nation's capital.

With Washington equal to 100 these sample cities have the following indices:[1]

Bamako, Mali	133
Bangkok, Thailand	110
Brazzaville, Congo Republic	142
Caracas, Venezuela	125
Conakry, Guinea	135
Dakar, Senegal	135
Kabul, Afghanistan	120
Mandalay, Burma	115
Moscow, USSR	120
Port-au-Prince, Haiti	110
Singapore	105
Tunis, Tunisia	105
Vientiane, Laos	125

When the itinerant tourist sees the obvious poverty around him, when he buys an alligator handbag for a ridiculously low price, when he finds the American resident is paying his cook $15 a month, he simply cannot believe any set of figures that show Washington to be *less* expensive. With such a low level of economy, much of it perhaps little beyond the barter stage, how can the State Department figures be accurate?

Aside from special cases of economic imbalance due to political troubles, financial irresponsibility and similar factors, the reason for the high cost of living is that the American is trying to live like an American in a country that cannot support such high standards. In fact, the country completely lacks most of the appurtenances now taken for granted as part of the American standard of living. This applies not only to food but also to clothing, housing, education, medical care and the rest. Most of the things the American uses while in the hungry nation are imported at prices that must include such items as transportation costs and high tariffs.

In reverse, if the government worker in Washington, say Grade 8 in the Civil Service ($5885 to $7370) had to pay the same percentage of his salary for food as his opposite number in Dakar (19 per cent for the American versus maybe 80 per cent for the Senegalese), then indeed there would be few appliances in his house and only one suit of clothes for his back and no car at the door.

"The culture of a people is inversely proportional to the time and effort required for their subsistence." [2]

Rich people and poor people. Rich countries and poor countries. The bountifulness of the food on the table is as good a criterion as any to show up the two ends of the economic pole.

In the United States one farmer now feeds twenty-six people. Food is so cheap it is no longer the number one expenditure for the average American family, the first time this has ever happened in the world's history (housing is now the principal cost for Americans).

Only fifteen years ago the average American family spent 26 per cent of its after-tax income on food. Today it spends 19 per cent. In Great Britain the corresponding figure is 30 per cent. In Italy it is 45 per cent; in Russia 60 per cent.[3]

Yet for the United States, at least, its present figure of 19 per cent will soon be out of date. "Technological developments of the magnitude projected by researchers may make it possible for the U.S. consumers to spend as little as 12–15 per cent of their income for food within a decade or two."[4]

In Guatemala, although corn represents 70 per cent of the national diet, corn costs frequently two or three times more than in the United States. Again, this is due primarily to the comparative productiveness of the land. The average yield per acre in Guatemala is only 11 bushels, whereas in Iowa 160-bushel yields are not unheard of. Furthermore, far more man-hours are needed to produce the 11 bushels than the 160.

I was living in a small town in Guatemala, thirty miles from the capital, when Castillo Armas in 1954 overthrew the communist-oriented regime of Arbenz. It was an exciting experience to be isolated there with my children, what with the shooting at my doorstep and the hiding in my house of Guatemalan friends hunted by the communist-type police.

In retrospect, I have always felt the role popularly attributed to the American Central Intelligence Agency (CIA) in this affair has been overestimated, despite the oft-repeated accusations of hostile Latins and CIA's smug, but silent, acquiescence to the charges. It is difficult for me to accept that Castillo Armas could "invade" Guatemala from Honduras with a ragtag "army" of about a hundred and sixty men and overthrow Arbenz's well-equipped forces.

A factor overlooked in the press reports of the day, and since then, was that the price of food in the months preceding the revolution in June had been rising drastically. Hunger was cutting into the bellies of the Guatemalans more than normally. The cost of corn had doubled the previous month. When Castillo Armas and his hundred and sixty men crossed the border the people were in no mood to support the Arbenz government and neither were the armed forces. What did they have to fight for? Their families were hungry and everyone was disgusted with his impoverished lot.

Thus, the *timing* of Castillo Armas, though probably by coincidence, was apt. To me, the nationwide high cost of corn was the secret of the success of the invasion by this scraggly revolutionary army.

The duties of the American agricultural attaché in the embassies around the world, as defined by the Congress, are to determine markets for United States farm crops. Nevertheless, the wise ambassador should have him study local crop decreases and climatic variations in order to predict discontent arising from food shortages. The only time I have observed this utilization of the agricultural attaché, however, was while I was stationed in Moscow towards the end of the war and Ambassador Averell Harriman considered his attaché, Dr. Lewis Michael, to be one of his chief sources of knowledge of the probable political disquiet of the masses throughout Russia.

In the hungry nations the rich are not rich and the poor are destitute.

Yet the alien writers and the alien officials, and also the local demagogues, so often condemn the "concentration of wealth" as causing the economic inertia, the rigid class lines, the lack of mass education, the violence of the political "outs" toppling the "ins."

Unfortunately, these observers are looking merely at results, not basic causes.

The basic, unvarnished, unemotional reason is that poor countries have poor resources. The resources from which stem the national wealth are scant.

In an Iowa town of, say, 25,000 population it is rare not to find at least one or two persons who can be classified as millionaires.

In all Honduras with a population of 1,900,000 it is difficult to find a dozen persons with an income of as much as $25,000.

Yet the spread of wealth, the pyramid, in Iowa and Honduras is probably about the same. It is just a difference between a big, rich pyramid and a little, picayune pyramid. And the difference is in direct proportion to the comparative resources of the two regions.

Nevertheless, it is the few rich in the backward countries who are criticized and blamed for throwing off balance the economic and social stability of the nation. Hence the efforts, both by Alliance for Progress policies and by national regulations, to bulldoze down this little pyramid to the level of the surrounding rocky plain. Unfortunately, the empirical record of the socialistic experiments in the undeveloped countries indicates this does not solve the nation's economic problems. The paucity of local resources remains the controlling factor.

By doing away with these old-line families a stable element is eliminated. As the nation totters forward to catch up with the twentieth century it eliminates what is probably the only educated class and the only group accustomed to provide leadership in economic ventures. All that this levelizing seems to do is to replace the educated, traditional entrepreneurs with a new government bureaucracy where, too often, a new sort of structure of wealth and privilege rises up – but it is a structure that is itself knocked down with each change of government.

Instead of a socialistic bulldozer, there is needed in those few, very few, countries where the entrenched families may indeed be a curb to the economy merely the institution of sensible laws, such as a proper income tax properly enforced, regulations compelling landowners to cultivate their lands with modern methods, tariffs prohibiting the import of unnecessary luxuries like automobiles, sport clothes, liquor and the like, plus restrictions preventing the use of foreign exchange for unnecessary travel abroad.

Where the so-called wealthy families do, in fact, need disciplining, the foregoing restrictions will be true hardships on them. Yet the restrictions will not do away with the usefulness of the only class at hand to lead forward the development of the nation's resources and the development of the nation's economy.

I offer the opening lines of a number sung by the currently popular Kingston Trio:

> They're rioting in Africa,
> They're starving in Spain,
> There's hurricanes in Florida,
> And Texas needs rain.
> The whole world is festering with unhappy souls . . .[5]

The woes of the world are many, yea, they are many indeed. In these chapters I do not concern myself with the troubles of the comfortable parts of the world. I limit myself to the hungry nations, and now, forthwith, go beyond their chief worry: the next meal. If they are to progress they must produce more than they themselves consume. This excess is the only source of capital for their development. Before blaming the local rich for the nation's lack of capital, ask: How rich are they, really? How much extra surplus do they have? Probably not enough to make any significant difference in the economy.

Ask, next: Where are the nation's resources to provide a national surplus, an excess, to provide capital?

Part II

4

Common Sense Can Move Mountains: Actions a Hungry Nation Can Itself Initiate

HERE IS NOW a set of basic hypotheses, or guidelines, for reducing the despair and privations of a hungry nation. They do not form a program full of details and specifics. They are merely guidelines suggesting the way forward and admitting that for each nation the rocky road will be different.

The goal, nevertheless, is the same: to lead the people upward to a reasonably comfortable level of twentieth-century living.

The course of action to achieve this goal is based on a single precept: make the nation's resources produce more than the people themselves use.

Only with the production of surpluses can living standards improve.

All the nation's efforts, all its capital reserves and foreign exchange, all its internal and international policies must be devoted single-mindedly to this one project: make the nation's resources produce surpluses.

Surpluses mean savings. No surpluses can accumulate if the nation's earnings, derived out of the resources, are frittered away on imported luxuries like foreign clothes and canned fruit or are squandered on stadiums, public buildings and status hotels.

The hungry nation must realize it is hungry not because of assumed mismanagement by its leaders, not because of alleged meddling by its neighbors, not because of past indifference of colonial rulers. The nation is hungry because its resources are limited. Its resources do not permit the relatively luxurious life that the rich nations today enjoy out of their rich resources.

Yet each nation does have *some* resources. Otherwise the area would be truly uninhabited. These resources must be developed and developed fully. And the increased income thereby earned must be saved and wisely plowed back into further development, not casually spent on this or that. The income must be *saved,* as a private person saves. The individual who does not save remains poor all his life. The same applies to nations.

When the citizens realize their standard of living is based on their income as generated out of the national resources – and not based on the things they see in store windows or bazaar stalls – then that country is well on the road to progress. From such a foundation all other factors of community well-being ought to develop naturally.

Paraguay. Uganda. Nepal. Sierra Leone. Albania. Jordan. Mongolia. Algeria. Haiti. Bulgaria. Nicaragua. Jamaica. Sudan. Somalia. Ceylon. Etc.

These diverse sovereignties have several items that link them together at the bottom of backwardness. Each has a vote in the United Nations as a full member of the club, although in a proper gentlemen's club one or two would be posted for non-payment of dues. Each is, in the new language, an emerging nation, although some, I note, are in the second century of puberty, making them rather long in the tooth for the tolerance and kindnesses extended to adolescents. Each is a mass of rising and excitable expectations that, at least in most cases, twist political and economic problems out of any saneness. Each has an exploding population that absorbs like a sponge whatever accumulation of capital their resources do develop. And in each a large proportion of the populace is undernourished and desperately hungry for a comfortable life, for the modern life.

Also, each is discouragingly poor in resources.

Each, I suppose, has a five-, seven-, or some-year plan produced with much bureaucratic labor, with or without the help of foreign aid people, to guide hopefully the nation's onward and upward surge to modernity and the abode of the blessed.

All such plans that I have seen will, I state flatly, miss the target. And by missing the target they will dissipate the capital and energies of the nation. Therefore, they will be retrogressive.

I propose they be tossed into a dusty filing cabinet and the following guidelines substituted.

If my comments here and elsewhere sound opinionated, I can only admit that I am impatient and contemptuous of the shotgun effect of most economic programs now on the planning boards; the buckshot goes every which way instead of concentrating all money and energies strictly on the specific target: to develop the nation's resources and thereby build a base for raising the standard of living.

GUIDELINE 1

Don't Wait for Political Stability.

Always heard in the hungry nation is the lament, voiced equally by nationals and foreigners, that nothing can be done until a degree of political stability is achieved. Such an attitude perpetuates a hopeless, do-nothing economic policy, while all hands continue centering their attention on politics.

Certainly, instability is the hallmark of a hungry, underdeveloped country. It is unstable financially and unstable socially. Any turn of events may set off a reaction that can upset whatever balance of living has been achieved temporarily.

It is wrong, however, to assume that a low standard of living, or, rather, a low level of modern comforts, is in itself the primary cause of political instability. Contemplate for instance, the political troubles, but not economic, of France in the last half-century, including all those newsreel shots of prosperous bourgeois throwing rocks at gendarmes on the Champs Elysées.

In the hungry countries the typical jockeying between various groups, so often erupting into street riots and periodically into a full-scale revolutionary donnybrook, is due basically to economic factors, not political – although I grant the two are everywhere inextricably mixed together.

Every citizen with ambition in these countries is acutely aware that the best opportunities to make money, the surest source of prestige, and the direct route to influence and power lie within the government. Those will be the rewards when the "outs," by fair means or foul, topple the "ins." In the comfortable nations, on the other hand, where stability rests on a broad base of developed resources, there are many avenues to money, prestige and power. Often, government position is the least effective route.

So, since you cannot get rid of instability in the hungry nation, forget about it and go ahead with the means at hand to increase present stores of wealth and to generate new ones out of the area's resources. Stability in political development may, we can all hope, be a dividend that results naturally from a sensible organization of available resources.

It's a grand asset, this political stability, if you have it; if you don't, get going anyway. Light your candle, stop cursing the darkness.

Guideline 2

Face Up to Reality.

I was traveling across Jordan through one of the country's few sort-of-pleasant agricultural spots. Elsewhere that day we had been in a desert, empty except for a few dilapidated camels and sheep and starving shepherds. It had been a desolate, hopeless countryside. The Jordanian city boy with me, perhaps overcome by the sudden greenery now around us, said, "You know, this is the richest country in the world. We have the finest agricultural land in the world, raise the best grapes and apples in the world. It is only because our government is corrupt that we are poor."

This Jordanian, and all the others like him in these countries, typically load the blame for their poverty on their government, on the school system, on poor health, on the distant

Americans. Shifting the fault to such emotional areas is, of course, an easy exercise whereby the reality of the country's lack of resources can be ignored.

These citizens must realize that Allah has not endowed their nation as bountifully as He did the rich nations, that their nation is *hungry* because He, for some reason, has granted to it only a paucity of resources.

Therefore, a primary step that the nation must take on the long road upward to the better life is for the leaders, the school teachers, the editors, all the populace to look in the mirror each morning and say, "We are a poor country. We are poor because we do not have the rich resources of a rich country. But we *can* improve conditions over what they are now. So how do we get started? How do we make proper use of the resources we do have? Let's begin by . . ."

GUIDELINE 3

Create a Minister of Resources.

This official, on whom the entire success of the nation's development will rest, should have cabinet rank and be second only to the president or prime minister in importance.

He should not be a lawyer. Nor an army colonel. Nor an obstetrician. Since resources are chiefly agricultural, that should be his background. Do not rely on an untrained person to do a specialist's job. Success will be based mostly on his ability to talk with experts and to coordinate their separate fields, plus the knack of maintaining public and political support. Thus, ideally, our Minister of Resources should also be skilled at getting funds out of parliament and at propagandizing the public.

Unfortunately, as every employer knows, the ideal man is an ideal never found. So he taps the best man available and tells him to get on with the job. Let us try to install in office, however, an agriculturist who at least knows what the talking is all about.

GUIDELINE 4

Don't Waste Time Making Surveys.

Now to work. The new Minister of Resources is sworn into

office with the panoply of ceremony his importance merits. He has, hopefully, the backing of the politicians currently in power, plus the enthusiasm of the country as a whole.

His first inclination will be – and every new aid administrator gets the same fever – to organize a survey which tots up the known resources of the country, where the minerals are, and the forests, and the shrimp beds, how much water power, etc., etc.

This can be, as a matter of fact, a facile way to gain time before coming to grips with serious decisions, but it is not necessary for starting the job at hand. For one thing, various surveys are probably already waiting in the files for someone to use, or pertinent surveys are available from international organizations. The Food and Agricultural Organization of the United Nations has over four hundred detailed reports from their specialists working in Latin America alone. Some that I have read are excellent, but it is rare indeed for any official of a Latin American nation actively to make use of them. And most surveys around the world receive the same fate.

Guatemala has the most complete soil survey of any country in Latin America. Of all the types of surveys, this is probably the most valuable, because it indicates which acreages can be used for agriculture and how they can be used. Yet I have never heard that any planner has ever used this survey, which is now thirteen years old.

So forget about the surveys. Everyone else does. And don't worry about the land which is not being farmed and the mineral deposits which are not being mined – if the land could be profitably farmed at the present time, farmers would be doing it; if the ores could be profitably mined, concessionaires would be competing to do it.

Adopt this philosophy as your creed: the resource you are going to develop is the resource now in use.

Guideline 5

List Your Resource Problems.

So here is the first order to your staff: make a list of the *problems* responsible for the low yield of each type of resource now in use and the *problems* hampering full productivity.

The staff consists, ideally, of experts in the various production routines of the nation. Nevertheless, don't wait for such an ideal staff to be built up – especially as experts are in mighty short supply in the nation. It does not take an expert to listen to a rice farmer tell about his difficulties, or a tuna fisherman, or a logger. All it takes is a good listener; rather, an intelligent listener with a notebook in hand.

The Minister will have to steel himself, I warn, against the type of complaint which most farmers and producers will call "problems." These complaints will be centered around the cost of marketing, the cost of shipping on poor roads, the high cost of gasoline, the lack of storage facilities, the need for price supports to allow competition in the world market, the closing of frontiers against competitive products, and so on. By giving too much credence to this type of man-made, often temporary problem, the Minister will overlook the basic fact that the enemies of low production costs are the poor soil, poor climate, poor seed, poor insect control.

When the Minister learns that a rust disease in corn is reducing yields, he can turn this problem over to plant pathologists (probably brought in under contract as explained in a later chapter). When he knows there is an insect attacking the cacao, he can turn the problem over to entomologists. When he knows that the rains frequently come too late to allow an early planting of rice, he can turn a team of plant breeders loose on finding an improved, early maturing variety. When his fishermen cannot find shrimp beds that are known to be there, he can bring in experts to show them how. The low fertility in cows. The high mortality in chickens.

Does this sound obvious? So obvious that of course everyone already knows what should be done? So obvious that all this would have been done long ago if it had been possible?

Don't fool yourself! This is probably the first time anyone in a high position in the capital city of any of these hungry nations has actually faced up to cataloguing the problems hindering productivity and doing something about them.

GUIDELINE 6

Face Up to a Time Lag of Several Decades.

As for the time lag, each development project should be drawn up on a two-generation basis. If the public cannot let itself think further than a soft five-year "improve-everything" plan, then the intellectual leadership of the country has failed to do its job of leading.

I suppose the eager-beaver propaganda official will now rush to the microphone with the appeal, "Sacrifice Now So Your Children Will Have the Good Life." Actually, I wonder if such a slogan, iterated so fulsomely in Russia during the massacres and artificial, political famines of the '30's, is really necessary for adults in a democracy. They know full well the tragedy of their present plight. They will sense, at least usually they will do so, when their leaders are sincere in offering plans that will produce, some day in the future, higher standards of living. The realization that at last, after all these years of inertness, practical plans have been formed and action begun should provide enough stimulation to carry along public support during the initial stages until results do finally begin to emerge.

The main problem, obviously, is to restrain the emotional ones who declare it is impossible to wait years for visible results, who shout that the good things must be presented to them right away this very minute. This, it seems to me, is primarily a political problem, often the "outs" versus the "ins."

For a while in Washington, I was involved in promoting economic ideas to make the Baghdad Pact, the Middle East military alliance with which the United States maintained economic ties, more widely supported by the people in the member states of Turkey, Pakistan, Iran and Iraq. It was a rather thankless task, inasmuch as the foot-dragging was in Washington (for political reasons), not out there in the middle of the Cold War blasts. Then, in 1958, the communist-supported Kassem overthrew the Iraq Government via some of the most barbaric rioting that even our violent century has witnessed, and the pro-West king and the prime minister, Nuri al Said, were killed. Aside from putting the kibosh on the Baghdad Pact, although perhaps only temporarily, the riot-spawned new regime also killed off the nation's carefully prepared development plans that were in steady progress toward fruition. Iraq has a huge income from its oil fields. Here, of all countries, it ought to be possible to make long-range plans and to hope that living standards and modern comforts and an abatement of hunger can be achieved. Yet the stormy winds of politics have not allowed this. In retrospect, it is easy to point to the personality failings and misjudgments of the old prime minister, Nuri. Yet the basic failure must be due to the immaturity of the Iraqi citizenry themselves, who allowed the "outs" to poison the air with their rantings that all progress, all luxuries, a car for everybody, two chickens in the pot, must come right away without anyone being inconvenienced by waiting, by working, by saving.

Few people are so proud of their past (ten centuries ago) as the Arab people. If now, with these sudden oil bonanzas, they are unable to use the income for proper development, then surely a generation from now the rest of the world will regard them as the most contemptible of races. So far, there is little indication the Arabs are organizing their countries on a long-range basis so that hunger and misery will be tempered in the years to come; much of the oil income is being dissipated on quick nonsense. Yet the Arab wailing for more free money from the aid countries is ever louder. It is, of course, anybody's guess how long the cornucopia of oil income and of free aid income will continue to flow.

As for the time lag involved in development, think of the Pan American Highway. Here, if anything can be, is a popular, easy-to-grasp project. Since the United States has been willing to pay for most of the construction costs, one would think that the local governments could have resolved the internal political and external treaty details with ease. Not so. Not so.

I drove from Mexico City to Texas in 1932, when that section of the highway was under construction; it was only one dirt lane wide, and passing an oncoming bus was a ticklish affair considering the hairy drop-offs down the mountainsides. At Valles, the only town of importance in two days' travel, there was no hotel and I slept on a billiard table – after the local sports had folded for the night. On arrival in Monterrey I bought a Mexican magazine with a fine article forecasting the delights of driving to Panama almost any time now. All during the '30's came the magazine stories on driving to Panama "pretty soon," and also during the '40's and in the '50's. Finally, in 1963, at last the articles say that *now* the average family car with the average type of driver can safely drive to Panama. Note the time lag of three decades.

The complex and trouble-ridden Helmand Valley project in Afghanistan has already been mentioned. The latest government report to come to my attention about it contains this paragraph: "In looking back it is easy to see errors and perhaps the greatest error of all by both U.S. and Afghans has been that too much was expected too fast. Experience around the world as well as in the U.S. shows that such projects take from 20 to 30 years to reach their full potential." [1]

During the span of life of the development plans initiated by the Minister of Resources the government will be changed many times. Thus, the vital factor must be a hard core of intellectual leadership able to prevent sabotage, in the name of political expediency, of the initial stringent plans. An altruistic hope? Of course. Yet the public usually, not always – as Iraq demonstrates – can spot the phony appeal when the subject is as close to them as raising their wretched living conditions, provided they understand the facts involved. India would seem to illustrate that a nation can maintain its development plans despite the temptation to yield to extraneous pressures.

To repeat. It is up to the aforesaid intellectual leadership to see the public does understand the facts of development. But the leadership must itself face up to a time lag of several decades.

GUIDELINE 7

Develop Your Resources Develop Your Resources Develop Your Resources.

This theme is the anvil on which the nation's progress must be forged.

In my use of the term "resources" I keep emphasizing primarily agriculture, and also forestry and fisheries. Mining always seems to be able to take care of itself. When a deposit of marketable ore is discovered, or rumored to be discovered, or it is faintly breathed that maybe ore might be somewhere about, a peculiar but numerous breed of foreigners will zero in. Arriving will be qualified and unqualified mining men anxious for concessions and otherwise glad to help the local leaders develop the new mineral find. So let the foreign expert develop them for you with his money, while you turn your attention to other things. Don't, however, overlook this truism I have heard several mining men repeat, such as, recently, an aluminum company official: "There is no shortage of bauxite in the world. There is only a shortage of good governments with whom we can deal in order to get out the bauxite."

If the country discovers, on the other hand, a new way to utilize nitrogen fertilizer in the production of rice, nothing, but nothing, happens in the way of outsiders rushing in to help develop the new process. It is up to the nation's leaders to do their own developing and to locate abroad whatever advisers are needed.

So if you have minerals, use them to the hilt, and also any other special resources like strategic canals, ski runs and pink sand beaches.

Yet even the country that has such assets must fall back on its agriculture as the only resource that will raise the standard of living of all citizens. Nearly every economic transaction in the economy is traceable, in every nation, to an agricultural transaction.

The essence of agriculture is that it means tilling at regular intervals the same piece of resource. It is a continuing, ever renewing routine — until the resource is destroyed through faulty methods of tilling.

Thus far everyone, presumably, has been nodding his head sagely in agreement that of course resources must be developed; of course that is the road to prosperity; of course modern methods must be used.

But what methods? It is at this point that suddenly there is a surfeit of impassioned advisers each advocating his special techniques for saving the world. The Keynesian wants to borrow. The road expert wants to build fine highways. The banker wants more lending facilities. The tax man wants to jivvy with the imposts. The industrialist wants to do everything under a corrugated iron roof with happy, cheap laborers happily toiling. The socialist wants to level everyone down. The capitalist wants everyone but himself to keep their cotton-picking fingers off. The public health man wants no disease anywhere, not even a corn on the little toe. The educator wants everyone to study and study like the very dickens.

And so it goes.

Most of these pressure groups I consider in later chapters. Any or all of their methods may work fine in the comfortable countries. But in Dahomey? Syria? Burma?

Guideline 8

Set Up a Productive Land Utilization Program.

This does not mean, great God, land reform! Agitation for land reform, in one shape or another, is common throughout all the hungry nations. Therefore, the new Minister of Resources is going to have to cope with this agitation. Unless his philosophy in this emotional area is sound, the result can be catastrophic. Perhaps more economic atrocities have been committed in the name of land reform around the world than under any other single slogan.

Nevertheless, the people are in the throes of this agitation. It cannot be ignored.

A sound philosophy in this respect might be as follows: the Minister of Resources, who has dedicated himself to the development of the nation's resources, must look on land reform, land utilization, rural rehabilitation, or whatever the term may be, as a means of *increasing the productivity* of the land. His goal is to make sure that each individual piece of land produces its maximum, regardless of who owns it and regardless of who farms it. If this means redistribution of that piece of land, then that is what he should favor in this particular instance. If it does not mean redistribution, then he must somehow sell his point of view to the people and quiet their agitation.

I later devote a section of this book to my views on land reform problems and offer a plan for peaceful redistribution of the nation's land which should lead to maximum utilization and productivity. Preparing such a program and inaugurating it will obviously require a period of time during which, we all hope, the agitators will relax and wait for its publication.

The preliminary job of the Minister of Resources, therefore, must be to instill confidence among those who own the land that any redistribution will be done fairly and gradually, and at the same time convince those who are clamoring for land that a just program will eventually be installed. This is obviously a complex psychological job, but it is largely a matter of persuading all levels of the population that this reorganization of agricultural land will be both effective and peaceful, both humane and honest, and that the land redistribution plan will increase production, thus lowering the cost of living for everyone – helping all, not just those few lucky enough to get a new piece of land.

Guideline 9

To Industrialize, Begin with a Little Acorn.

That mania to industrialize! The citizens of the hungry countries have it like the rabies. Their economic aid advisers are equally afflicted with this emotional frothing. Industrialization, all, all agree, is the life force, the vital fluid, the wonderful mystery that so miraculously will produce the fabled life of the Champs Elysées right out here under the coco palms.

Enviously, they stare hypnotized at the sprawling plants in the United States and Europe and the supertrained men running around within their innumerable specialties. Yet common sense should tell the leaders and especially their foreign aid advisers that the undeveloped nation is poorly fitted economically, physically and mentally for the type of big factories everyone is yearning for.

Parallel with this absence of common sense is the forgetfulness that many important manufacturing processes are actually very simple and often require only commonplace materials prepared by unsophisticated workers. The know-how for making pickles is really not so mysterious, but nobody would ever guess it by visiting a super pickle plant with its assembly lines, belts, and hundreds of employees doing the oddest things.

What the small nation needs is not the assembly line, many-engined factory. It needs merely a *shop* using the simplest tools.

What it needs, and all that it needs for many years to come, is a village type of industry pattern that can lead to the manufacture of items for the local markets and thereby reduce the necessity for using foreign exchange – and can accomplish this without artificial rigging of special tariff concessions. The goal is to produce items for sale on the local markets more cheaply than similar imported items.

Sometimes there can also be included the first step in the processing of local raw materials before they are shipped abroad, but this depends on a juxtaposition of favorable economic factors that, unfortunately, does not exist in many of the hungry countries.

Guideline 10

Stop Using Government Funds to Aid Private Industry.

The fate of private industry under this program will be: no government money. Private enterprise will be left to its own devices to get a new can opener factory built and running, or the textile plant, or, if ever, that steel mill.

Government help can, however, come in the form of special tax write-offs, a workable labor code, and, if absolutely necessary, a five-year temporary protective tariff. These are major aids, and if a businessman cannot succeed with this help, either his project is commercially unsound or he is a poor executive.

Money, the cash, the government will not provide. It will hang on to its hard-earned tax money and it will keep its little store of foreign exchange. This cold cash will be channeled only into items which will support the government's resource development program, such as a nitrogen fixation plant for fertilizer, and items which are too big or too risky for private business to handle. Whether such a nitrogen plant should be wholly government-owned and state-operated, or leased as a concession, or financed by a joint stock company is left to the exigencies of the moment.

But that proposed cement factory? Considering the initial cost, would it not be better to import the rather small amounts of cement that the government requires? If private business has expanded to the point of needing a cement plant, let private business build it, not the government.

I intentionally use a cement factory as an example because it represents the type of industrial project which the Minister of Resources should recognize as dissipating his objectives. The items that require large amounts of cement, such as paved highways, government and office buildings, and apartment houses, are not directly oriented to resource development. Thus, leave it to the private entrepreneur to tackle the cement plant.

A new telephone system? A frill, gentlemen, a frill. When there is enough private money floating around to support dial phones in decorator colors, private money will be delighted to provide. Of such is the essence of capitalism.

Guideline 11

Cut Out Nonessentials.

A nonessential, Confucius doth say, is something that is not necessary. It may be nice to have, but when all is said and done you can go your way without it.

A first job of the new Minister of Resources is to go through the budgets, both national and provincial, and strike off every nonessential – or rather, to set up a hopeful time program of getting the public (i.e., the politicians) to support him as he strikes off every politically entrenched nonessential.

For him the definition of a nonessential is anything that uses up the nation's limited capital without generating new capital, which is to say making the resources produce more.

Public health programs? Most are nonessential.

New roads? They are nonessential unless *present* traffic, not future, absolutely requires them.

Sending students abroad? Sometimes yes, often no.

Embassies?

Automobiles instead of buses?

The army? The navy? The air force?

Imported canned fruit cocktail instead of local mangoes?

The Minister of Resources and his staff must, obviously, play it by ear in determining when public opinion will support the elimination of a nonessential, such as the beloved canned fruit or the army or a proposed paved road. Unhappily, the law of nature can only be: no sacrifices, no higher living standards.

I wish a foolproof Gallup Poll formula could be devised to inform the Minister of Resources as to when the public will support him or when the public needs more propaganda juicing.

The only advice I can offer in place of $E=mc^2$ is the wisdom of the ages: "Faint heart never won fair lady."

Guideline 12

Cut Public Works to the Bone.

Regardless of political pressures from various groups, every public works item should be eliminated unless it definitely contributes to the development of the nation's resources. A public work that generates new wealth from the present stock of resources is all to the good, but give it a tough examination before granting a passing mark.

Let's look at that dam, for instance, that everyone says is going to produce cheap electricity – and it probably will. Upon examination, will this dam generate, however, new local capital or even bring in new capital from abroad?

The cheap electricity may merely mean that the people will now have more electric light bulbs in their homes, or have electricity where before they used oil lamps. The need to buy imported bulbs, wiring, switches and so on can actually lower the standard of living by diverting foreign exchange from projects designed to develop new sources of capital.

New electricity will not generate new wealth unless it is geared to resource development, such as reducing the cost of mining or the cost of fertilizer, or stimulating new artisan shops and the processing of local products.

Cheap electricity is a pleasant thing for any nation, but food in the stomach is better. Food is not produced via wasting resources on luxuries like electric light bulbs of even fifteen-watt capacity. Any individual, including whole cities, can get along without electricity if necessary.

And I speak here personally from the chore of living in various "exotic" locales with only candles at hand, plus, sometimes, those balky, imported Coleman lamps that endlessly consume, like Moloch, imported mantles which only the rich can afford.

An electrical plant with power lines and wiring into each room and grass shack is an expensive, extraordinarily expensive, affair, even with a percentage of the poor secretly tapping their lines into the outlets of the rich – or are you familiar with this common fact of living in the hungry areas?

Note that I do not argue against constructing the dam and creating new sources of electricity. I do argue that the new, so very expensive electricity be evaluated *not* on the basis of the comfort or pride of the region's inhabitants but strictly on the basis of the probability that the area's resources can be developed more profitably – profitably, that is, after the huge costs of the new dam and the new power lines and the new wiring have been deducted.

Guideline 13

Cut the Nonsense Out of Education.

A hungry nation cannot afford elaborate educational programs. Yet today each such nation has embedded into its life many school courses and many institutions – such as, probably, a useless national university – that merely drain away money from more valuable educational chores. Any hard look by the Minister of Resources at the country's educational system will expose the units that can be eliminated until such time as the country's prospering will warrant their revival.

How much education can a community afford to give its young? What kind of education will best produce the men needed to pull the country out of its pit of misery? These are questions to be answered coldly and objectively without sentiment and without nonsense.

Education along lines of self-contentement is a luxury it cannot afford. Only the comfortable country can prate, "Let's give everyone a high school education." "Let's be sure everyone has six years of science." "Let's develop the whole child."

GUIDELINE 14

Forget International Prestige.

The things about which a citizenry can go overboard in the name of national pride are a constant amazement to the traveling foreigner. Governments of new nations often dissipate their few resources because they are anxious to prove, both to foreigners and to their own citizens, how important, how up-and-coming they are. Hence the foolishnesses of deficit-laden national airlines, showy hotels, and sumptuous embassy buildings abroad, all eroding large amounts of the limited national funds away from developing their resources. For its embassy to the United Nations, Mali purchased an estate in the New York suburbs for $300,000. Indonesia paid $350,000 for one of the great show houses of Washington for its embassy.

"In Tanganyika, President Julius Nyerere has issued a presidential order to 'stamp out the disease of pomposity,' which will take some stamping out, particularly in Africa, where the President of the Ivory Coast has just built a $10 million marble palace and the President of Liberia has appropriated $12 million to build himself one." [2]

At a meeting of the Foreign Aid Appropriations Subcommittee of the House of Representatives, the testimony disclosed a yacht presented to Emperor Haile Selassie of Ethiopia in the guise of foreign aid. The yacht was a converted seaplane tender that had been mothballed. To remodel the ship into a status worthy of a royal yacht and to train a crew of Norwegians (!) had cost the American Government $3,100,000.

A committee member asked, "Are we going to have to furnish a flagship for every ruler around the world now? This gets to be a matter of pride."

The laconic reply of the foreign aid officials giving the testimony was merely they had not received any more of such requests "yet." [3]

That the American taxpayer feels it politically advisable to give the Ethiopian emperor this yacht is not of importance here—such regal gifts have been part of intergovernment relations since the beginning of time. The point I make is that the hungry Ethiopian taxpayer must now annually pay for the upkeep and operation of this vessel, including those Norwegians, in the name of national pride, of international prestige.

Guideline 15

Put the Military in Their Place.

A gendarmerie or a constabulary to maintain law and order is one thing. The military is quite a different mulligan stew. One of the first items each new nation usually does, after shucking the apron strings of colonialism, is to create generals, first lieutenants and military attachés, all in the name of national pride. And the military immediately hanker after baubles like jets, rockets and officer club swimming pools.

Sometimes an ambitious lordling (Nkrumah of Ghana and Sukarno of Indonesia come to mind) may build up an army for apparent aggrandizement against his neighbors, who then must, I agree, build up their own military as self-protection. If only the United Nations would hurry up with its international police force!

Yet it is surprising how many countries around the world are firmly at peace with their neighbors and have no need for a national defense unit. These are the ones I talk about here.

For example, what do Brazil, Chile, Mexico—to name three in Latin America with big forces—have to fear from across their borders? The answer, we all know, is that their militaries are deeply entrenched in indigenous politics and are active with other pressure groups pulling and hauling at the government. Getting these groups out of the pork barrel will, obviously, require a major revolution in itself.

Hans Morgenthau in his widely read article "A Political Theory of Foreign Aid" calls military assistance a form of "prestige aid." The jet fighters given to some nations are certainly not to perform a military function, but simply to help strengthen the prestige of the recipient group that happens to be in power.[4]

Should the leader of a hungry country, when offered these soon obsolescent jet planes and whatnots, accept them in the name of his nation's present temporary prestige, or should he decide that a comfortable standard of living sometime in the future is a surer basis for prestige? This seems like a simple question with a simple answer, but apparently not, judging by the success of our military aid lobbyists.

For Americans, perhaps one of the most conscience-pricking practices of our officials abroad is the hard sell job of our military and naval attachés with regard to our surplus military hardware. Often it seems that an attaché's reputation at the Pentagon is made or broken on the amount he succeeds in getting his host nation to accept in the name of "national prestige" – or, expressed differently, that he arranges with the Pentagon administrators to give to that nation as "good will."

The bigger the pieces of equipment, the more expensive their operation, which means less money available for the effective development of the country.

And so Brazil jauntily sails its navy up and down while hundreds of thousands of Brazilian citizens continue to exist under as awful conditions as there are anywhere in the world today.

The communist bloc activity in this field of military aid is particularly pertinent because it uses up more of the hungry country's resources, relative to the quantity involved, than the American. American military equipment is virtually an outright gift; the receiving country normally pays for only the operation and upkeep. Communist military equipment, and also their training services, must, on the other hand, generally be paid for. Thus, this cost must be diverted out of the hungry country's resources, which otherwise would be channeled into economic development.

"In order to keep six transports, a helicopter and two biplanes given by the Soviet Union, Laos must support 60 Soviet pilots and technicians at a monthly cost of $75,000. That's just about what the country earns from its exports each month." [5]

A discouraging fact about these militaries of the backward countries is that almost everyone involved knows the armies and navies really could not fight their way out of a paper bag if a war should come along.

In 1955 Nicaragua invaded Costa Rica. Through the years Nicaragua had spent a large proportion of its budgets to build up what was generally regarded as one of the best armies in Latin America. Costa Rica had abolished its army in 1949 and established a well-trained Guardia Civil of two thousand men to maintain internal order. Costa Rica, for the record, has developed one of the highest living standards in Latin America; Nicaragua's remains close to the bottom.

When the invasion came, Costa Rica's police force, plus the zeal of the populace, stopped the highly touted Nicaraguan army cold in its tracks.

I do not recall any military unit in any backward country anywhere in the world, except the occasional palace guard used for show purposes, that was not bedraggled, unkempt, dispirited, and, in a word, unmilitary. The higher officers may be charming guests at embassy cocktail parties, but the men under their command are indeed sad parodies of fighting units. Rather than adding to their country's prestige, they are the butt of jokes from every passing foreigner. The fault, needless to say, is not that of the unhappy soldiers. The fault is that the nation does not have the money – that is, resources – to clothe and train them adequately and in military fashion.

To summarize: when the leader of a hungry country is offered these obsolete pieces of hardware by American, British, French, Russian, etc., attachés, all he needs to do to save money for his country is to say, "No." That's all it takes. "No."

Guideline 16

Forget Your Boundary Claims.

No foreigner ever understands the emotional crisis of another people, least of all such things as boundary claims. Even if there is validity to the claims to these pieces of real estate (which are so often pretty well empty of any visible wealth), the crises generally seem, to the foreigner, created to distract attention from the political faults of the group in power.

It is, I know, wrong for an outsider like me to criticize the emotional involvements of another people. Nevertheless . . .

One case is the Moroccan claim to the territory of now independent Mauritania. I was in Mauritania the year before this dispute developed and thus was interested in following the headlines. Modern Morocco, incidentally, does not even border on Mauritania, although "border" is a figure of speech out there in the empty sands. I have read the official brochure issued by the Moroccan embassy in Washington on the Mauritanian claim. Its assertions of contacts with that remote area a century or more ago seem as tenuous as the vagrant caravan trails, but the desire to expand Moroccan boundaries, whether due to emotional or ethnological reasons, can be accepted as real. However, when France had decided on independence for its Mauritanian colony and the other powers concurred, it would appear to be common sense for the Moroccan Government to face reality and turn to the urgent problems within its own boundaries. If the time and effort and cash outlay spent by the government on this claim had been channeled into a specific development project, at least one step forward to progress would have been achieved.

I was also in Afghanistan during the period of the birth of India and Pakistan out of the old British Raj. Afghanistan pressed for an autonomous border state of Pathunistan within the new Pakistan for its blood brothers the Pathans – at least, they are brothers to the Afghan ruling clans, although not to the other components of the country. Here Afghanistan did have technical legal rights and also valid emotions, and my sympathies are fully on the side of the Afghans in this dispute. Yet at no time has the government had the remotest chance of success in behalf of this nebulous Pathunistan. Nevertheless, for the past decade and a half the nation has subordinated its economic development efforts and its international political influence to this quixotic crusade. It has created an enemy of its originally friendly, coreligionist neighbor Pakistan, resulting in periodic blockading of the only practical trade routes out of Afghanistan. Facing up to reality should have dictated discarding the chimera of Pathunistan at the very beginning, or even now. But the Afghans, for emotional reasons of national pride, continue to cut their own economic throats – and bleat for bigger foreign aid charity handouts, which, it seems, are O.K. with national pride.

The latest boundary troubler is brand-new Kenya, so new no one even knows what its real problems are. Yet it refuses even to discuss realignment of the boundary with Somalia, a boundary that the stigmatized colonial regimes laid down for their temporary colonial purposes.

> Logically, the Nairobi Government ought to be glad to get rid of the useless, costly, contentious chunk of desert whose inhabitants are Somalis, not belonging to any Kenyan tribe. Instead, there is a crisis; a state of emergency has been declared . . . Kenya – which has been independent for two weeks – is saddling herself with one of those irritating, gnawing, interminable border disputes that will make no practical difference however it is resolved.[6]

The Moroccans, Afghans, Kenyans and the several other boundary claimers around the world are not facing up to realities in their politics or in their economics.

GUIDELINE 17

Forget Foreign Help: It's You, Only You, Who Can Get Things Going.

One often hears the argument that the United States itself would never have developed so rapidly if it had not been for loans from the British and other Europeans. Similarly, the steady flow of nineteenth-century European capital loans into Canada, Australia, Latin America, India, China and Russia is also emphasized. The largest portion of this capital went into railroad construction to further agricultural development.

Here various points are pertinent:

(1) The economics of the nineteenth century have little relation to those of the mid-twentieth. The undeveloped areas were usually still virgin territories rich in unused resources; colonial governments were stable; even in the independent Latin American countries the property rights of investing companies were respected; and nowhere were there population pressures as we understand them today.

(2) The European countries had generated within their own borders entirely by themselves both the capital which had initiated their own industrialization and the capital which they exported (except for the gold and silver from Spanish colonies).

(3) The countries receiving the loans were helped by this inflow of European capital, but "it is more accurate to think of it as accompanying and reinforcing their growth than as preliminary to it." [7]

(4) Private investors have a different viewpoint than government (foreign aid) investors. The former plan to get back a profit from their investment; the latter are interested in political and diplomatic objectives. The advantages of wanting a good interest return, good dividends, good security on capital, rather than merely the consideration of temporary national policy, almost automatically insures that private lending will be more economically productive than government lending.

(5) Insofar as Russia is concerned, do not forget that the huge loans it received before World War I (some sets of statistics show it to have been the largest borrower of all) were cagily repudiated by the communists. Thus Russia had the advantage of receiving the capital but not the inconvenience of using its resources to repay it.

(6) Japan borrowed only an insignificant amount of capital during this period, except for a short flurry as a result of the cost of her 1907 war with Russia. Japan is an excellent case history of a country generating its own progress out of its own quite limited resources. A hundred years ago Japan's agricultural yields were no higher than they are today in most of Southeast Asia. Yet by now Japan has increased its yield 300 per cent, but, significantly, without any important increase in the area of land under cultivation. It is this increase in productivity, even without an increase in the area of land in cultivation, that has allowed Japan to feed her urban population and to develop industrially. Large amounts of foreign capital were not required.[8]

To repeat, don't rely on foreign aid; it's your own resources on which you must build.

GUIDELINE 18

About That Foreign Aid, Be Canny.

Just the same, since that nice stuff, foreign aid, is already coming in, don't turn it down. Please, however, try to channel it into increasing productivity, no matter how the donor country may press for this or that quick-time propaganda, "impact" project.

Since the donor gives aid money to achieve certain political advantages, namely propaganda good will, the Minister of Resources is obliged to adjust to the situation. Ordinarily, this need not mean compromising national emotions and aspirations.

The right way to handle this touchy problem, it seems to me, is for the Minister of Resources to select from his master list of problems to be solved those items that will both further his own development program and at the same time redound to the propaganda advantage of the aid donor. Unless he has ready at hand his own specific proposals and unless he is firm in using the aid money for true development progress, it is likely the aid officials will prevail with their own ideas. Those ideas, need I add, are colored with the current aid fashions prevailing in the donor's capital and may have little connection with the requirements of the Minister's own country.

For instance, Washington for the past several years has favored projects that can be *seen.* This is one result of the furor over the successful Russian bakery and paving of the main street in Kabul, successful in a propaganda sense because they could be *seen* by the Afghan public. Alliance for Progress officials talk of development planning for programs requiring several years. Go behind the talk, however, and you find the emphasis on quick projects that can be finished and *seen* within two years.

So, if that is what the donor insists upon when he gives his free money, it is up to the Minister of Resources to have at hand worthwhile proposals along that line and to insist that his proposals be the ones initiated, not the proposals from the donor's distant capital city nor from temporary aid officials residing locally on a two-year tour of duty.

Also, it is up to the Minister to assist the donor in getting his propaganda worth out of his aid money. Of such is an honest business arrangement.

GUIDELINE 19

Get on the Research Bandwagon.

Resources in the hungry country, as I emphasize so often, are few, marginal and far apart.

But there are some.

These resources, whether in the form of minerals, agricultural lands, fisheries or forests, may be inaccessible, they may be poor in quality or too small in quantity to bother with, or they may even be, as a matter of fact, presently unneeded.

The hungry country must, to make any progress at all, find some way in which the marginal, submarginal, unused resources can help in the nation's development. It must find some way to make those that are already producing produce still more.

Research is the way. It is the job of research men to overcome local handicaps and develop a profitable use for each and every resource.

In the field of research the primitive nation starts truly from the bottom. Probably no research at all has ever been carried out on any single item of the country's produce, at least not inside the country itself, although millions have been spent on other phases of the subject in Oxford, Utrecht, Heidelberg or Princeton.

Unfortunately, the hungry country seldom has the trained brains or the long-range stability to do the research itself.

Today, praise be, it is as if Allah-Jehovah-Buddha had especially provided the open sesame. The postwar world has developed a complex system of research organizations, both commercial and educational. These are located not only in the United States but in many countries in Western Europe and, in certain instances, in tropical areas. The research problems of the small nation can be turned over, by contract, to these institutions to solve.

I point out the intriguing fact that it ought to be easy to get a foreign aid grant from the country of which the institute is a national in order to take care of this research. It is already proven in many countries, such as Israel, Sweden, Germany, France, Japan, as well as the United States, that the money for a research project is mighty easy to come by, either from official or private sources, if one of their national institutions has the contract.

GUIDELINE 20

Cease Aping the Fashions of U.S. Main Street.

Nothing is so elusive as the reasons why people run panting after a certain fashion, whether a new-look dress, a new bubble bath salt, or fish fins on a Detroit sedan.

In the hungry countries the efforts of the upper classes, and often of the entire population, to ape what Americans and English dukes, or, on the other side of the wall, Russians and Castro *barbudos,* are wearing, drinking, and smelling can have a debilitating effect on the local economy.

Perhaps this quotation from V.S. Naipul about Trinidad best illustrates an attitude common in most hungry nations, especially those with a colonial background.

> Trinidad considers itself, and is acknowledged by the other West Indian territories to be, modern. It has night clubs, restaurants, air-conditioned bars, supermarkets, soda fountains, drive-in cinemas and a drive-in bank. But modernity in Trinidad means a little more. It means a constant alertness, a willingness to change, a readiness to accept anything which films, magazines and comic strips appear to indicate as American. Beauty queens and fashion parades are modern. Modernity might also lie in a name like Lois – pronounced Loys in Trinidad – which came to the island in the 1940's through Lois Lane, the heroine of the American *Superman* comic strip. Simple radio is not modern – commercial radio is: when I was a boy not to know the latest commercial jingle was to be primitive.
>
> To be modern is to ignore local products and to use those advertised in American magazines. The excellent coffee which is grown in Trinidad is used only by the very poor and a few middle-class English expatriates. Everyone else drinks Nescafé or Maxwell House or Chase and Sanborn, which is more expensive but is advertised in the magazines and therefore acceptable. The elegant and comfortable morris chairs, made from local wood by local craftsmen, are not

modern and have disappeared except from the houses of the poor. Imported tubular steel furniture, plastic-straw chairs from Hong Kong, and spindly cast-iron chairs have taken their place.[9]

High officials in the hungry countries, almost without exception, today wear Western business suits when in public. In the privacy of their homes they may or may not wear the traditional local costume.

At the conference of the heads of thirty African nations held in Addis Ababa in 1963 "almost no one wore tribal dress, though President Fulbert Youlou of Brazzaville, a defrocked priest, still sports his Dior cassock, and Nkrumah's new fashion gimmick is a Mao Tse-tung jacket in black serge, which neatly covers a bulletproof vest. For the most part, it looked like any international gathering. Pan-Africanism had come of age."[10]

The great ambition of all men of the lower classes is, naturally, also to possess a Western business suit. It is, in fact, a necessity. Any junior clerk with ambition must own one in order to attend a social function where his "betters" will be present.

In many nations this means that the cloth must be imported; often the entire ready-made suit is imported. It also means the proper shirts, ties, shoes must also be imported, or perhaps manufactured locally from imported materials. Can the hungry country afford the luxury of a two-button, slash cuff, roll lapel outfit as a replacement for the native aba, sarong or longyee? My opinion as an outsider is that it cannot, and the money spent this way should be used on something more vital to the development of the nation's economy. But of course, I already own a suit. I do not have to prove to my superiors or to my friends that I am *modern.*

My suggestion is that the president of the country and the cabinet members set the fashion of wearing the local costume in public and in pressuring the officials under them to do likewise. Other pressures, perhaps tariffs, can be placed on the importation of Western cloth and haberdashery so that the non-officials will also be affected. However, don't try to regulate this by law, as fashion *mores* cannot thus be controlled. The goal is to make the local costume the fashionable thing to wear.

Gandhi did this for homespun cloth so that even millionaires in India were wearing it, for a time.

A nation's leaders must face the decision where to draw the line in aping foreign customs. Each item imported merely because it is internationally fashionable or because Americans or Europeans use it cuts into the local reserves of foreign exchange that much deeper.

As for those business suits, think how the tourists will appreciate the substitution of the far more beautiful local costumes. And think of your own national ego; your officials really do look sort of funny in those suits designed for men of a quite different build and carriage. Also, when dressed in local costume the urge to import Western office gadgets and home decorations should lessen.

And, to top it all, the stupid suit is so gosh-awful uncomfortable.

I am here bypassing a discussion of separate provincial cultures within a nation. In the new nations it is often an extra problem to merge provincial loyalties and tribal jealousies into a national whole.

A Gambian told me, "One can always tell to which tribe a man belongs by the clothes he wears. The adopted Western clothes have speeded up detribalization and this is important in our new society. Preserving one's personal culture is necessary, but in some cases the cement, which made social cohesion through fierce tribal loyalties, should be disintegrated."

True enough, alas. The outsider can only wish that a Gambian "compromise" costume, comfortable in that hot, sweaty climate, could be evolved rather than the alien, unsuitable suits.

Mrs. Castillo Armas, wife of the Guatemalan president who tumbled the communist-oriented regime of Arbenz, accompanied her husband on a state visit to Washington. Guatemala is a country famous among tourists for its beautiful cotton textiles, yet the local elite, and, therefore, also the bourgeois, consistently ignored the textiles as peon stuff. Mrs. Castillo Armas, for this state visit, had her entire wardrobe made up of Guatemalan textiles, and a very beautiful wardrobe it was. The immediate result was a revolutionary change of attitude among the women; the local cloth has since remained a natural part of the fashion scene.

One of the discouraging features of modern life is the collapse of the profession of architect into a status of international mimicry. All new buildings on all continents now seem to look alike. Land at any airport, whether Bangkok, Dakar, Zurich, or Cleveland, and the traveler cannot tell where he is, not even on which continent he is, except by the identifying sign. For a country hankering after tourists, this "international style" is indeed a foolish sort of architecture to use. Yet it is indicative of the lack of cultural standards in these cities, including Cleveland, as the leaders spinelessly continue to authorize buildings that look like everybody else's. For the hungry nation such foreign-style buildings form one more deadening influence that molds the citizens into aping foreign doodads.

Kemal Ataturk's ruthless "Westernizing" of the dress and buildings of Turkey after the First World War served the purpose of jarring the country out of its lethargy, curtailing the power of the priests and emancipating the women. That policy has served its purpose, and I wonder if now is not the time to re-Turkify the leaders of the nation.

Turkey in the days of Ataturk was a special case. The need in the hungry countries today is not to get them out of their lethargy and into the modern world; the need is to restrain the headlong rush away from all facets of their traditional cultures.

GUIDELINE 21

Respect the Roots of Your Culture.

One of the rarest things in 90 per cent of the capitals of the world is a good restaurant serving native foods. Instead, when the local officials decide, "We must attract tourists and all that splendid money," the first action is to import a third-rate Italian or French chef for whatever passes as the tourist hotel.

May I suggest calling a halt to serving up third-rate foreign food, usually made into fifth-rate food because of the need to twist local products out of all reason, such as the veal scallopini

I once experienced in Bangkok made out of water buffalo meat. Water buffalo is good to eat, but only when cooked and spiced in the ways the locals found out long ago to be best.

Most national cultures do not, as a matter of fact, have enough variety in food to allow preparation of a range of different menus. It is one of the proofs of the poverty of the country. Yet there is no reason variety could not be developed for tourists able to pay the price. What it takes is effort and imagination.

Every patriot, every orator, every leader gives lip service to how wonderful the national culture is, and then, as I have already said, himself rushes off after whatever is fashionable in somebody else's culture. No one seems to do anything about supporting and nourishing and protecting the local culture, other than to forbid export of antiquities, to organize a self-conscious, arty folklore concert, to manufacture silly whatnots for tourists.

What is needed is to make the people of a country proud of their own culture and proud to make use of its component parts. Normally, the base of any culture is its agricultural products. These are the items that make the culture of a country different from its neighbors. Encouragement of the people to make use of their own products rather than import foreign ones should, therefore, be a natural part of the overall job of the Minister of Resources.

Creating a restaurant that serves local dishes to foreign visitors is not in itself of importance. Yet it would bring home to the local people that they do have, or could have, a national cuisine, and it would encourage the local consumption of local products by the local elite who set the style.

My thesis is that somehow – and the indigenous food is only one aspect – the citizens of a small nation must be made to take pride in their culture and in the agricultural roots from which it has evolved. Unless the citizens respect those roots, scarce reserves will be dissipated on superficial expenditures that will not contribute to national growth.

It is one way to bring self-respect to rural regions.

It is one way to keep city people relaxed in their own routines instead of hankering for ever bigger night clubs with imported strippers.

Appreciation of one's own culture will be expressed most clearly when the citizen guides his foreign visitor to the sights and customs which are clearly native to his country – instead of to the new angular concrete building. And when he takes him to the smelly bazaar instead of the "modern" store, to the teahouse instead of the chrome-plated "nice" bar.

Drink rum instead of scotch.

Drink the local fermented juice stuff, and my gullet still throbs, instead of gin.

GUIDELINE 22

The Intellectuals Must Get with It.

Often the peasants lack political power; the city folk have little conception of national problems; the business community is, due to the very nature of business survival, a selfish, self-centered group; the politicians do not plan beyond the next election; labor is the most shortsighted and narrow clique of all.

This elimination of groups that are powerful influences in every national life does, however, leave one remaining group, the intellectuals. It is my belief these can give the necessary emotional uplift to the program for developing the nation's resources and that they can keep the public's emotions keyed up during the several decades required to produce results.

It is difficult for Americans to understand the importance, and limited number, of those who are called intellectuals in most foreign nations. Actually, there is no counterpart group in the United States, chiefly because education is so widespread here and class lines are so vague and, in any case, so easily crossed.

In Russia the term has been debased so that now almost anyone who does not work with his hands is an "intellectual." It is almost equivalent to "white collar worker."

I am, obviously, using the term not in the Russian sense but as most hungry countries would apply it. In Latin America there are the highly honored terms *científico* and *sabio.* Such a person may know little about science or technology, but he does have an education, by local standards, and is interested in the outside world and in progress and literature and the arts.

Again and again in the most remote towns of the most primitive areas on all continents I have met up with these semicultured, keenly intelligent men of the type I mean. I recall a governor of Herat in northeastern Afghanistan, an administrator in the Bissagos Islands off the coast of Portuguese Guinea, a mahogany lumberman in Mindanao, Phillippines, a raja in Bali, a lieutenant in Ouarzazate on the Moroccan edge of the Sahara, the wife of a stall keeper in the Cholon section of Saigon, a school teacher in Amapala, the Pacific port of Honduras, and so on. Little traveled, they nevertheless had acquired books and they subscribed to a newspaper. In an American college town they would blossom like the thirsty desert rose.

People of this caliber receive substantial respect in their communities and often exercise considerable influence.

Although the intellectuals of a country are seldom a cohesive group, inasmuch as they are scattered throughout the political spectrum and often do not take an interest in local politics anyway, nevertheless they are a specific target that can be reached by persuasion (i.e., propaganda). Once they are convinced that a project such as our development program is truly in the national interest, then the Minister of Resources has a core of effective support. This core may be able to keep public opinion protecting and nursing his program through the succession of political governments.

Only the intellectuals can build within the country's educational system a propagandizing, nationalistic element that will make the students aware of the needs of the program and of the sacrifices that will be necessary – and keep them conscious of this when they become adults and voters.

Unfortunately, the intellectuals must first repair their own drafty think-house.

For one thing, they must train themselves to believe that hard work and honest sweat are proper.

In order for land, labor and capital to be used intensively and effectively, individuals must believe that work – growing, making, creating, serving – is a value of the highest order, something most devoutly to be sought. Individuals must believe that hard work, sacrifice and saving – the process of capital accumulation – represents not only a theoretical ideal but a practical guide to day-to-day living. Conversely, the value of leisure must be rendered unimportant or, for a country which wants rapid economic development, eliminated almost entirely from the culture.[11]

It is in this very area of faulty mental attitudes that so many intellectual groups in the hungry nations are remiss. This is especially so in the Latin and Arab countries. Fortunately, in African and Asian countries the attitudes are more realistic, except where contaminated by the artificialities of colonial life.

Hispanic culture has traditionally emphasized the value of ostentatious leisure (travel, patronage of the arts, ceremonialism in personal relations, oratory, conspicuous consumption). If leisure ennobles, work degrades, and there is generalized contempt for the kind of labor described in such terms as "manual, productive labor" . . . Thus, the highest status in society is likely to be accorded those who live in ostentation without labor of any kind . . . The *pensadores* (high level novelists, poets, essayists, intellectuals) attacked utilitarianism and materialism as inimical to the traditional values of Hispanic culture . . . The institutions of higher learning reflect the prevailing feeling. Although education is greatly venerated, it is sought more for prestige than for its values in utility and training. The most popular curriculae are those producing lawyers, medical men, writers, poets, politicians and others who demonstrate by their titles ("Dr.," "Ing.," "Lic.," "Arq.") that they have nothing to do with the inferior, producing classes.[12]

The methods by which the Minister of Resources enlists the interest and the support of a cadre of intelligent intellectuals and how he brings them down to earth from their drafty ivory tower must obviously differ in each hungry country according to local social customs and racial temperaments.

But it must be done; yes, it must be done.

Guideline 23

Allow the Poor Guys a Couple of Human Frailties.

If a luxury, such as a stadium, is built, thus taking away funds and man-hours from projects that could directly assist in the tedious economic march upward, this fact should be acknowledged publicly. I do not argue against the stadium. I merely want everyone, both leader and lowly citizen, to recognize the new item for what it is, a luxury paid for out of stringently restricted resources. Instead of a dedication plaque at the stadium entrance reading: "To the Memory of Our Heroric Heroes Who Died So Gloriously in the Defense of Our Glorious Magnificent Homeland," I suggest: "To the Joyous, but Transitory, Relaxation of Ourselves While We Forget About the Needs of Our Needy Homeland."

Psychological lifts to maintain the spirit of a struggling people will always be required. However, the emphasis in public statements, newspaper columns and radio talks must be on the long, long climb ahead. If this is not done there will always come quickly to the fore at each lull in public support a self-interested group urging a luxury in the name of "national prestige," like an international airline, an automobile plant, a paved road in lieu of a graveled one.

Nevertheless, all of the preceding harsh guidelines add up quickly to an admittedly Spartan, heartless, ironhanded, stern, austere and mighty boring regime. Surely, people ought to be allowed a couple of good things while they toil so hard to pull their nation upward.

I have denounced all those luxuries everyone wants, I have cut out all the unnecessary things that are so nice to have around, I have lambasted the normal human weaknesses. Surely there is something left which poor people, and poor nations, can enjoy while they consume irrationally. Surely the savings of surplus and the tight guarding of foreign exchange can be weakened here and there.

So I now back down somewhat from the stringent plateau of my foregoing suggestions.

I recall this quotation, with extraneous sentences omitted, from *A Tree Grows in Brooklyn,* the novel by Betty Smith of a childhood in the bitter slum area of Williamsburg, New York City.

[Coffee] was their one great luxury. Mama made a big potful each morning and reheated it for dinner and supper and it got stronger as the day wore on. It was an awful lot of water and very little coffee but mama put a lump of chicory in it which made it taste strong and bitter. Each one was allowed three cups a day *with milk.* Other times you could help yourself to a cup of black coffee any time you felt like it. Sometimes when you had nothing at all and it was raining and you were alone in the flat, it was wonderful to know that you could have *something* even though it was only a cup of black and bitter coffee.

Mama poured out Francie's coffee and put the milk in it even though she knew that the child wouldn't drink it. Francie loved the smell of coffee and the way it was hot. From time to time, she'd smell the bitter sweetness of it. That was better than drinking it. At the end of the meal, it went down the sink.

Mama had two sisters, Sissy and Evy, who came to the flat often. Every time they saw the coffee thrown away, they gave mama a lecture about wasting things.

Mama explained, "Francie is entitled to one cup each meal like the rest. If it makes her feel better to throw it away rather than to drink it, all right. *I* think it's good that people like us can waste something once in a while and get the feeling of how it would be to have lots of money and not have to worry about scrounging."

This queer point of view satisfied mama and pleased Francie. It was one of the links between the ground-down poor and the wasteful rich. The girl felt that even if she had less than anybody in Williamsburg, somehow she had more. She was richer because she had something to waste. She ate her sugar bun slowly, reluctant to have done with its sweet taste, while the coffee got ice-cold. Regally, she poured it down the sink drain feeling casually extravagant.[13]

What can be used in the hungry country as a luxury-feeling equivalent for Francie's chicory-bitter, watered-down hot coffee?

In Morocco it is the charming tradition for the guest, or even friends meeting in the bazaar, to remain until the third glass of mint-flavored tea. Or, if he stays longer, to remain for the sixth or the ninth. Never the second or fourth or the seventh. In principle, this leads to excessive consumption. But who would want to alter this pleasing social custom?

And who would advocate banning the importation of tea, coffee and tobacco because they use up needed foreign exchange?

The soft drinks like Pepsi-Cola, Coca-Cola, Seven-Up consume a certain amount of the precious foreign exchange in the importation of the drink essence and the bottles and in the payment of franchises to the parent company in the United States. But let us leave them there as a satisfying form of Francie's coffee.

Similarly, movies use up foreign exchange. Yet anyone who has sat on a hard bench in a slum area's smelly theater or in an open air clearing in some lost valley knows full well the pleasurable excitement of the audience as it cheers and stomps in tune with the hero's troubles and triumphs. Their easy immersion in such movie joys has now mostly been lost to modern Americans and Europeans. Too bad. I suggest the traveling tourist forego what passes for the "proper" theater in the capital city and make the effort to visit a movie where the audience lives and dies wholeheartedly at each performance. It is indeed a fine variation of Francie's coffee.

And that's about it.

I can hear shouts that if these are all the "extras" I am going to allow then I surely lack compassion. The critics forget that in the hungry countries today the majority of the population do regard these as luxuries, not necessities. By removing items like automobiles, imported clothes, imported canned fruit, and all the rest I am not depriving the people of things they already have – except, obviously, for the elite few who, in any case, probably need to have brought home to them the local facts of life existing in their own hungry nation.

The hungry nations are poor nations, and the simple pleasures of the poor are not to be measured in terms of the rich.

Guideline 24

Be Ready to Limit Population When Science Finds the Way.

The subject of population control has by now come out of the dark corners of international discussion. It is a subject that the Minister of Resources and other leaders must understand and be able to confront openly. It is not a matter of rushing to initiate birth control measures, because science has not yet achieved in this area a plane of firm knowledge and facts. Rather, it is a matter of determining what can be done to prepare public opinion for facing intelligently their population problems.

The year 1963 saw two reversals in public opinion on population problems. They were, in fact, major breakthroughs.

(1) Regarding birth control, suddenly in the United States people were discussing it openly. The subject broke free from the isolated, embattled small rooms of pioneer sociologists. It also came down from the abstruse level of scientists as the American public in general became concerned about what was worrying the experts.

> The events of the past year [1963] have left such old-time campaigners as Planned Parenthood and the Population Reference Bureau happily stunned with success. After years of shouting in the wilderness, their industry and perseverance have paid off in a way that might be characterized as the "end of the beginning." In line with this, Robert Cook, head of the Population Reference Bureau, which is an invaluable collector and disseminator of population information, commented . . . "If three years ago I had predicted that 1963 would turn out as it did, my friends would have told me that I was crazy and I would have had to agree with them."[14]

In 1959 President Eisenhower, under threat of difficulties with the Vatican, had forbidden the executive branch of the United States Government to have anything to do with the problem of birth control. "That's not our business," he stated,[15] as if social legislation and social research were something new to the federal government.

Pressure of catastrophic reality forced changes, however.

In 1963 the Congress adopted a foreign aid bill which provided that funds could be used to conduct research into problems of population growth in underdeveloped countries. The Agency for International Development (AID) announced it would welcome requests for population control assistance from other countries, and it set up a small part-time staff to consider any population problems others might present to it.[16]

This change of attitude about the open discussion of birth control and the need for government participation in control measures has not yet extended much beyond the United States, however, except for a few earlier pioneers, such as the Scandinavian countries, Japan and India.

(2) The other breakthrough concerned the general realization among the world leadership that the statistics of the global population explosion are, alas, only too true. Heretofore, many prominent segments of international thought down-played the statistics as the work of scarifiers.

The world census program of 1960–1961 was the second world census. For many countries this was the first opportunity to measure systematically, rather than to estimate, their population growth. The truth hit them between the eyes. The previously disparaged statistics for the hunger belt were found incorrect only on a frighteningly not-pessimistic-enough basis. Ghana had thought its population growth was at the rate of 2.3 percent per year; now it was determined to be 4.9! This meant that instead of the population doubling, as anticipated, in thirty-one years, it would double in fifteen.[17] This is such a drastic change that possibly Ghana's figures from the first census were in error. However, countries known to have good data are valid examples. Venezuela discovered that its population would double in eighteen years rather than twenty-six; Korea, in twenty-five years instead of fifty.[18] During the same decade India's population increased by 21.5 per cent compared with 13.3 per cent the preceding decade.[19]

It was the rare nation that did not have to acknowledge an ominous population growth rate. Now these statistics are, on the whole, admitted realistically into the committee rooms of the leaders.

These were two breakthroughs. Another major one has yet to come.

When will world leadership and public opinion accept as realistic the forecasts which state that population increases are now wiping out the food production increases in the hungry nations? As of 1961, for instance, output of grain per person in Latin America has fallen 16 per cent since the mid-1930's.[20]

I published in 1954 a paper that used as an illustration a large coffee *finca* in Guatemala which my friend Arturo Falla Cofiño manages for the family. It then had a total population of 476; that is, the workers and their families. The custom, as elsewhere in the area, is to give food and housing as part of the wage system. Although the original workers had, in years past, been hired on the basis that the output of the *finca* required their labor, by 1954 the owner was having considerable difficulty finding work for the ever-increasing number of descendants. In the *fincas* and *haciendas* and *estancias* still remaining in the hemisphere, the owners seldom are able to discharge any of their working force and send them away. It is not primarily a matter of national laws; the owners themselves feel obligated to "take care of" all those born on their property. It is a way of thinking, a tradition-bound relationship between the *patrón* and "my people." Whatever may be the injustices and inequalities of the system, at least the worker has job security and the assurance of food and housing of the traditional quantity and quality.

In that paper I asked, "If with 476 people [the owner] now has problems when working conditions and government climate are ideal, what kind of problems will he have within ten years when he will have over 600?" [21]

I recently wrote Arturo and asked if my forecast of 600 had turned out correct. His reply was: "Hell no! You missed the mark by 25 per cent. I now have almost 800 on the *finca*. I never stop building houses. I never stop worrying how to divide up the corn crop. Until your letter I had forgotten about the Golden Age when there were just 476 here, only nine years ago." [22]

Eighty per cent of the 500,000,000 new extra mouths this planet has acquired in the past ten years are in the hungry nations.[23]

Each reader of this book, it can be taken for granted, himself uses reasonably successfully, or has used, some form of birth control in his personal life. Thus, it may be a new idea to him, one beyond his comprehension, that *there is no effective method of birth control now known that will work in the backward areas of the world.* When a government or foundation or social agency introduces into a hungry, backward village or valley any of those same techniques that the reader may use, gives everything absolutely free of cost, carefully instructs the people, continues the program for several years, there is still no appreciable decrease in the birth rate.

Why? The outsider often puts the blame on the low or nonexistent level of education, the lack of domestic privacy, the inability of the indoctrinators to "communicate," and so forth.

Actually, the situation seems to be a paradox that cannot be explained rationally. On the one hand, there is the local psychological resistance to the idea of birth control. The man, universally, takes pride in a large number of children, especially sons, as public evidence of his sexual power. The woman, universally, wants at least one child as public evidence of her fertility. Other factors involved include looking upon children as a sort of old age pension – at least one of them will look after the old folks. On the other hand, there is the very real problem of abortions in these same villages and valleys, and not at all just among the unwed, as evidence that large sections of the populace *do* want to control their parenthood. Yet the village birth control program, no matter how well organized and financed, seems always to end in failure.

The existing techniques and knowledge that are effective in the advanced societies fail in the primitive ones. Could this be one way to measure the primitiveness of a society?

Ghana's leaders and nationalists would, I am sure, consider it a deep insult if the epithet "primitive" were applied to any phase of their national life. Yet the country's population growth rate of 4.9 per cent, if correct, must be accepted as a sign that the people there are on the whole primitive in the absolute lack of ability or awareness to control population growth. The so-called developed countries do have their own population increases, but not with such an outlandish statistic, and the reason, it now appears, does not lie wholly in higher education or the money available for contraceptives.

Why this should be still remains unknown. Call it the paradox of factor X in human relationships.

There are exceptions, however, in the backward areas.

Two hungry places seem, according to the latest statistics, to have found a way to lower their birth rates. Singapore lowered its from 45 per thousand in 1952 to 34 in 1962. Nationalist China, which operates a government-supported birth control clinic program, lowered its birth rate from 46 to 37 in the same period.[24]

Why only here? How? Only sociological research will give the answer.

Eventually, science will discover a properly effective method of birth control. This method, unfortunately, will have minimal usefulness unless the primitive societies can understand and want to adopt it.

In addition to the laboratory research of scientists in birth control matters, there is needed a major research effort and grass-roots investigation to learn why a primitive society continues stubbornly to maintain a high birth rate even when given the same physical accessibility to birth control methods as the advanced society.

Until that fine time when we have both the effective method and a population ready for it, there is much the leaders of a hungry nation can do to condition the attitude of their people toward willingness to follow birth control procedures.

In preparation for legislation needed to clear away traditional, legal and religious obstacles encrusted in custom, superstition and rigid dogma, the leaders can purposefully seek out the facts that can be used as evidence when the public campaign later becomes feasible.

Demographic experts must be hired to determine and tabulate birth and death statistics, separating facts from gossip.

The universal problem of abortions can be faced up to squarely and openly now, as has happened in Chile. There it was found that for every 100 live births occurring in the hospitals, there are 31 hospitalizations due to induced abortions; for every 100 general admissions into emergency hospitals, 42 are for complications arising from abortions; out of every 100 liters of blood used in transfusions, 27 are expended on abortion cases.[25] The economic costs to Chile's health services are enormous. "Abortion competes in a growing fashion with [scarce medical facilities], consuming an urgently needed quantity and quality of resources."[26] "Induced abortions occurred in 35 to 40 per cent of all pregnancies in Chile."[27]

It is probable that such a critical situation exists in other countries as well. However, the government bureaus do not seek out the data in order to learn what is going on.

Chile has met its crisis halfway (fullway, I suppose, would be to make abortions legal and to supply qualified doctors in sanitary hospitals) and has set up family planning advisory clinics. (In Nationalist China these are called "prepregnancy clinics" in order to avoid the troublesome phrase "birth control.")

To the leaders of the hungry nations are already available experienced advisers from abroad and much direct financial and technical help from the nations that have recognized the benefits of family planning, such as Sweden, and, now, from the newly authorized service of AID. Several foundations are also geared for direct help.

But the initiative to obtain such help must come from the leaders themselves.

I recall one writer whose synonym for "babies" was "disasters." In his statistics he would say a certain number of "disasters" per thousand died for lack of proper food, or that so many "disasters" reached the age of fourteen suffering from malformed limbs due to lack of calcium.

Such a term as "disasters" may help clarify the thinking of the Minister of Resources. In one way or another the Minister is going to have to accept openly and honestly the sad fact that population growth is an impediment to the economic development of his nation.

It will depend, I suppose, upon the controlling religion of the nation as to how, and whether, the Minister can prepare the public for the use of the effective birth control method that science must surely soon discover.

Mongolia is a highly mineralized region, but extracting the ores has been forbidden through the centuries. It is against the Lamaist religion to disturb the spirits of the underworld. The present communist, atheistic government is now proceeding with large-scale mining plans and the prospect is that this industry will become the principal source of revenue for that barren nation, the principal base for giving it a modern economy.[28] It is easy to understand the tragedy of a people whose religion has been taken away from them. It is not so easy to comprehend how a single dogma of that religion can press back so tightly the economic well-being of an entire people.

John D. Rockefeller III, chairman of the Rockefeller Foundation, has stated, "Private groups can contribute much in the way of information, specialized knowledge and trained personnel, but population problems are so great, so important, so ramified and often so immediate, that only governments, supported and inspired by private initiative, can attack them on a scale required. To my mind population growth is second only to the control of atomic weapons as the paramount problem of our day."[29]

5

Ideas Are of Greater Value than Fine Gold

MONEY, no matter what, is not everything. Ideas are coactive. Yet even the ideas must be practical ones.

And even the practical ideas for national development must be fruitful and lead to positive results. That job of the Minister of Resources is no sinecure. It is hard to find *practical* ideas and it is hard to make the practical ones *fruitful.*

Before getting out into the field where hands are calloused and backs are bent and stomachs unfilled, it is unfortunately necessary for me to detour into the high, airy halls in the capital cities where the high, airy officials kill off – smother is a better word – the ideas before they can sprout out of the seedbed.

I refer, but of course, to the propagandists.

Today's top officials propagandize worthwhile ideas to the death, to the very death. This is a major reason, in my opinion, why the general public has so many misconceptions about development work, why parliaments fluctuate to such extremes of support and condemnation, and why so much effort and cash thereby drift away into the thin air.

Each time the country's leaders decide on a new development project the first act, absolutely the first, is to rush out and organize a PUBLICITY OFFICE to start the drums of propaganda beating. Similarly, each time Washington or London or the

United Nations decides on a new phase of aid giving, the first step is to start shouting from the marble domes.

Is there a better example than the Peace Corps?

I consider the Peace Corps a fine organization because it enables idealistically inclined youths and adults to channel their efforts for a while into useful work before settling down into the mechanics of earning a living back home. Certainly most of the Corps members should return to the United States more knowledgeable and more mature citizens than when they left. It is thus a worthwhile organization from the American point of view.

But is the Corps so important from the point of view of the receiving countries?

It is hard for me to see that these young Corps members are doing much effective work in terms of fruitful economic development in the hungry countries. Of course, it is interesting to note that they are a form of the technical assistance "know-how" which was the basis of President Truman's inauguration of American (Point Four) foreign aid. Today American aid is swamped and sinking with sociological projects and billions of appropriated dollars that must somehow be quickly spent each year, and the old line technicians are the least important, the least-listened to men on the aid missions. It is all a far cry from Truman's original proposals. The Peace Corps is, to a degree, a return to Point Four basics, but instead of our sending expert men to the backward areas, there go these youngsters equipped with a few months' crash indoctrination course.

Even the publicized role of the Peace Corps members living actively and successfully in a remote alien village and "making friends" is a temporary, soon forgotten thing in that village.

Yet it does no harm. It probably does produce, for a while, good will locally in behalf of the nebulous, far-away United States of America. Such good will in a remote village, however, is thoroughly diluted by the time it is transferred to the power circles of the capital city. Nevertheless, this does no harm, except for one factor.

The publicity office of the Peace Corps is constantly flooding both the American and foreign public with overt press handouts and covert influencing of publication media about how successful the Peace Corps is. In this fashion it beguiles the public into believing that development progress is simple and easy to achieve; it misleads the Congress; it misleads the administrators, both American and native, who handle development funds.

The harm is that just the opposite is the real truth. Development progress is a complex and long-drawn-out process. It is *not* simple. It is *not* easy.

So when the hungry nations still continue hungry, in direct contrast to the quick, easy triumphs reported so loudly by the various propaganda machines (and that of the Peace Corps is only one among many), the public is rightly confused. They blame innocent government officials and, in the end, condemn all development projects as useless and believe no money at all should be put into these fruitless foreign aid programs.

And, of course, each new government agency, each new high official must produce even more startling propaganda reports of successes than their predecessors in order to catch the jaded eye of the newspaper, magazine and television editors.

Once it was the hallmark of success in Washington officialdom to have a rug in the private office, then it was two telephones, then a private toilet. Now it is whether or not you have a staff photographer accompanying you on inspection trips in order to provide the publicity office with "human interest" material.

And now down to the level of working ideas.

Any area in the world could be used as source material for examples. The first draft of every development program everywhere is a mass of ideas presented for consideration. The final draft is pockmarked with the ideas that were discussed and discarded.

For my examples here it seems best to limit myself to one area. I can then accentuate that a lot of people are worrying about how to develop it, and yet, even with the best intentions, the work of trained experts does not guarantee advantageous results. I now talk, therefore, solely about the hungry nations of Central America.

Jicarito is a highland village of twelve hundred people, an

hour's drive from Tegucigalpa, capital of Honduras. The crude adobe houses have earth floors. Cooking, sleeping, sanitation and the rest of living are carried on with the simplest of facilities. The community is spread out helter-skelter on a rough, gravelly slope. The inhabitants have no land that can be tilled.

The town originated a few generations ago with laborers who worked seasonally on the farms in the valley below. Honduras never had the large, feudal type of *haciendas* of some other sections of Latin America. Here most farms are worked by the owner plus a varied number of hired hands; hence the gradual growth of Jicarito.

Only one thing distinguishes it from hundreds of other villages of the Central American uplands. The American-endowed and -administered Panamerican Agricultural School (better known as Zamorano) was established here in 1941 and its land cuts into and around the town. Most of the inhabitants are, in fact, pseudo-squatters inside the school's boundaries.

As director of this school, I was, in a sense, the acting mayor of this impoverished town for five years.

The only building of consequence until recently was the old customs house of indeterminate age. The Nicaraguan border is fifty miles farther along the road, which, however, still degenerates into a mule path before it reaches the frontier. The customs house marked the limit of Honduran police control up to about twenty-five years ago; marauding bandits were common, and this or that culprit was hanged by his thumbs from the branches of the mango trees.

The farms in the valley have experienced varying degrees of prosperity. After World War II cotton was profitable but insect pests increased to the point where they destroyed the profits. The farms and the village of Jicarito have languished ever since. As I said, just a typical uplands village.

Except for the Zamorano School. The school hires about two hundred of the inhabitants in varying capacities. Note the large percentage of adults this leaves permanently unemployed. As director, I knew most of Jicarito's population. I wanted to help the village, to encourage its development economically and psychologically.

By unobtrusively pulling strings in the background, I managed to get a fine elementary school built in Jicarito, financed from Honduran and American sources and constructed on land donated by Zamorano. The citizens of Jicarito provided the free labor ("sweat capital") to build it and a fine stone wall surrounding the area.

This was their first civic project, and full credit is due the entire population for their effectiveness in accomplishing it once the outline was clear to them. The task included trips by a planning committee, elected by the villagers, into Tegucigalpa to review the project with high government officials – an exciting psychological adventure without precedent in the town's history. It also included the arranging of proper living quarters for the new teachers.

As always, the outsider is amazed at the talent and latent energy in what at first has seemed a totally dispirited and hopeless community.

Despite the new school, the finest in *all* rural Honduras, I looked upon Jicarito as my personal failure. Here at hand, ready for use, in contrast to other similarly destitute villages in Central America, were my own agricultural training and the varied technical resources of Zamorano's professional staff. Also, Zamorano's students would have worked closely with the villagers in whatever project could be initiated.

Nevertheless, I never was able to come up with a practical idea for improving Jicarito's economic lot.

You see, it was not physical stuff, like money and muscle, that was lacking here, but *ideas* for developing a village which has not a single resource.

Among other efforts, I visited the administrator for CARE (Cooperative for American Relief Everywhere) in Honduras, Robert Anderson. Anderson had had a couple of years' experience in Honduras and several more elsewhere in Latin America; he spoke Spanish well and was one of the few foreigners in Tegucigalpa who had traveled widely throughout the rough, backward areas of the country. He was an authentic expert.

When I explained about Jicarito, Anderson was delighted at my interest and immediately said, "What do you want me to do to help?" I said I had not come for physical help because Zamorano could supply that, but for *ideas* on how to aid the village. He could only shake his head and say he was sorry. He had worked hard on the same problem of the plight of the upland villages, had had special experts come to visit the area, but no effective project had yet been suggested. Together we reviewed a long number of possibilities, but on examination each became obviously impractical in view of our own personal knowledge and experience.

This dead end led to my asking him to arrange for me to discuss the problem at CARE headquarters in New York City. I hoped their top officials, with their wide international experience in rural community development, might generate a spark of a new idea that could help my Jicarito.

The New York meeting was interesting. Dr. Ralph Greenlaw was waiting for me with several of his associates and said they were eager to hear my plan for the development of Jicarito, because through the years they had not been able to find any way to develop those villages which do not have any resources. "What, Mr. Paddock, is your plan?"

I had to tell Greenlaw and the others they were mistaken as to the reason for my visit. He was to tell me, rather than my telling him.

The conclusion of the meeting was that no one knew of any way to help Jicarito. CARE's own efforts to promote projects in villages throughout the world consistently ended in failure when there was no local resource that could be developed.

The people of Jicarito are practical souls. They have their own solution to their insolubly hard life: make sure that their children get to the fine new school and get there every day and get the maximum education available in it. Afterwards, the half-grown youths and girls can be sent away from Jicarito to the slums of Tegucigalpa. Maybe, because of the extra advantage derived from this elementary education, they can survive the destructiveness of slum life and raise themselves to the next higher level of urban acceptance and send money home to the old folks. Perhaps not all of Jicarito's citizens send their children to the school regularly, and probably none have thought this through as a set plan. Yet this is what is happening. Few of the school's graduates will stay in Jicarito.

The village, however, will not wither away. The inhabitants will continue to exist somehow, and the population figure, like that of all Honduras, will continue to go up and up and everyone will get hungrier and hungrier as they divide and then subdivide the available food.

I give this long space to Jicarito to illustrate the many, the oh so very many, places around the world that have not one idea, absolutely not one idea, working fruitfully in their behalf to overcome their troublous state.

There is no solution to their poverty. There is no local resource that can be developed. Instead, one of three alternatives can be selected by government planners: put the inhabitants openly on a public dole; or move them, lock, stock and barrel, to city slums; or forget the area and abandon it to its primitive fate.

Spending money for development in these places before the right idea appears is merely dropping it into quicksand.

From this working level of no ideas I now move to another working level of false ideas. Here everyone is loaded with ideas and everyone is listening avidly and everyone is awfully anxious to put the ideas into operation, but right away quick like.

I was once given eighteen hours to prepare for an aid program, a plan for spending $450,000 on grain storage. The country had just had a revolution and the White House policy was to show immediately its good will toward the new regime. I said the plan could not be prepared in such a short time. The Chief said it had to be done because those were his orders from on high. Accordingly, during eighteen hours of nonstop work I did devise a rather reasonable plan without, however, too much regard to such basic factors as whether the storage bins should be located on farms or in towns; whether the grain storage should be under the control of community cooperatives, the central government or private firms; how the grain was to be brought to the bins in the first place; and, in the very first place, how the grain was going to be purchased. My storage plan became lost in the aid program shuffling and I never heard more about it. However, other projects drawn up just as hurriedly did survive, which is why I sidestep naming names here. Why criticize the wrong men? Aid personnel are generally truly dedicated people. They are also intelligent. They are aware of the difficulties facing any adopted project. It is not their fault if politically influenced orders come from on high to start up programs no matter what, come what may, in areas where the laws of economics and common sense are disregarded.

As every American citizen must know by now, the amount of foreign aid money channeled abroad since the last war by all agencies, both government and private, is astronomical. The normal mind is unable to visualize $103 billion already spent by the U.S. Government nor comprehend the billions more that are planned.[1]

By now the literature of foreign aid could fill a library. Everyone has had his say, the politician, the general, the admiral, the hard-working technician in the field, the consultant who never saw dirty fingernails, the newspaperman, the professor, the religious, the contemptuous, the superficial, even the indigent native. Everyone has had his say.

American aid officials report their astounding successes year after year for submission to the budget hearings. And year after year, hard-bitten Congressmen deflate these successes – or sometimes are surprised to find them genuine. It is all on record in the public domain. Beautifully phrased, deeply analytical reports from big-name scholars and foundations are available from which anyone can draw valid support for whatever procedure he advocates, whether five-year plans or no plans, free trade or tariff walls, aid based on Christian principles or aid based on political opportunism, military aid, colonial exploitation, people-to-people friendship. Also at hand are the volumes detailing the history and the philosophy and the apologies of foreign aid, plus columns of any kind of statistics you want, all of which I gladly omit here as extraneous.

After all, we are now in our third decade of this form of

bountiful giving. United States Government aid to Latin America began on an annual basis back in 1942. Aid through the Export-Import Bank began in 1934. Enough field experience, enough professional analysis, enough thoughtful forecasting surely have by now been given to this subject so that, one would think, a set of pertinent rules could have been formulated. Both the policy makers in Washington and the aid officials in the field ought by now to have a clear-eyed knowledge of how the aid dollars work in actual practice in the receiving country.

Unfortunately not. Perhaps there have been too many voices on the subject, too many publications, too many Congressional hearings.

> The chief handicap faced by all is the impatience of the modern fast-moving world – expressed in the impetuosity of youthful nations seeking in the next few years to jump gaps of decades or centuries; expressed in the desire of philanthropists (individual, foundation, national and international) for concrete evidence of the good they are doing; expressed in the hope of the specialist, during a tour of one and a half or two years, to leave a permanent mark upon the culture that has been evolving for one and a half or two millennia.[2]

One thing is for sure. We have ideas by the millions for spending the dollars. The tragedy is that the record now clearly demonstrates that yoking multitudinous ideas with multitudinous dollars does not assure progress for the hungry nation.

From this working level of false ideas – false, that is, because the ideas are proffered in the careless assumption that tossing them into a gold-lined pot and stirring madly will help solve a hungry nation's problems – I move to the working level of fruitless ideas.

These fruitless ideas are really healthy and sound, not at all foolish. Yet somehow, even with all the good will in the world and the strongest efforts, the ideas fail to bear fruit. What is wrong with them? Often the most careful analysis fails to show what caused the failure.

I could tell of the failures of others, but why do so when the list of my own fruitless efforts is at hand?

For instance, me and my arracacha.

Once I thought I had the food problem of Guatemala licked. I still believe this product I tried so hard to promote could be of major benefit to the hungry people there. I still do not know what is keeping my beautiful, wonderful idea so fruitless.

Arracacia zanthorhiza is a root plant that is an important food crop in Colombia. The roots (like overgrown parsnips) weigh up to several pounds each and are high-energy carbohydrate food.

During the 1930's the United Fruit Company imported some arracacha into Guatemala. A few years later Dr. I. E. Melhus, my predecessor at the Iowa State College – Guatemala Tropical Research Center in Antigua, acquired some of these arracacha and planted them in experimental beds. Upon my arrival there I became fascinated with the possibilities of this plant. It looked as if ten tons of arracacha roots could be grown per acre. It outgrew every other plant in sight. Why should the Guatemalan Indian farmer struggle with eroded, worn-out corn fields when this fine arracacha, so full of carbohydrate, was at hand?

When our crop was fully ripened I remembered a Guatemalan official who had visited the Center and said his family ate arracacha and loved it, but it was hard to find in the marketplace and expensive; at times he paid a dollar a pound for it. Great! Here was a chance to earn some fast money for the Center. I asked an assistant, Marcial Barrios, to take a fifty-pound sack of arracacha to the market women in Antigua. Maybe he could get twenty dollars for it. Hours later Marcial returned; the women would not buy it; there was no market for it.

I decided to try the market in Guatemala City. *There* the people must be familiar with arracacha. Marcial and I loaded two hundred pounds of it in the back of the car and drove to the capital. With a sack over each shoulder, and after being tabbed a fifty-cent fee for permission to sell in the market, we went from stall to stall and squatting Indian to squatting Indian. They bought and sold everything from pineapples to red peppers to used razor blades, but none would buy our arracacha.

I now remembered that the Guatemalan official, whom I never

saw again, came from somewhere on the Pacific coast, quite a different area climatically from that of the capital. Marcial and I drove to Escuintla, paid a twenty-five-cent marketing fee, and again tried to sell our arracacha to the vendors, and again no luck.

It must be the clever market women, I thought, taking sly advantage of the young *gringo*. I gave up my attempt at wholesaling and went retail. Marcial and I now squatted down among the others and tried to sell direct to the housewives. Didn't sell a damn one all day.

Back in Guatemala City the next day I tried retailing again in the big central market, again squatting all day on the moist cement floor and again not selling a single arracacha.

The housewives knew nothing about this new root and were not interested in spending any of their limited *centavos* to try it out.

That Guatemalan official who was "familiar" with the arracacha must have been merely displaying the traditional Latin politeness in humoring my enthusiasm about my pet plant.

I continued to talk up the virtues of arracacha during the rest of my time at the Research Center and, after it was closed, during my tour of duty with the American aid mission in Guatemala City. I was never able to interest anyone in it. I still think it would make a fine crop for that nation. I still do not know how to go about introducing it to the Guatemalans who must watch every penny they spend for food and who cannot afford to indulge in some new exotic product.

Another fruitless endeavor of mine was teosinte. This is a relative of the corn plant and grows as a weed in southern Mexico and Guatemala. Recently, Dr. Melhus, one of the world's great plant scientists, showed that teosinte is particularly rich in protein, having nearly twice as much as corn and of much higher quality.

Although the plant is a real stinker to work with — the hull is hard as a rock and there are special agronomic difficulties — plant breeders could, if necessary, probably overcome these factors. Anyway, I became excited about it and looked forward to its becoming a useful food plant and one that would be profitable for Guatemalan farmers to grow.

The teosinte path, to cut details short, led Dr. Melhus and me to a meeting with the board of directors of H. J. Heinz Company, the one with the 57 food varieties. We pointed out the advantages of teosinte, the board members were definitely interested, they thought it might make a useful geriatric cereal, supplying the high protein required by elderly people. The discussion then turned to the cost of introducing a new breakfast cereal on the American market. Their advertising manager said it would take a million dollars in development and publicity to put the first box of the cereal on the market. Was teosinte worth this gamble? The decision was no. And certainly they were right, inasmuch as teosinte cultivation is still experimental.

Someday, I still hope, research and proper marketing can establish teosinte as an important agricultural product in Central America. But when, or how, this will come about I do not know. Until then teosinte remains a good idea, but a fruitless one.

A substitute for milk was developed a few years ago by the Institute of Nutrition for Central America and Panama (INCAP). Called Incaparina, it is composed of an all-vegetable protein mixture of cornmeal, ground sorghum and cottonseed flour, fortified with calcium and vitamins. The product could be of immense value in supplying protein to populations in many parts of the world. An article about UNICEF's use of Incaparina said, "It is providing a lifesaver to milk-hungry babies in Central America." [3]

The verb tense, unfortunately, is not quite correct. It could later on prove to be a lifesaver, but it is not so proving today. The consumption of Incaparina remains at a low level. Yet a trained expert was hired by INCAP just to publicize the product and to push its distribution and sales by various techniques of promotion.

I hope INCAP continues its endeavors with Incaparina, for it is an excellent idea. The reports of its great success (and the number of papers written about its development and prospects is truly legion) seem unfortunately to come only from the researchers who developed it. Incaparina, in spite of more than eight years of testing, has not been a success with those distributors with whom I have talked. The person who has probably given it the most thorough trial is Francisco de Sola, a managing partner of H. de Sola e Hijos Sucesores, which has had the manufacturing rights for El Salvador. He made an active effort to have his countrymen adopt it. He told me, "Incaparina is a failure here and I can find no evidence it has been a success any place else. It has so little flavor or palatability that people just won't use it." His firm finally gave up manufacturing it in 1963 and would have done so before except for its desire to carry the product as a public service.

Another excellent INCAP idea was tortillas enriched with powdered ramie, produced by its researchers in the early 1950's. Tortillas, made from ground corn and limestone water, are the equivalent of bread in most of Central America and Mexico. Ramie is normally used as a fiber plant in southeast Asia. INCAP's research men determined that ramie, when powdered and mixed with tortilla flour, made a product high in protein value. It was a long and difficult project. Voluminous reports were written on its development. It was discussed and encouraged by aid groups in several of the countries of this area.

And so the day came when research ended and the ramie tortillas were introduced on local markets. Everything was fine, except for one detail which apparently no one had considered important until then. The ramie tortilla turned out green – not a pleasant green, but a bilious green. The Central American housewives were properly horrified. The ramie tortilla remains a fruitless idea.

Some day Incaparina and the green ramie tortilla – and the many similar products science has already developed – may become incorporated into the diets of these hungry countries. But when? And how?

My suggestion is that if it costs a million dollars to introduce a new breakfast cereal on the American market, then officials should face up to this fact of human nature. Make the acceptance by the local population an integral part of the cost of the original research project.

A friend from Malaysia, now a Woodrow Wilson student at Princeton University, has reminded me of one peculiarity of mankind that is as true in Penang as in Milwaukee: in marketing a new food get the town's elite to start using it at a snobbish price and the under classes will crave it no matter how odd it tastes. His comment: "Expensive food usually does taste sort of funny."

So hit the cocktail party circuit with the bilious green ramie tortilla and soon the market women will carry it as a staple. At least, this kind of operation has worked with other products.

Nevertheless, I point out one disturbing factor that all these illustrations of mine have in common. All are new, exotic items without any roots in the population's customary habits, including my own favorite arracacha and teosinte.

Research money expended on increasing the yields of crops *already in use* by the people will almost surely pay off more than trying to get some new, exotic product accepted.

Ideas are wonderful things. But they have to be tried out. Neither the thinkers nor the doers can subsist without the other. Like the yang and yin halves of the Buddhist symbol, each is sterile without the other.

And when the effort ends in failure there is no alternative, unfortunately no alternative, but to pick up the pieces, gird the loins, grasp the staff, raise the eyes, take the first step of the first thousand *li,* and follow the ancient adage of man's experience: try, try again.

The trick is for the outsider, whether an American striving in an alien culture or the native official from the capital city faced with the blank stare of nonunderstanding by his compatriots in the boondocks, not to become downhearted at the vagaries of his fellow man.

In one country steel plows are introduced where previously a pointed stick had served. The farmers accept them with polite gratitude and use them as ornaments but not for plowing. Why? These plows require two hands and the farmers are accustomed to using only one, the other being used to guide the bullock. A more productive variety of rice cannot be introduced in part of Nepal, where it is needed and very well suited to climate and soil, because the grains cling a bit more to the stalk and a new threshing technique would be used. But threshing is a family or community undertaking involving social and ritual as well as mechanical activities. Running water in people's houses is not accepted because the village well is the social center as well as a source of water. Cookstoves designed to conduct smoke out of the house through a chimney are not acceptable to Hindu housewives in place of the open smoky *chula* now in use because religion requires that all parts of the stove (including the chimney if there is one) be cleaned after each meal. It would not be difficult to put together a large list of such minor failures nor to include in it some major ones. If these seem improbable or easily overcome, the reader might review the introduction of an innovation, say the fluoridation of water, into our own technologically highly sophisticated society. He might also consider the willingness with which Christians, out of Christian motives, will help to reduce infant mortality and disease in a distant non-Christian country and how unwilling they may then be to help control the population explosion that inevitably results.[4]

Against this background of the constant pressure of political exigencies, pressure of pressure groups and pressure of constant, deafening publicity, against this background of no ideas, of too many ideas, and of fruitless ideas, against this background of many diverse groups sincerely and intelligently and earnestly working to help the hungry countries of the world and yet finding themselves stymied and frustrated, I now enter the field of actual development programs.

The projects in these programs, regardless of which part of the world they are inaugurated in, fall into a half-dozen general categories, such as public health, education, industrialization, transportation.

I now want to show that each group of such development projects has, or seems to have, a malign tumor embedded within it. Otherwise, the results, after all the money and time and dedicated effort spent on these programs around the world, would not be so thin.

Many observers are continually pointing up the faults of these development programs, whether initiated by local governments or foreign aid funds. All kinds of reasons are given for failure.

Usually the reasons, it appears to me, point up only the showings of failure, not the inlying causes. Perhaps I can now indicate the causes of these failures.

I call them fallacies.

Part III

6

The Fallacy of Slum Clearance and the Remedy

BY "FALLACY" I mean something embedded in a development program that brings to naught the efforts expended.

The human element – that is, human failing – is not involved here, although the fallacy can lead to a way of thinking or an atmosphere of public opinion that in itself affects economic development goals adversely.

No, the fallacy is endemic within the program. Even before the first step is taken, the first shovel turned, the program can end only in failure. Rather, the specific project can be a success, but the goal of raising a nation's standard of living is foredoomed.

Slum clearance, as included in a nation's development program, is an easy fallacy with which to start. Everyone wants to get the slums of the cities of the hungry countries cleared away. Everyone believes that with the slums gone a lot of social and economic problems will be resolved. All will be happy. All will be well.

Alas, whatever slum clearance may do for places like New York, St. Louis, Manchester and Milan, there is a sad fallacy within this wishful thinking insofar as the hungry nations are concerned.

The low-rent housing and apartment centers presently so favored by most government leaders and American aid officials are not always intended as "slum clearance" in the strict sense of the term. Nevertheless, the aim of these new clusters of buildings is to lessen urban congestion – to decompress the bodies in the city alleys. Thus, it seems proper to include in the overall term of "slum clearance" these new urban developments, both those financed by local governments and those financed by foreign aid allotments.

Nearly every writer on foreign subjects, certainly every prosperous American tourist, at some time weeps over the horrendous slums he finds in his travels.

This same person, most likely, has never in his entire life walked through a true American slum, such as the backwash of Brooklyn, Harlem, Chicago and, really, almost any of our cities. Yet the American slum would be paradise indeed for the unfortunates he sees in the *bidonvilles* of Casablanca, Bogotá, Cairo, Bombay.

Thus, the American writer or tourist who is ignorant of his own slums is doubly shocked when confronted with the squalor abroad. There is no need to repeat here their accounts of the filth, the stinks, the emaciated body propped exhausted against a wall and, worst of all, the despair and hopelessness of the humans abandoned to these hells by the disinterest of their fellow beings, their church and their government.

City slums are not, of course, a modern phenomenon. They have formed a counterpoint in the life of every city in the past. Ancient Rome, famous for so many beautiful palaces, was also famous for its awesome slums – and for the street mobs that erupted from them.

The new element today is that man, for the first time, dreams of cities where slums do not exist. In this "age of rising expectations" slum mobs riot when their hopes are frustrated and, like mindless pixies, stone the American embassy but not the Russian.

As with any complex subject, the reasons why slums exist are many. Obviously, the basic reason is that the people living in them do not make a decent enough living to afford something better. As people flood into the cities from the country districts unequipped for city life, their earning capacity is low. The city is as ill prepared to receive them as they are ill prepared for the city.

When rural areas become depressed, from such causes as crop failures or overpopulation, then the surplus members of the farm families or the discouraged ones or the ambitious ones migrate to the cities. Boredom and the hope for a better life also lure the rural population. The slums of the city constantly ingest fresh victims.

We now know there is even a social law involved: the more the city raises its own standards, the more the rural people will migrate into it.

Housing projects to eliminate slum areas merely make the city more attractive to poverty-stricken farm area inhabitants.

The only sure way to reduce slum areas is the herculean task of raising the living standards of the farm regions to those of the city. This is approximately what has happened so fortuitously in Scandinavia and New Zealand. It would also be the situation in most of the United States were it not for depressed conditions in the South and Puerto Rico. Cities in the North and Middle West might be able to catch up with their slum problems were it not for the steady influx of Southern whites, Negroes and Puerto Ricans; how can city officials stem the spread of slum areas with housing projects when a never-ending additional supply of hungry mouths arrives each day by bus, jalopy and chartered plane?

If Americans with their wealth, aggressiveness and their tradition of striving always for a solution have not, so far, found it possible to eradicate slums, or even to lessen their area, consider the infinitely greater difficulty this problem poses for the officials of unwealthy Latin America, Asia and Africa.

This situation was well summarized by correspondent C. L. Sulzberger after a tour of the capital cities of Latin America:

> In most lands steadily mounting metropolitan attractions suck human energy away from a gradually stultifying countryside . . . As the cities boom the rural areas drift ever further behind. The cities get richer; the countryside gets relatively poorer; and the gap widens, with all

its obvious and inherent political dangers . . . If Lima is attractive to [the rural Indians] in the form of [its slums'] waterless, lightless shacks scavenged by swine, how much more attractive will it be with some slum clearance . . . The necessity for slum clearance appeals to our decency and benevolence. But in overall planning does this really merit high priority? Cruel logic dictates a negative reply.[1]

Slums are the result, not the cause, of national economic and social breakdown.

Slum clearance in the hungry nation is nonproductive. It does nothing to further the development of the nation's resources. It merely makes the few who are lucky enough to get apartments in the new buildings feel better. It is a luxury.

Worse, even those small sections that are improved at such great cost are immediately replaced by new slums in other marginal areas. Even if the entire city were rebuilt and the old one destroyed, new congeries of shacks, shanties and lean-tos would be procreating within a year as the rural population continued to swarm in from the discouraged countryside. Herein lies the fallacy that brings to naught the sums of money spent on slum clearance and urban development in the hungry countries.

Yet slum clearance is a wonderful, showy political gimmick. It can be *seen*. It can be completed within two years. It has propaganda impact. Hence the irresistible attraction it has to foreign aid officials.

The first three projects for which funds were allocated by the Inter-American Development Bank under President Kennedy's new Alliance for Progress were:

(1) To Panama City, $7,600,000 to help finance 3000 houses in a low-cost housing development.

(2) To Caracas, $12,000,000 to help finance 21,000 low-cost houses.

(3) To El Salvador, $2,000,000 to help finance credits, mostly of medium- and long-term duration to small-scale farmers.[2]

So $19,600,000 of the first $21,600,000 went to slum clearance in its various forms. Within the next eighteen months the United

States had given Latin America $300,000,000 in loans, grants and investment guarantees for housing.[3]

I hasten to emphasize I do not criticize the Alliance as a political gesture. The publicized goal of the Alliance, however, is not politics but to help Latin American countries to overcome their backwardness.

There is a second unfortunate result from improving slum areas. Despite chaotic conditions in these areas, the population is organized sufficiently, even in the most primitive cities, for public health departments to control epidemics. There are often such things as mobile TB units. Even the slum's grocery store, or bazaar equivalent, sells penicillin. You can walk behind the counter, drop your pants, lean over, and someone will give an injection. The city water is pure enough to form an adequate safeguard against contagious diseases. It may not be pure enough to protect germ-protected Americans from, to select some synonyms at random, Delhi Belly, Aztec Twostep, Djakarta Jumps and Turkey Trots, but the purity is sufficient to become a major cause of lower death rates and soaring population statistics.

Regardless of our compassion for the sick in these nations, high death rates are almost the only factor preventing even greater starvation and misery among the not-so-sick.

The rock-hard, dead-end trouble with slum clearance in the hungry countries is that the job is so enormous it cannot be done via housing projects. It is estimated that Latin America now has from 12,000,000 to 16,000,000 houses that do not provide "decent living."[4] Yet William Vogt, a student on the subject, says it is likely that urban areas in Latin America will increase "more than 50 per cent in population within the next ten years."[5]

In India for "the extra housing that will be needed by 1986 if the present rate of population growth continues, exclusive of rural areas or even of improvement of existing housing in such cities as Calcutta, the total investment required is estimated at approximately $25,000,000,000," said Eugene R. Black when president of the World Bank. "If you find the figure difficult to grasp . . . it is well over four times the total lent by the World Bank since it started business sixteen years ago." [6]

So why waste time and — more important — waste precious government capital in this morass? Leave it to private money to build what it can at a profit, as was the procedure before government-financed housing came to dominate everyone's thinking.

The only way the government can itself alleviate the pressure of slums in these nations is to rehabilitate the rural areas sufficiently so the attraction to the cities is lessened. The problem is to keep them down on the farm and not let them migrate and congest the cities' unemployed and unemployable.

The overall goal is to make the rural areas more attractive to live in. A higher income through improved agriculture is the most effective method, but this is also the most complex and takes the longest time to achieve. Yet it can be realized if sufficient effort is given to solving the problem.

The technical problems of maximum land utilization and rural rehabilitation I take up later. Here, since slum clearance is a sociological matter, I offer some intangible sociological suggestions for making the rural population more aware of their own importance and for making life more pleasant, less stultifyingly boring. Cancellation of the smallest slum clearance project on the drawing boards will more than cover the cost of most of these.

Community centers in the villages. Not an antiseptic new hall. Just make certain the smelly *cantina* or teahouse or *serai* is enlarged to have a couple of pool tables and, horrors, a jukebox. Extending credit facilities to the *cantina* owner might be enough to set this up.

For the women provide a well with some stone flagging around it, or a cement laundry place with a roof, so they can congregate to wash the clothes rather than string out along the rocky banks of whatever rivulet passes for a stream.

Weekly movies. Not in an expensive new theater, but at any sort of open air spot. All that is needed is a $250 projector inside a waterproof shack on stilts. Come the rains and you will find the audience will be there just the same, each person with a poncho or umbrella or something over his head. Arranging these movies is not primarily a matter of expense but of organization. A highly successful advertising operation of an aspirin company in Central America was to send company trucks on regularly scheduled rounds to villages to show not advertising documentaries but regular commercial films.

Sports. I hesitate to suggest intervillage leagues, considering the explosive incidents that so often occur when sportive passions get out of control, such as those international imbroglios when rioters stone embassies and Ministers of Foreign Affairs sniffily break off diplomatic relations. Nevertheless, few things can develop a community's spirit so strongly as a good team. I once lived in Nebraska; it was then said the only thing that held together that spread-out state was the university's football team. I have already mentioned the village of Jicarito. There the greatest excitement was generated when the new soccer team acquired uniformly colored, tattered T-shirts. When the President of Honduras was due to visit the village, the team practiced running along the highway so they could act as escort for the presidential cortege.

New industries. When it has already been determined that a new factory is to be erected in a nation, the Minister of Resources should consider the advantage of helping it to locate not in the capital but in a rural area. This is one method of decreasing the number of persons migrating into the city. Perhaps special concessions in the form of transportation rebates or waiving of taxes can be established so that the new factory can compete with those based in the capital. But beware of the advocates of cottage, handicraft industries. Unless carefully thought out and organized in advance, these artificial efforts seem regularly to end in failure. A CARE official told me of the time he gave three sewing machines to a village in southeast Asia, brought in a sewing teacher, and established a class for making dresses and other clothing for sale in the capital city. The majority of the women, as soon as they learned this trade, immediately packed up, left the village and their husbands and moved to the city. They knew they would have a better living there as seamstresses. The poor CARE official had no idea how to solve this new problem of the wifeless village, for which he was, justly, blamed.

Taxes. A head tax might be levied on city inhabitants. This would at least emphasize to the prospective migrant to the city that living is more expensive there.

Better education. One attraction of the city for parents is the schooling available for children. It is urgent that rural education receive the same attention and monies spent in the cities.

Visits of high officials. One tangible way to create community spirit in a village and to develop a feeling of importance within rural areas is visits by the president of the country and by other high officials. It is also good politics, as many an expert executive has learned. Among those who have demonstrated that tumultuous city folk can be downgraded if the rural areas are calm, Magsaysay and Nasser come to mind. The only examples I recall that ignored the agricultural population in favor of city workers were Stalin and Perón.

Japan was able to recover from the emotional and physical chaos, after the war, largely as a result of rural stability.

Ubico, the dictator of Guatemala (1931–1944), based his political support on the rural districts and almost completely ignored the citizens of the capital. At every opportunity he made trips through the countryside. It is still a legend in many places how Ubico would suddenly appear, where roads had never been built, riding his own motorcycle up the rocky mountain trails.

Lázaro Cárdenas, President of Mexico (1934–1940), developed and maintained his firm political support by countless, and I mean countless, hard physical trips into the most difficult, remote areas.

My first post in the Foreign Service was in Mexico City during the regime of Cárdenas. My ambassador, Josephus Daniels, elderly and seemingly frail, often accompanied Cárdenas on these trips and, equally important, often went off on similar rough trips by himself. Usually Mrs. Daniels, also elderly and also seemingly frail, went with him. They did more traveling around the country than the rest of the embassy staff put together. During those difficult political days of the Mexican expropriation of the oil companies' properties and the land-reform cutting up of large *haciendas,* including American-owned ones, this steady traveling of the ambassador was a major factor in lessening the anti-American feeling and keeping it within manageable limits.

I emphasize these points because I want to accentuate the importance of the agricultural areas in the political life of most backward countries. Remember: these countries are *agricultural.* Usually, the capital is the only city.

The government's primary goal should be to give the rural areas a feeling of importance, a feeling of pride, that they do indeed form the backbone of the nation. Once such a feeling has developed, the pull of the city for the rural population may be less magnetic.

The poor in the cities are concentrated in their slum areas. They are easily aroused by orators and easily led into demonstrations and rioting. They are a physical, tangible force whether active in the streets or latent under police controls. They can needle a government on a violent, temporary basis, whereas the scattered inhabitants of the countryside do so only on an intangible long-range basis. But any political scientist will affirm that almost always it is the long-range influence that prevails.

Also pertinent: the poverty in the rural areas makes less impression on the casual visitor. It is not readily seen. Often it is difficult to determine, as one passes by, whether a farm is relatively prosperous or relatively impoverished. In the cities there is no doubt. Slums make dramatic magazine photos; farms are merely picturesque.

In the policy-making rooms of Washington, voices are constantly raised that this or that type of aid project, especially slum clearance, is vital because it will gain the good will of the urban masses. The voices argue that this is where lies the fulcrum that controls the country's political life. Usually, it would seem, these voices are frightened by the headlines of the latest riots of university students. It would also seem that this is one more example of American officials extending their own modern urban background into the quite different environment of the hungry nations. City bosses and ward machines and labor unions, even of the currently fashionable "clean-cut" type of the United States, do not dominate the life in the hungry nations. These nations are *agricultural.*

The chairman of the United States Senate Subcommittee on Housing, Senator John Sparkman of Alabama, has announced that what foreign aid needs most is more housing projects. When he appointed a team of thirty-six "scholars and housing experts" to prepare a study of international housing, he said, "Our foreign aid economists should modernize their thinking, recognize housing not only for its social purpose but for its economic impact, which, in the United States, has made it the fifth largest industry." (Note here, again, the unquenchable dogma that what has been good for good old U.S.A. is dandy for everybody else.) "Too often in the past housing has been relegated to the bottom of the totem pole in our foreign assistance programs. I believe the American people would have a great deal more sympathy with our foreign aid program if it were oriented more toward direct assistance to the people, such as housing." [7]

Senator Sparkman made no mention specifically of slum clearance, but neither did he talk of adobe and/or palm-thatched huts complete with dirt floors. In the hungry nations any house with solid walls, a tile floor, a roof that does not leak, and a total of three rooms – one a kitchen lean-to, one a parlor, and one a bedroom for momma, poppa and the seven kids – any house of such grandeur is strictly for the bourgeoisie. And yet is this not what the Senator's team of "scholars and housing experts" and the slum clearance planners are aiming at?

A community development worker who had spent most of his life working for the Friends Service Committee told me that in tropical America and Africa tile or cement floors are not as sanitary as packed dirt floors. For families that do not look on cleanliness as does an American or European middle-class family, a dirt floor allows the children's urine to filter through. The puddles left by children, dogs and other animals do not persist. Also, in his view, a roof that is good enough to protect the inhabitants from rain is all that is needed to make any house classifiable as acceptable. Would such a house fit Senator Sparkman's standards?

I would not be so foolish as to say people prefer to live in hovels. However, it is also foolish to try to synchronize the feelings of a middle-class American concerning life in a hut with the feelings of an Indian who has known nothing else all his life.

Sociologists have noted that most American welfare workers and ministers come from our middle-class families where cleanliness is next to godliness, where it is not *nice* to fight with your fists, and where it is not *nice* for parents to sleep in the same bedroom with the children. Yet these are the welfare workers who deal with slum families where reverse standards are accepted. One result is that legislation (in our case, foreign aid allocations for slum clearance) is oriented towards putting the straitlaced *mores* of the American middle classes onto the alien lower classes. These lower classes, nevertheless, have their own firmly entrenched, strictly moralistic standards. Who is to say which set of morals is the better?

An article in the *National Geographic Magazine* included an attractive photograph of a new government housing project in Athens. The caption said that these neat, balconied apartments were sold on twenty-year terms to urban dwellers at $0.13 per month (thirteen cents, just to make sure you do not misread the figure).[8]

Who would not rush to the city pell-mell when he has the chance to buy a fine new apartment for $33.20, including interest, in payments spread over twenty years! Wouldn't you?

When the steady migration into the cities is lessened, the dead-hand pressure of the slums on the economic life of the cities will decrease. Agitation for slum clearance should similarly decrease, but the slums themselves will remain – indefinitely.

Meanwhile, leave the construction of new housing to private capital so at least some money profit can come from it. Channel government capital (tax income) into development work that will redound to the national advantage.

7

The Fallacy of Public Health Programs—You Can't Afford the Luxury

PUBLIC HEALTH is an area where both the general reader and the Minister of Resources can grasp easily the harsh realities and rock-ribbed principles I want to emphasize.

Every general development program has money and personnel assigned to an assortment of public health items. Most officials, both foreign aid and local, take for granted – unquestioningly they take for granted – that public health programs should be a part of aid giving and a part of all locally initiated development programs. Arguing against public health for the hungry nations is to argue against motherhood, liberty and apple pie.

When faced realistically, nevertheless, it will be recognized that public health actually damages the economy of a backward nation and definitely delays, if it does not eliminate, hope for a rise in living standards until population control is effectively organized.

A nation's standard of living, when all is said and done, is derived by dividing the nation's production among the total number of its citizens. The production is generally agricultural. To make the picture simpler, divide up the agricultural output among the number of mouths in order to arrive at the standard of living.

For a person in Washington, Oslo or Sydney to argue otherwise is merely to demonstrate how far removed he is from reality as he relaxes in the comfortable surroundings of food surpluses which allow him to acquire assorted luxuries as the evidences of *his* standard of living. He is removed from that tenuous existence where people are hungry, hungry every day, where all a man's thoughts are devoted to finding food for himself and his family, where each day he knows not what new belt tightening the morrow may bring.

In the backward, primitive nations today, the majority of the population lives in this state of emergency, even though the countryside may appear pastorally peaceful and the cities have a skyscraper or two and some people have new autos and everyone accepts the surrounding poverty as the "natural" norm of living. The population is numb to the threat of starvation, as the citizens of comfortable nations are numb to the threat of atomic disaster.

Each slight falling off of agricultural production — such as lack of rains or excess of rains or anything at all — reduces the margin of existence and headlines hit the world press and the compassionate send in relief supplies.

Such events are obvious for everyone to see. Yet they are unimportant compared to the insidious eroding away, year after year, of the food supply available per person as the number of months increase year after year.

If production remains constant, then each year the standard of living, the amount of food available per person, is reduced as the number of mouths increases.

And the cause of population expansion is not a rise in birth rates; it is a decrease in death rates.

Herein is the fallacy of public health programs: they decrease death rates without curtailing birth rates.

Birth rates have remained more or less constant in all the undeveloped countries for centuries, and probably amount to the same rates as existed in the United States and Western Europe until there came about various forms of birth control and, probably more important, new standards of living in an industralized society.

The new element has been the new means of saving the lives of newborn babies and extending the life-span of adults.

To illustrate: During the last war two visitors happened to suggest to the local health officer in Georgetown, capital of British Guiana, that he use DDT to reduce the insect-borne diseases which were partly responsible for the high infant mortality, 350 deaths out of every 1000 births. The health officer did this. The flies were killed. The disease rate fell. Infant mortality dropped to 67 out of 1000 births.[1]

What the uninitiated person does not understand is the terrifyingly incredible efficiency of modern public health procedures when introduced into a backward area.

To put it on the simplest basis I can think of: a public health team can visit a village in Tunisia, stay a single day, teach a small group of housewives to boil water and persuade them to do so as a matter of habit. From this small group the practice spreads through the village. The population of the village can conceivably double within a decade.

On the other hand, when skilled scientists discover a simple improvement for a food crop, which may increase production 10 or 20 per cent, it will take twenty years, on the average, to develop that discovery into a usable procedure.

The results of public health improvements skyrocket like a jet. An improvement in food production plods forward on foot.

The physicist who invents a new nuclear weapon shrugs and says the misfortune of its misuse is not his responsibility.

The doctor who prolongs a slum dweller's life for further wretched existence washes his hands and says the patient's fate is not his concern.

The official who spends millions on public health says it is not his department how the increased population divides whatever food happens to be available.

In Africa an official with whom I discussed my point of view about this problem of public health expenditures said, "All very well. But without a big campaign to develop public health my nation will always continue to have squalor and dirt. The blind, the lame and the halt will always be with us. The people will remain sick and weak and unexciting. The nation will remain unadventurous."

What he said is true, but the flaw still remains that until population control reaches the level of an effective science, and so far it is far from that level, the rush of extra bodies must continue to press back the nation from progress. The majority must continue to live in squalor and dirt.

Who is there to argue against health for the sick? Who is there to argue against life for the newborn babe? Who is there to say no to the foreign aid officials who, bearing free money, pressure the acceptance of gifts of hospitals, clinics, mass inoculations, DDT sprays?

This someone must be the Minister of Resources. Somehow he must, with the support of the president and the intellectuals, convince the nation that money must not be diverted into public health programs. There is not enough food to feed the rush of new mouths that will result, nor will there be enough food for decades to come no matter how successful the overall agricultural development program may be. In most of the countries with which we are dealing here it is physically impossible to increase the supply of food fast enough. Good health for all the citizens is a catastrophe, not a boon.

He must somehow convince the nation that the surest and the fastest route to the good life, including health, lies via the long and difficult and tedious route of resource development. Only when the resources start to generate a significant surplus will the nation be able to absorb the increases in population resulting from public health programs.

No other course makes sense. Unless the Minister of Resources can get his nation to go along with this philosophy, his program is doomed to failure.

I do timidly make one concession, although I realize it favors the well-to-do of the nation rather than the masses, and thus goes against the grain of all modern thinking. If private citizens want a hospital, maternity clinic, medical care for workers, and so forth, let them pay for it out of their private incomes. This means that group medicine must be paid for in full directly by the contributors. If people want special clinics for retarded children, if they want homes for the aged, and if they are willing to sacrifice from their private incomes to get them – as, for instance, members of a labor union paying from their own wages – let them go ahead and do so.

But the Minister of Resources will not allow the national monies, the reserves of foreign currency, the tax income, to be diverted from resource development into the area of public health.

After all, this private medical routine prevailed everywhere, including the comfortable countries, until a few decades ago, when the doctrines of socialism and statism came to the fore. Those early restrictions on the spending of government money must have been a contributory reason why the comfortable nations were able to build up their surpluses and thereby cease to be hungry.

Americans seldom realize that in the hungry countries the medicine and doctors, insofar as there are any, are usually provided free to the population – at least, they are free if the sick person can get himself to the door of the clinic.

In Portuguese Guinea I often saw groups of people straight out of the jungle who waited at the clinics in the provincial towns and larger villages. The Portuguese Government, so maligned by African nationalists, has developed here a quite elaborate system of weekly visits by doctors and nurses, and all treatment is free. It is not the complex medical care of trained specialists with elaborate equipment (in fact, there was no surgeon in the entire province when I was there). Yet the staff who make their weekly rounds obviously have pride in their work and they deal with the sick with kindness and sympathy. Certainly it is a humane service. Nevertheless, looked at coldheartedly, is this service vital to the welfare of the area?

In the former British colony of Gambia, below Dakar, I visited a hospital at Bansang, a hundred miles inland from the coast. Here were a couple of hundred patients from a dozen tribes scattered throughout several of the new nations of West Africa. The rural people preferred to come to this hospital, located square in the bush country, rather than to the too sophisticated coastal capitals. All treatment was free, even to the non-Gambians, and here the standard of medical care was high and the operating room was, it seemed, a nonstop affair. As an example of how removed these patients were from modern life, the doctor in charge said the previous week he was suddenly alarmed to note that the hospital's water supply from the tanks was rapidly vanishing. He finally found that in one ward the patients had discovered a water faucet and were turning it on and off as one of the most delightful sights in this world. In their own villages they probably had to walk a mile or more for a bucket of water. The doctor was sincerely regretful he had to turn off their "TV" entertainment.

I, too, am sincerely regretful to urge that public health programs, free hospitals, and weekly visits of clinic staffs be curtailed. I am thankful I personally can afford good medical care in my own American town, and when I travel I sure hope there is a doctor around if I get sick. I wish everyone in the world had the health I enjoy so much.

Yet the cold facts of life do not allow it. All the doctors and clinics in existence cannot bring permanent health to a man who is semistarved. Even if a hospital fills up the man with vitamins, it is a temporary, no-time affair. In a week he is back again at his old gaunt level. And next year, with another additional mouth in his family to feed, he will be still more gaunt.

So the medical treatment in the hospital is free. So what? What good does it really do in the long run? In the comfortable country when a patient is cured he stays healthy until the next sickness. In the hungry country the patient's ill health is merely alleviated for a few days, an ill health probably brought on in the first place by malnutrition.

Medicine is a frighteningly expensive business. It is also a big business. For those who live behind the times in America, note that *Newsweek* reports: "Health may now be the nation's third largest occupation, surpassed only by farming and building trades . . . Of every thirty Americans now holding jobs, one is a doctor, dentist, nurse, lab technician, pharmacist, or a worker in some other part of the field of public health or private medicine."[2] By "other part" is included, I dare say, those necessary souls who create TV commercials that drip, drip, drip acid into stomach recesses. All, all are vital to the great American dream of no ache, pain, pang, crick, kink, or twitch in this best of all physical worlds.

Such an emphasis on a life without ills is not, I repeat, for the hungry countries. It is a luxury they can afford only when they cease to be hungry.

The world of medicine is stupendously, intricately organized. A new disease crops up somewhere and all sorts of organizations are geared to worry about it. The more esoteric the disease, the more the worry.

Hemorrhagic fever is one of many such lesser diseases, although, granted, it is a terrible affliction to the person knocked out by it. This fever has appeared in India, Thailand, the Philippines, Argentina and Russia. An epidemic in Korea in 1951–1952 resulted in about 160 deaths out of 1600 cases.

A hemorrhagic fever outbreak occurred in the Beni region of Bolivia. Over a period of a "few years" one hundred thirty deaths resulted; the mortality rate was 30 per cent.[3] News reports spoke of "Bolivian and international medical teams" studying the fever in the villages there and special laboratory work in the Middle America Research Unit of the United States National Institute of Allergy and Infectious Diseases. Eventually, the virus was isolated and presumably a cure will be forthcoming. I do not know the overall cost of the work involved in this medical research both in Bolivia and in the United States, but it must be high. Most of it, I suppose, was paid from American funds.

My point is that the medical world is so organized that immediately upon the first whiff of the outbreak of this disease special teams — and, apparently, adequate funds — were able to go into immediate action. Yet it is indeed a minor disease (only 130 deaths over a period of a "few years").

It is a blind spot of the modern world that organizations are not similarly geared, similarly attentive — and with adequate funds — to the diseases that affect food crops.

When the hemorrhagic fever is eradicated from the Beni, how healthy, how unhungry, will the villagers be?

A standard excuse for public health programs is that healthy people can produce more than sick people and thus the standard of living will rise. It sounds logical. Yet a number of times I have tried to find statistically accurate examples of this, and I have never succeeded. Public health devotees have yet to prove that a healthy population generates a higher standard of living than a sick population.

It stands to reason that a man who is not racked with yaws, who is free from syphilis and internal parasites, will be able to plow more rows of corn a day or produce more tons of ore than the man so afflicted. But on an overall community, regional or national basis, public health measures prolong the lives of people and lead to population increases that more than wipe out any food increase which might result from individual workers becoming healthy.

Thus, I maintain, the theory has yet to be proved that a healthy community in a hungry nation achieves a higher standard of living in the long run than a sick community.

It is startling to note that this theory is repeated so often and is so widely believed. If it were true, surely the proof, based on empirical statistics, would be at hand to justify the vast sums of money spent on public health measures around the world.

Development groups, especially foreign aid missions, often include nutritionists who arrive at their posts equipped with long lists of calories, proteins, and so on. With the greatest of ease they can say exactly what each human must eat in order to keep his health (if we are talking about a healthy American) or to keep on breathing (if we are talking about the starving native of a hungry country).

On an aid mission abroad surely this is a useless, hypothetical exercise. Don't bother to tell the hungry man what kinds of food he should or should not eat. He will eat whatever he can get his hands on and be thankful to get it. Also, he is not going to get enough of any sort of food ever to achieve a "balanced" diet.

The proper milieu for the nutritionist is in the comfortable, well-stocked country, taking in hand, for example, those American teen-agers living on a diet of Cokes, burgers and malts.

As for the population of the hungry country, first get some food on the table to get the stomachs filled. If there is not enough food on the grass mat on the earth floor, then the fault – assuming the false assumption that the country is not overpopulated – lies with the low productivity of the soil. The primary job is thus to find out how to increase that productivity. The core of the job is to worry about the nutrition needed to increase the harvest of the plants and animals that feed the humans, not about the hypothetical nutrition/calorie charts of what ideally fed humans should or should not eat.

The trouble with the nutritionists is not that their work in these hungry countries is pointless; it is that they absorb money and man-hours that should be utilized for the vital problems of resource development. More money can be spent by an aid mission for this theorizing by the nutritionists than for the entire area of developing the know-how to grow two ears of corn where only one now grows.

A word in behalf of the administrators of foreign aid programs is in order. I have already said these programs represent political (propaganda) goals.

Certainly we cannot expect the U.S. Coordinator of the Alliance for Progress to come right out and say that Latin America should not have good health. He cannot win friends and influence people that way. It would seem possible, however, for him to lament that although the United States would like to put money into public health projects, although it would like to build a great new hospital, support new drinking water systems, and so forth, unfortunately there is not enough money to go around to include these. He should say the United States welcomes the desire of the hungry nation to better its health, but, alas, the citizens of that nation should use their own private money and not American money for this purpose. Any other approach will cancel out the great sums of money the United States is spending to help these nations, as it already has canceled out much of the huge expenditures of the past. If you need proof of this statement, read the plaintive questions in almost any of the Congressional hearings on foreign aid budgets: "But where have you used all this money?" "Where are the results?" "Why now do you need so much more?" "Why are these countries not yet showing any development?" This is what I mean by canceling out.

There is one area of public health which the Minister of Resources can back with all the strength and dedication at his command. And backing it will placate, to some extent, the clamorers for other types of public health programs.

When a natural resource cannot be developed because it is located in an area where unhealthy conditions prevent people from working, then the Minister has just cause to step in.

Thus, a malarial or tsetse fly region will need a control program; otherwise its development will never take place. Good agricultural land is scarce, and development as a result of disease control and insect control is as justified as development by the application of nitrogen fertilizer.

Nevertheless, there is, surprisingly, no statistical evidence that even malaria control is directly responsible for increases in agricultural surpluses. Dr. Victor Arnold Sutter, assistant director of the Pan American Sanitary Bureau, Regional Office for the Americas of the World Health Organization, told me that this office has long tried to demonstrate conclusively this correlation, but so far has not found it possible. Any time there is an increase in health, there is an increase in the number of mouths to be fed; any increase in production immediately disappears into the maws of those new gaping mouths.

It isn't that everyone has not tried to show this relationship between good health and economic progress. Quite the contrary. Economic development is today's glamor sphere and the medical profession has no desire to be left out in the cold.

Dr. Walter Salant of the Brookings Institution has stated:

> It may be argued that such studies would have little practical value because public health expenditures are made for humanitarian, not economic, reasons and would not be influenced by the results of any study . . . I am disposed not to accept [this] conclusion. One reason is that so long as resources are scarce, choices must be made among alternative forms and amounts of such expenditure and economic consequences are relevant to the choices . . . Another reason that I do not accept the conclusion is that even if the undertaking of public health expenditures is not affected by their economic consequences, these consequences should be known if economic planning is to be conducted intelligently.[4]

And J. George Harrar of the Rockefeller Foundation:

> It is impossible at the present time to make any precise or authoritative statement bearing on the relationship between disease prevention and economic productivity.[5]

But you keep hearing the statements.

For instance, the *New York Times* cited the wonders malaria control had brought to Guatemala: over a period of five years "the value of agricultural output has increased 60 times" in an area covering 42 per cent of that nation.[6] How fine such a thing would be if true (and how ignorant the editor was of the slowness of any form of agricultural increases). In my frequent travels to Guatemala I have never heard about any increase in agricultural production as a result of malaria control; when I read this I checked with the pertinent desk officer of the Department of State and he also had heard nothing.

Nevertheless, there is the dramatic example of Sardinia, long the "hell-hole of the Mediterranean" because of, principally, malaria. A massive effort at malaria eradication did reduce, although not eliminate entirely, this disease. So the island is now rated as healthy. Now it is not only attracting tourist money but is partaking fully in Western Europe's prosperity. Malaria control can be said to have been responsible for this revolutionary new level of living, at least on this island.

Thus, if it is to assist land resource development, spend money on malaria and tsetse fly control. Similarly, silicosis should be controlled in the mines. Such expenditures further national development.

In contrast, investing public health funds in projects simply to make people feel good is going to pay dividends only in more stomachs to fill.

The following is not offered as a solution to this impasse. Yet I wonder how extensive would be the ripples of action on a still pond if a leader of the proper caliber and prestige from a hungry nation, such as Macapagal, Senghor, Eric Williams, Nyerere, Bourguiba, Lleras Camargo, Haile Selassie, Mohammed Reza, Mohammed Zahir or Hussein, would speak forth forcefully and candidly on this subject from the rostrum of the General Assembly of the United Nations:

"I *demand* that you, the scientific and medical community of the world, come to my country. I *demand* that you repair and alleviate the havoc and misery which the results of your uninhibited research on human mortality control have created among my people. I *demand* that you study on the spot in my country and aggressively initiate research on human fertility control so the citizens of my nation can look forward to a future free from the hopelessness of overpopulation. I *demand* you grant to them the hope of the shining future which other branches of science can make possible. We are powerless to fend off alone the catastrophe you have inflicted upon us. It is your responsibility to rectify the tragic results of your heedlessness. I *demand* that you come."

8

The Fallacy of "Surplus" Food Shipments—Down the Drain

A CATASTROPHE OCCURS and it is the natural reaction of civilized man to want to alleviate the distress. Each year brings calls for compassion and help.

Following my line of earlier reasoning, I believe that help should come after a one-time, one-shot catastrophe like an earthquake or flood, and that the area should be restored to its former economic activity as swiftly as possible.

The catastrophes of drought, however, are usually recurrent. The headlines come every few years from the same country, and no amount of relief aid is going to change the threat. Such repeated headlines prove that population pressures have forced the farming of submarginal land. Until that country gets its population back to a livable ratio with its agricultural farmland, or increases the agricultural output of that land, then it is no favor, really, to send in relief food. This merely postpones elimination of surplus population and keeps the entire country again hanging on the cliff edge of will-the-rains-come-this-year-in-time-or-won't-they. And so the rains don't come and those farmers, who are farming where they shouldn't, begin starving and again the appeals go out for charity food. The food sent in will not restore the farmers to true health; it merely keeps them breathing in the full misery of semistarvation until the next drought.

How often in a decade do we read about famine in Communist China, in India, in the Near East?

Yet the world continues to accept as temporary or unexpected those emergencies which are nothing more than the standard pattern for the country involved, the pattern of poor agricultural conditions. Surely, this is the case of the repeated calls for help from Pakistan — and the repeated huge shipments of food the United States has sent in response ($637,700,000 from 1955 to 1963, plus cost of transportation, with more than $375,000,000 already scheduled in advance to be delivered by 1965).[1] Except for the transitory political factor of keeping the Pakistanis friendly to the United States in this Cold War, just what good has sending these foodstuffs done for Pakistan? It has merely postponed death for a certain portion of the population who will remain continuously at starvation's door no matter how much foreign food is sent. It means that Pakistan officialdom continues to postpone coming to grips with its serious agriculture problem — right now! It means that a portion of America's own resources, gleaned from the not inexhaustible soils of the Middle West, have flitted away into useless nothingness over the horizon.

Everyone loves a kitten. No one wants a cat.

Namely, the world emotionally rushes to help hungry children. Yet the world remains callous toward the conditions in which those same children must live after they become adults and are still hungry. Incredible amounts of food are shipped every week from the United States to feed children and pregnant women. Yet little regard is given to the children when they become hungry men and to removing the causes of that hunger.

One of the first acts of the new United Nations was the organization of its Children's Fund (UNICEF). A representative of the fund came to Kabul, Afghanistan, in 1947 to organize a local committee which would arrange contributions to be sent to the United Nations headquarters.

I was astounded by the response. It was the first time anyone had ever come to this remote country — much more remote then than now; at least now it has airplane connections — and asked its people to contribute for the benefit of the needy of other nations. Here was the international spirit of the United Nations at its best. Here the Afghans could act as the equals of the other sovereign nationalities. A committee of women was quickly formed — even though the purdah seclusion of the women was in those days very strict — and effective results achieved.

Work in behalf of the children of the world rises above Cold War politics and above national insularities. Probably in many communities, in addition to Kabul, this work for the Children's Fund was the first contact the local people had had with the exciting new international postwar world, the first realization that everyone, including purdah-limited women, can participate in international assistance.

By now there are many diverse kinds of international organizations designed specifically to feed the children of the world, almost always using foods supplied free from the United States.

One of the exciting sights I have visited as a tourist is the ruins of Petra in Southern Jordan. It was a long, dusty drive across the desert to a small fort where horses were rented for the couple of hours' ride to the hidden chasm where the fantastic Rose City is carved out of cliffs. This was a caravan crossroads on the edge of the Roman Empire, where for a few centuries merchants created a sumptuous city.

All that day on the way there I had seen few signs of life, usually only a cluster of nomads around one of the few springs, the only source of water throughout the entire area. There was almost no water in or near Petra (the ancient city was supplied by an ingenious aqueduct now in ruins). These nomads were as wretched a group of dismal people as I have ever seen anywhere, mere bones and skin, and the gleam of life long gone from their eyes. I felt hopeless and lost as I looked at them, and they looked hopeless and lost as they looked at me. All day the sight of these scattered groups of dejected people dispirited me.

But once I was among the magnificent sights of Petra I forgot them as my spirits soared with the imagined splendor of this fabled city of the caravans. As I went admiring from sight to sight, I came, without any advance warning, to a cave which bore a nicely lettered sign, "Save the Children Fund." I opened the door to the cave and entered a room where the walls had been painted white and everything looked clean and sanitary. Here was a young American doctor.

"What in heaven's name are you doing here?" I asked.

"Just what the sign says. Keeping children alive."

"How?"

"Well, I give the kids a shot of penicillin, put a little Mercurochrome on their bruises and bandage them up. However, the principal job is to give powdered milk and rice to the families for use by the children as they come to the clinic."

"Does that really help them?"

"Not directly, of course. The nutritional level of the people here is way below any acceptable standard. But this is to be expected. There is really no hope for these people unless we can raise their nutritional level, and this is what we are trying to do."

I enjoyed meeting this dedicated and sincere young American in this final, dead-end point of the world. Truly, he is to be admired for carrying on his work there. Petra is an exciting place for a visit, but to live there must be rugged and lonely in the extreme.

Yet surely his work was the epitome of uselessness, except for the fleeting satisfaction of bringing momentary comfort to the children with their bruises and cuts.

Is he, or anyone else, making any effort to show these nomads how to acquire a bit more food so that when the children grow up they can live as decent human beings?

Everyone loves a kitten. No one wants a cat.

For four years my wife worked in a group of eight women who acted as agents of CARE in the distribution of food to two hundred fifty persons in a small, desolate village in Central America.

My experience with CARE has convinced me it is a well-administered organization and is efficient at verifying that its food is distributed to needy people. Its accounting system to keep track of this food is detailed, honest — and onerous.

Not generally known is that the food is distributed by volunteer workers. In these backward countries the volunteers usually are the type of civic-minded, conscientious women who in the United States are active in various social welfare organizations. Generally, in the remote areas this type of satisfying public service is not easily accessible to the local women. Hence they welcome the opportunity to act for CARE.

On TV in the United States recently my wife saw that the ten-millionth package that CARE had shipped abroad was being sent to Colombia. "Look!" she said. "Packages! Real packages! If we could only have seen one such package!"

The food received by her group for distribution arrived in large boxes or sacks or five-pound cans. It was hard physical work to open these and measure out the exact amounts per portion. The women claimed the cans were made out of cast iron and could be opened only by a blowtorch. Yet the cans had to be opened and the cheese sliced, the powdered milk measured out, and the beans and the rice. Have you ever measured out powdered milk for two hundred fifty people? Every Thursday? For four years?

Have you ever stood in a line of two hundred fifty persons waiting for a food ration? At each distribution without exception there would be fights. Children would fight. Women would fight. Big children would push aside little children. A woman would suddenly erupt in a fight over gossip about whose man was sleeping with whom. There would be arguments over the size of the piece of cheese received. If a woman did not get the amount of powdered milk to which she thought she was entitled, it would not be unusual for her to throw it on the ground or even, once, at one of the women distributing it.

Never, but never, was this a scene of joyous thanksgiving. The women distributing the food were often irritated because of the hard physical work and the lack of thanks they received.

Only their sense of duty kept them there. Often they were accused of profiteering. Every three or four months a letter would be printed in the newspaper in the capital city of the country — which one of the persons receiving the food had presumably written — accusing this group of women of maltreatment and of stealing the food given to the village.

The people who received the food came to look upon it as their birthright. They never understood from where the food came and did not care anyway. They usually assumed it came from the president of the country as a personal, political gift, although in fairness to him he had never in any way tried to give such an impression, as I am told has occurred with executives in some countries in regard to American free food.

After four years the spirit of compassion toward the needy was exhausted and the eight women resigned. There was no one else in the community to whom CARE could turn over the job of distribution and so the service in this village ceased.

In reviewing their work the group decided that yes, it was likely some persons had been kept alive in this hungry village who otherwise probably would have weakened and died. Yet they agreed they had never improved the *health* of any person, nor had the village as a community been helped. This distribution of CARE food for four years had not, in their opinion, engendered any good will on the part of anyone among the villagers and definitely not the slightest iota of good will towards the United States.

During these years the group of women repeatedly had held meetings to determine how they might distribute the food so that good will, or rather a sympathetic understanding, might be developed toward themselves, toward the CARE organization, or toward the American people who support CARE. No way was found.

Today Americans are giving some form of supplementary food ration each day to more than 100,000,000 persons abroad.[2] Note again that figure and think of the logistics involved — 100,000,000 persons each day receiving a plate or package of food shipped all the way from the United States. This food accounts for about a third of our total farm exports.[3]

Aside from the political advantage occasionally, very occasionally, gained from this program by the United States in the recipient country, does it really accomplish anything?

To a peaked school child the daily "lunch" probably seems a fine treat. Perhaps statistics can be drawn up to show some sort of weight advantage from these meals. The program does not provide health, however. In no sense is it a balanced diet needed by a growing child. When he finishes his schooling, he will begin his adult working life (whether at the age of ten, twelve or fifteen) still undernourished, still half emaciated, his bones still short of calcium. The lunch program is, in fact, spread too thin to do any good. Expressed differently, the selfish Americans are being too niggardly with their gift food when they give only one paltry ration a day to 100,000,000. And, in fact, that was the teñor of many speeches of President Kennedy and the New Frontier.

In 1954 Congress enacted Public Law 480 (reentitled by "public image" staffers as "Food for Peace"). Basically, this law enabled the shipment of American "surplus" foodstuffs abroad for free distribution to the needy or for sale to local governments for soft currencies which had to be left in the recipient countries. It has been a popular law. The do-gooders like it, the officials propagandizing foreign peoples like it, the politicians like it because it postpones their taking action on America's unbalanced modern agriculture, and the farmers like it because the politicians can postpone taking action on America's unbalanced agriculture.

Since enactment of the law, $12,000,000,000 worth of corn, sorghum, butter, cheese, wheat, rice and other basic foods have been shipped abroad under the program.[4] In my opinion, only a naïve person blinded with rose-colored glasses would claim that the United States has received anything of value in return, either economic or political.

An official connected with this work said to me the amount shipped currently is now about $1,600,000,000 a year plus freight expenses of $170,000,000. He added, in all earnestness, "Try as we do, we can't seem to increase the amount of food being shipped more than $100,000,000 above these amounts. I am afraid that this may be the maximum, but everyone is working hard to find new methods for shipping more food to the starving people abroad. It is a policy set at the highest levels in the government."

As a sort of footnote to the foregoing, and as an example of the constant barrage of emotional journalism reports that constantly overwhelm the American public, I quote the following story in its entirety from an American mass publication magazine. It is no different from many similar reports in other magazines of all types, although few refer to the program as "modest."

Despite the discouraging news about the lagging Alliance for Progress, the U.S. could find a lift last week in the record of one relatively modest but highly successful program. In 1954, the U.S. started shipping surplus food stocks to Latin America for use in a free school-lunch program. So far, under the Food for Peace program, the U.S. has sent thousands of tons of surplus flour, cornmeal, edible oils, cheese, beans and powdered milk. Distributed by private relief agencies and local officials, the food will help feed 8,300,000 children this year, or 25% of Latin America's school-age population. Another 5,400,000 babies and pregnant women get at least one square meal a day.

In Washington, Food for Peace officials have coined a name for the project — Alianza para los Niños, meaning Alliance for Children. The food is credited with helping to double Peru's rural school attendance since the program began: school absenteeism in Bolivia has dropped from 38% to 2%, and students now make sure to be on time since late comers go to the end of the lunch line. Each day in Mexico, more than 1,000,000 school children receive the donated food. "The lunch is the only reason a lot of parents send their children to school," says Djalma Maranhão, mayor of Natal in Brazil's impoverished Northeast. In Brazil alone, some 3 billion glasses of milk are distributed in 25,000 public schools. At the end of a three-month period, reports one Brazilian teacher, most of her pupils gained at least five pounds. With plenty of surplus food where this came from, Food for Peace Director Richard W. Reuter expects that within a year the U.S. will be helping to feed one-third of Latin America's schoolchildren.[5]

This is, as hits the eye, big business. The cost is a mighty big pile of the American taxpayers' money. In no sense is it "modest." But I am most worried by the phrase "With plenty of surplus food where this came from."

The agricultural wealth of the United States is not inexhaustible, as proven in many a worn-out, thoroughly exhausted region. This can happen also in the Middle West, although research is keeping ahead, for the time being, of the steady draining away of the heritage of soil nutrients and of the virgin topsoil.

The agricultural value of Iowa farmland, it is estimated, is deteriorating at the rate of 1 per cent a year in relation to its inherent productivity of soil.[6] Conservationists often claim the American standard of living has been bought by a permanent destruction of one-third of our topsoil.

The soils and nutrients in the soils of the Middle West are not inexhaustible. Remember how often writers used to say the forests of the United States were inexhaustible, the iron ore of Minnesota, the water supply for the cities, the buffalo, the passenger pigeons. Today one reads that the fish of the sea are inexhaustible food for the world's exploding population – when actually the expert knows how limited and capricious the fishing banks are.

I respectfully point out that the only genuine inexhaustibility in this world of ours is the use of the word.

If this "surplus" food being sent abroad produced tangible results either for American international policies in the Cold War or for financial returns to the national economy, there would be little cause for protest. But is it producing such benefits? If so, where? Egypt? Brazil? Pakistan? Indonesia? Mexico?

A gradual shift in the use of a portion of these exported "surplus" foods has, it is true, been taking place. Some of it now goes, via a routine of selling it for local currency, to feed the workers on development projects financed by the United States. Even in this fashion it usually turns out to be a free gift, inasmuch as the local currency rates used are often, shall I say, diaphanous. In 1963, for instance, the American Government agreed that the Indonesian official rate of 45 rupiahs to the dollar would apply to this surplus food. The rate at Djakarta's leading hotel for foreigners paying in dollars was 500 to the dollar. The rate in Singapore for Indonesian rupiahs was 1300 to the dollar.[7]

Also, the Congress has tied what it thought to be a big string to this food by requiring the majority of it to be "sold" to the recipient country. The sale is made in the local currency, almost always a soft one unmarketable internationally. The United States Government agrees not to withdraw this local currency. Instead, it is loaned back to the local government or else it is used to finance American activities, such as construction of an embassy building or of U.S. exhibits at local fairs, and also to pay local expenses of American officials. Unfortunately this stock of local currency (including the counterpart funds from other sources) piles up in some countries so fast there are not enough valid excuses to make use of it. It piles up higher and higher as American officials wade deeper and deeper to find something to use it for.

In 1962, the amount of this money sitting around waiting to be used totaled more than $2.8 billion. In Brazil, for instance, there were $168 million, in Chile $21.9 million, in Indonesia $148.7 million, in Spain $166.1 million, in Syria $28.5 mllion, in Ecuador $10.6 million. Even Guinea had $4.5 million.[8]

My suggestion is that all funds derived from the shipment of American "surplus" food be channeled into supporting local agricultural research and local agricultural education, to the end that these countries can become self-sufficient in food, to the end that the United States can phase itself out of the charity business. What these countries need (and want) is not charity but the kind of development that will produce two heads of grain where one is now grown. Research and the adaptation of modern technologies to local conditions are the only way to achieve this.

It ought to make sense to turn the local currency reserve gained from "surplus" food into a form of endowment; this endowment could finance, for instance — with the local government matching the money — an agricultural experiment station with the equipment and facilities needed to make it capable of solving at least some of the nation's food problems.

We are all sorry the hungry nations are hungry. Yet simply by feeding paltry food rations to children and pregnant women the United States is, in a very real sense, making the recipient nation more, rather than less, dependent upon our bountiful exhaustible Middle West.

No Congressman or other American official ever intended, when this free food program began in 1954, that the American citizen must maintain this burden of "surplus" shipments for ever and ever and on and on.

And it is not necessary — if the recipient nation can be forced to make itself self-sufficient in food.

My point, however, is that neither the American taxpayers nor the hungry-nation officials should fool themselves that much health is coming from the food which is shipped at such great cost halfway around the world and up the jungle river to the dirt-floored school.

Yet to protest shipping this food to hungry children and to emphasize that the real problem is to develop the resources of these nations to the point where the adult receives three good meals a day, all this, I lament, is to shout to the wind. Logic has vanished through the window.

Everyone loves a kitten. No one wants a cat.

There is an old Chinese proverb: Give a man a fish and he will eat for a day; teach him to fish and he will eat for the rest of his days.

9

The Fallacy of Education— How to Germinate the ABC's

NOTHING RAISES the hackles so high among so many as a proposal to change current patterns of education, as any teacher anywhere can testify. Everyone, suddenly, is an expert.

In the hungry countries there is the extra factor that universally, among all classes, education is today the magic key to economic and social betterment, both on the individual basis and also with respect to one nation's status over and against her neighbor's.

This attitude is not so different from that found in the United States, especially in families whose child has only average grades and is facing that eye-of-the-needle entrance into the overcrowded "college of his choice." The family is fully aware that education at a well-known college will almost automatically later assure their child a satisfactory financial income and social acceptance.

The schools of a nation, or of a single community, are today the thing to which the people point with pride. In former times an outsize church or mosque or temple provided the mark of prestige for a community.

I think that some of us have turned to education as we turned in times past to religion – to help us handle our fears and anxieties. We are no longer terrified by mysterious plagues or earthquakes, but by the irreconcilability of political systems, the very real danger of nuclear explosions, the inevitability of overpopulation. Most of us feel that the only hope lies in new knowledge.[1]

The hungry nation suffers similarly, although perhaps for differing reasons, from this fanaticism that education is a cure-all for the future. The United Nations held a conference on science and technology for the developing nations in Geneva in 1963. The head of the United States delegation later made this comment:

> If you take any U.S. educator who has the most extreme attitude on the very great importance of education in the development of an underdeveloped country, you would find that this extreme attitude was really a conservative attitude in comparison to that held by the delegates from the developing nations.[2]

And so a large portion of a hungry country's national budget, supplemented by aid funds, is spent on education.

The amount spent by some nations is often, as a matter of fact, enormous. Mexico devotes 15 per cent to education, Costa Rica 25, El Salvador 21. Peru goes so far as to require by law that the national budget must allocate not less than 12 per cent to education, but actually spends 20 per cent.[3] "In many African states over 40 per cent of total government revenues are spent for education."[4]

The Bolivian constitution states that "education is the highest function of the State . . . attendance at school is compulsory from 7 to 14 years of age." [5] This, like many such laws in countries too poor to provide the necessary funds, is unenforced.

My criticism is not against the large sums spent in the hungry nations on education. I protest the current school programs on two counts: that the officials so often believe education is the cure-all to the economic ailments of the hungry nation; and that so much of the education money (in most countries nearly all of it) is spent on the wrong kind of schooling.

I claim the education now given does not provide the propulsion for a national effort to develop resources and thereby raise the standard of living and decrease the backwardness. Rather, the type of education now taught is education merely for the sake of education. It, therefore, is regressive to the national welfare.

Herein lies the fallacy of education budgets.

Senator George Smathers of Florida has written about a visit he made to a village in Nicaragua. He tells of talking with a Nicaraguan carpenter who was forced to teach his seven barefoot children himself because there was not enough room for them in the schoolhouse. The Senator pointed out that Nicaragua was spending 20 per cent of its budget on education and that even this was not enough for the task at hand. He said, "Ignorance breeds poverty, denies people the chance to gain a better life, keeps them tied to a primitive economic system and makes them ready targets for the false promises of Communism." [6]

This picture of the carpenter eagerly and bravely teaching his seven children the rudiments of learning illustrates the craving of the people in all these countries for education. Senator Smathers, nevertheless, is using faulty reasoning. He misses the point that the poverty of the carpenter and of Nicaragua is due not to lack of education but to lack of resources. The lack of education is simply one of many evidences, one of many results, of the poor resources.

Iowa, despite the wealth of its soil, could not in the early years allow her children to be off the farm nine months of the year. It was not until 1902 that Iowa passed its first compulsory education law. Parts of the American South did not have similar laws until the middle of the First World War. In contrast, Massachusetts, with its accumulated savings, had compulsory education as early as 1858.[7]

It is not the Spanish colonial exploiters and the later *filibusteros* who have held back Nicaragua, nor lack of education. The land itself has done this.

A poor country is made up of poor people, and poor people must use every available minute to make enough money, or its equivalent, to feed themselves. This means their children must also work. This means they cannot afford to have their children in school nine months a year.

Education in present-day European/American style is a luxury.

Only the comfortable countries can afford such a luxury. For the poor country another kind of education is necessary.

The aims of the educational system of a hungry nation should be: (1) to produce leaders able to lead the nation forward, and (2) to produce a citizenry trained to make use of the full range of the nation's resources.

Education for the sake of being "educated," for the sake of being cognizant of the humanities, arts, philosophies and other pleasant things of the outside world, is a luxury. It can also be an albatross hanging dead weight around the country's fragile neck.

Chile is a clean-cut example.

In the decades around the turn of the century Chile received large numbers of immigrants from North Europe, especially Germany. These were imbued with the traditional European attitude toward education. The professor who lectures on an erudite point of philosophy has great prestige. It is education for the sake of education. It has no relation to teaching a man how to earn a living other than that, in theory, it is supposed to train his mind to be facile. Anything that will train a man for a business or agricultural life is for the lower classes – the prestige professions are in law, medicine, architecture and engineering.

Simultaneously with this immigration Chile luckily found itself to be a most favored nation financially because of its huge nitrate deposits, which were then virtually the only source of nitrogen in the world. These came to provide 60 per cent of the government's income. Thus, it had plenty of money for an educational system designed in the German manner.

Rather, only the aristocratic features of the German educational philosophy program were adopted; the quite practical aspects that developed German technical efficiency and scientific brilliance were excluded as being plebeian. Science, when taught in Chile, is "pure" science, which is quite different from practical, applied science.

Chile today has perhaps the highest rate of literacy in Latin America. It also has the greatest number of trained scientists per capita in Latin America. The university system is the finest in

Latin America. Also, the universities are not dominated by student shouters to the degree found elsewhere.

Nevertheless, on a recent trip to Chile when I had long talks with a number of professors in these universities I was disheartened at their complete lack of interest, or even desire, to orient their classes or their "pure" research toward solving Chile's economic problems.

For today the nitrate bonanza is long gone. Synthetic nitrogen has replaced Chile nitrate in the world's gunpowder and fertilizer industries.

Today Chile is a pauper country. It is a begging nation. Since World War II the United States has allocated over $700,000,000 to Chile.[8] It ranks sixth in population in Latin America but is second in the amount of aid money received.[9]

As for Chile's education system, a Peruvian told me, "It has trained the Chileans well in the arts of speaking persuasively with foreigners to obtain their aid money."

Chile has myriad problems. A basic one is that its educational system has not taught its leaders nor its common citizens nor its intelligentsia how to grapple with these problems. But in Santiago you can have a delightfully stimulating dinner conversation on Kant versus Sartre, Picasso versus Klee, and the thought processes of Dr. Zhivago. In Copenhagen such dinner conversation is the proper dividend of a prosperous economy. In Chile it does not seem so proper when outside the door one out of every four citizens suffers from serious malnutrition.[10]

Education has not solved the problems of Chile. Yet the aid planners anywhere else in Latin America or Africa or Asia would be delighted if they had around them the literacy and educational standards that prevail in Chile. In fact, it is just such false standards and just such a false educational climate that they are striving so hard to achieve in these other hungry nations.

Egypt is another backward nation that is similarly producing the wrong kind of skills out of its educational system. This quotation sums up the situation there.

> Egypt represents certain countries (among them India) that seem to be spending more effort in producing high-level skills than is justified by their present stage of development . . . In proportion to its

population Egypt has more students in universities than Britain and twice as many in secondary and higher education as West Germany. Egypt has an alarmingly high rate of unemployment among university graduates, and the government is hard pressed to find jobs for them as junior clerks and minor functionaries in the already overstaffed ministries.[11]

The educational systems of Egypt and Chile are retrogressive forces because they mistrain the human element and thereby fritter away vast sums of money. This money is capital that these countries cannot afford to invest in training its people unless the investment pays off in increased resource production.

Spend, therefore, the money on education, but spend it where it will give impetus to resource development. Above all, do not fall into the false thinking that a country is backward because the people have lacked education in the past. A country is backward because it does not have resources, or does not use fully what it has.

If the entire population held university degrees this would not, in itself, change the situation. All that could be hoped for is that such a group of educated people would apply their knowledge effectively to improving the use of those resources they do have. With the Chilean, however, this has not been the case – the more he is educated the farther down the path of "culture" he meanders.

Africa is more rural than any other continent. Between 80 and 95 per cent of the population live in villages and depend on agriculture, pastoral activity, fishing or the forest. What is needed for them is primarily (if by no means exclusively) a rural and technical education program. Only if the large masses in agriculture can be brought to produce more, especially to produce more food for themselves and the growing market in the towns, can the first tentative steps be taken towards African prosperity . . . The African future (and Western influence in Africa) depends absolutely on a peaceful yet speedy transformation of African agriculture; and a rural renascence is inconceivable without a revolution in rural education. . . .

African countries feel committed to adopt the conventional European educational system. Anything else would seem "inferior." There must be elementary schooling from six years onwards, a conventional complement of secondary and higher education housed in modern buildings — like the African universities which have already been erected, with salaries at levels comparable to those current in almost fully developed countries . . . A tolerable standard of life for the African masses cannot be assured without a break with these traditional attitudes. All they can do is to produce a discontented class of white collar city-dwellers, who cannot be given work because funds for much needed development schemes cannot be found.

The nonsense of the situation is obvious. These educational programs have been devised without any thought for the organic relation of education to social structure and economic needs. Welfare and administrative services must not claim the whole of the resources available for development, otherwise they will be self-defeating (Upper Volta is a case in point: half its budget comes from foreign aid, and a quarter of it goes to educate 7 per cent of the children of school age).[12]

Education for education's sake is, to repeat, a luxury the hungry nation cannot afford. Money spent on education that will never be used in behalf of the country's development is wasted, the same as the money spent on a highway that leads to nowhere. This, I emphasize again, is the fallacy that defeats the educational programs of these countries and that defeats the various educational projects financed by foreign aid, both governmental financing and that of churches and foundations.

Yet properly educated people are needed in these nations, urgently needed.

So how do we organize and administer an educational system designed specifically for the hungry nations?

First, the money problem.

Education is costly! Look at the budgets of most of these hungry nations today to see just how costly.

The tragedy is that so much of this money is spent without obtaining even partial return from it. Nevertheless, the lesson to derive from these lavish budgets is that the voters are willing, they are eager, to pay the high costs.

If a community is going to have a *good* school, it must attract *good* teachers. Such teachers are a scarce commodity anywhere and, therefore, they can demand higher salaries and proper working conditions, which in the hungry countries means work only in the capital city. The patriotic satisfaction of knowing that their work is important for the welfare of their country may at times act for a few of them as a substitute for high wages, and this "psychic income" may persuade them to work for a while in an isolated village. This happens rarely, however, and usually only during the first couple of emotional, nationalistic years after independence or a popular revolution.

The extraordinarily high cost involved in a good school with good teachers is beyond the comprehension of anyone except a school administrator. At the Panamerican Agricultural School (Zamorano) in Honduras, to which I have referred before, the annual budget was close to a half-million dollars for a student body of one hundred and sixty. Visitors always wondered why it was so expensive to operate the school, since the students produced most of their food in their field laboratory classes and since most other living expenses in this remote valley seemed nominal for both students and faculty.

The basic reason for the school's high budget was its high goals. I considered it at that time to be the finest vocational school in the hemisphere. An elaborate program of written and oral tests administered by faculty members traveling to fourteen Spanish-speaking countries recruited the highest type of Latin students, the cream of the crop so to speak, for the school's one hundred and sixty scholarships. The twenty-five-man faculty came from a dozen countries. In the subjects taught at Zamorano most of the courses were without equal in Latin America. Moreover, the faculty were all full-time, a most unusual situation (there were then less than seventy full-time professors in higher agricultural education in all Latin America, an area with 200,000,000 people). Furthermore, this faculty all had Ph.D's or master's degrees or at least four years of full-time teaching experience. Academically, no institution in Latin America could, at that time, match the faculty or the students' high performance.

Hence, the half-million dollars per year for one hundred and sixty students.

I have given this space to Zamorano, which would have been a small operation in Europe or the United States, to demonstrate how unique it was in the framework of Latin America — or Asia or Africa.

Even where the schooling is simple and goals are modest, any system of education is a complex process. There is the constant lack of teachers, whether good ones or poor ones. Salaries are too low to attract high-caliber people, usually, and in many countries the teachers have little prestige or career satisfaction.

School buildings are expensive when efforts are made to pattern the education on European/American lines. Even though the buildings may be a foreign aid gift, the cost of maintenance is a constant drain on the budget.

The tools of education (textbooks, laboratory equipment) are also expensive when modeled on European/American standards, and the worn-out tools must be continuously replaced.

All these costly factors are compounded when the education is carried on outside the capital city. The biggest difficulty is to get teachers to go to the villages. Living conditions are hard for them there and cultural stimulation is nonexistent.

Worse, the village teacher is constantly burdened with time-consuming, difficult chores totally unrelated to his job. Any time the government, or an aid official, wants to inaugurate a new social development, such as take a census, distribute free food, supervise a self-help adult education program, the job is imposed on the village teacher. Often it is difficult for him to find time to teach.

The intelligent village teacher senses that his teaching is wasted on his rural students. He senses, even though he is unable to explain why, that he is giving them the wrong kind of education.

But the money *is* available. The taxpayers are eager to provide funds. Latin America alone expects to spend more than $29 billion on education in this decade.[13] If only money could do this complex job!

Money, unfortunately, alone can not do it, neither local pesos nor free American dollars. Nor can any existing European/

American system of education do it in these backward areas.

The numbers of people to be educated are just too enormous for the number of teachers available – or for any conceivable corps of teachers who can be trained via current methods. South Asia, for example, has more than 326,000,000 illiterates, with the number increasing at the rate of some 7,500,000 a year. The enormity of the job of educating the masses stretches the imagination. Sixty-five per cent of the Near East is illiterate, as is 85 per cent of Africa and 45 per cent of Latin America.[14] Yet merely teaching the basics of reading and writing to illiterates is *not* education.

The fallacy of the present educational systems in the hungry nations is that the wrong kind of training is given for the needs of the people. The fallacy is compounded because no matter how huge the expenditures of educational funds may be, the results among the millions of population will always be inadequate.

The system gives the wrong education. The system is inadequate. Therefore, a new approach to education in these areas must be devised.

I proffer my own suggestions for such a new system. I know of no place where my proposals have been tried and only occasionally have I found parallel thoughts in pedagogical writings. In fact, I present not so much a system as a series of broad brush strokes of ideas that must be left to the activists in each hungry nation, such as the Minister of Resources, to adapt to local conditions.

Let me first emphasize there is no substitute anywhere in the world for the well-run school with well-equipped classrooms and well-trained, enthusiastic teachers with the time to give individual attention to each student. There is no substitute for this, but it is an extremely expensive, extremely rare school anywhere in the world that achieves these standards.

With that qualification disposed of, let us now turn to how the hungry country can develop an effective school system, effective in terms of serving the needs of the hungry country without concern as to whether European and American educators would approve.

The system to be substituted for the present faulty European/American one must meet four basic conditions in order to achieve success:

(1) The system must have mass appeal. Each community, each small village, must believe worthwhile instruction is being given to their children in furtherance of this education they so crave.

(2) The system must overcome the teacher shortage. More, it must put before the students teachers who are dynamic, capable and well-trained individuals.

(3) The system must be adaptable to the already existing schools in the capital city. Yet it must also offer the special education needed in the rural areas. This education must be so good that ambitious families will not feel it necessary to migrate to the cities in order to give their children an education. And, when the rural students have finished, their education must have given them *talents they can use in their own environments,* rather than, as is often the case today, talents that are usable only in the city.

(4) The system must constantly and automatically select and encourage those students ready and capable for advanced work. It must filter out the incapable and the uninterested, and yet at the same time allow the competent ones to rise to the opportunities that the national life will offer them.

Is even a single one of any of these four conditions being achieved today in any hungry nation? I know of none. Can any twisting of, and adapting and tinkering with, the European/American education format achieve these objectives? The answer is no.

Since the traditional methods used in the comfortable nations will not work for the hungry nation, it must turn to new ideas and new equipment. The undeveloped nation must leapfrog over the standardized educational systems of the developed nations.

Herewith I present such a new idea. If the initial cost seems great, recall the great proportion of national income nearly every country is already spending in the field of education. Yet the cost of this new method, on a per student basis, will be considerably less than is now being spent.

It is best to talk of the mechanical equipment to start with. First, television, the backbone of this "brush-stroke plan."

The operation of the big transmission station in the capital city is understood by most persons, even though commercial television has not yet arrived – and rightly so – in all countries. Generally unfamiliar, however, is the type of receiving set now available that is designed for areas without electricity.

When one stops thinking of electrical transmission via power lines and begins thinking of other methods of producing and storing electrical power, then a new world opens up for the rural communities of the hungry nations. The cumbersome, damnable walkie-talkie of World War II days has long since been buried with the dodo.

Today, if a village can accumulate – the key word is "accumulate" – a thousand watts a day stored in batteries, then it can operate three twenty-three-inch television sets, plus a television relay station, plus a dozen radios and even a phonograph. I slough off the details of the various ways batteries now can be charged as the data are available elsewhere. I like best the game whereby a schoolyard merry-go-round can be attached to a generator. The more the children whirl the more electricity. You can't beat that.

The mechanics of covering a country with a network of television relay stations beaming classroom material from a central station are relatively cheap, as prices are gauged in the educational world. Transmitters now cost $35,000 and the relay station ranges between $10,000 and $15,000. There is also a relay station on the market that sells for $3000, measuring less than half a cubic foot; it operates on a five-watt battery and has a radius of ten miles.

A twelve-volt, battery-operated, twenty-three-inch television receiving set built in modules can be ready when there is a market for it. Its repair could be so simple it would require merely a boy on a bicycle pedaling around with a batch of replacement modules, removing the faulty ones, plugging in new ones and taking the old ones back to a central repair center.

The purpose here is merely to demonstrate how simple and

cheap the mechanics of television and batteries are becoming and will become in the immediate years ahead.

The mechanics are simple, but as always the human element lags behind. Effective use of these new tools in education requires imagination, patience and plain old-fashioned drive, rare factors in any society.

My brush-stroke suggestions are these.

Teach by television and examine by correspondence school methods.

Let the Minister of Education concentrate in the best school of the nation, unfortunately probably in the capital city, a corps of the country's most dramatic and experienced teachers. This group will be the key personnel in designing and televising the course material to receiving sets in the provincial areas. The value of centering this work at this selected school is to measure immediately the impact on students of these televised courses and supervise any changes.

Preferably adjacent to this school will be the offices of those involved in the correspondence part of the educational system.

This is the teaching end of the proposed system, more or less as is already being developed piecemeal in various communities in the United States and even in some countries like Nigeria and Brazil.

The receiving end must be, however, something quite new. As far as the village schoolhouse is concerned, the building need have only a roof to keep out the rain and sun. Elaborate, costly schoolrooms with blackboards, form-fitting desks, laboratory equipment, supervised play and all the rest are hereby tossed into the trash can as not needed.

Instead of "schoolhouse," let us call this roofed-over place the "viewing center." In those countries that use chairs, let the students each bring his own; ditto for those countries that use mats. There need be no other furniture. Desks would be fine if they are already there, but let the children write on the ground or on work boards on their laps. Other things are more important than furniture.

Instead of a teacher at the viewing center we shall need a "monitor." His qualifications, aside from knowing how to read and write, are two: he must be true-blue honest, because he will handle the examination papers; he must be able to maintain discipline among the students.

Instead of traveling inspectors giving annual examinations, as occurs in many countries because of their European colonial heritage, we shall establish an "examination headquarters," presumably in the capital city but possibly with branch headquarters to service provinces. The examination headquarters will be staffed with "counselor-correctors." It is here the bottleneck will most likely develop. The most difficult part of the system will be the handling of the thousands of schoolpapers, correcting them, making pertinent comments on them and returning them to the students.

If the office management job at examination headquarters sounds complex, that is true. It is likely most nations have never attempted such an administrative job. However, the answer here is to get the advice of the big correspondence schools in the United States and of the even bigger correspondence schools of the American Armed Forces. Such advice possibly could be arranged as part of the American aid programs. There is also the experience of the Cambridge Certificate system in England and the state-wide placement and examination system now in use in some American school programs.

Anyway the administration is a purely technical problem, and somehow that never seems so difficult to straighten out as a human problem.

So much for the mechanics.

We now have the country's most dynamic teachers broadcasting from their classrooms and otherwise presenting their instruction via television. Even if we go no further into the proposed educational system, the students already are receiving a much more vital and stimulating education than they now are in their forlorn, primitive, poorly maintained schoolhouse from their forlorn, semitrained, frustrated teachers. Remember, this is a substitute for ideal schools with ideal teachers giving individual attention to each student. It is a substitute because that ideal cannot be achieved in the hungry nations, ever.

The use of television, however, opens up the hungry nation to much more than this. Available are not only the country's best teachers but also the teaching tools and techniques of the entire world. All the wizardry of Hollywood movies and New York and European television studios is at the nation's disposal in order to produce lectures with impact that will capture and hold the students' attention.

Here is an example of how a single course could be prepared — for instance, a course in biology for the equivalent of American sixth-graders. The Minister of Education (or AID) would sign a contract, probably with the American Institute of Biological Sciences (AIBS), Washington, D.C., the official organization of the biological scientists in the United States. The contract would call for the preparation of thirty half-hour presentations covering the principles of biology needed in a rural society for students, few of whom probably would go beyond the sixth grade.

These thirty units as initially outlined would be farmed out to pertinent committees. Each lecture would contain material consisting of dialogue for a teacher, clippings from the most striking films on that subject, plus teaching aids especially constructed to emphasize specific points. All of this would be organized and perhaps partially filmed at a television laboratory by producers experienced in preparing this type of documentary.

Simultaneously, AIBS would have the students' examinations prepared and adapted to machine-grading by the counselor-correctors.

The final material for this course in biology would now be sent to the contracting country together with a skilled television producer and camera crew.

There the material would be translated into the national language and placed on television film utilizing local teachers and local advisers able to convert the American examples into the local idiom — that is, using a water buffalo instead of a cow.

Ninety per cent of the work on this course would be done in the United States and can now be used in dozens of education-starved countries. The remaining 10 per cent of the work—translating and adapting it to the local conditions and filming it with local teachers—is all that need be done, and, because of foreign aid, possibly paid for by the Ministry of Education.

Such a course, I am told, probably would cost around $230,000. If it is true that the hungry nation will have to pay only 10 per cent, then the bargain is obvious. It is receiving a dynamic course prepared by the international leaders in that field. No single teacher, even at the best American school, could hope to equal such a presentation.

Note that this biology course would be only one of several courses being taught in the sixth grade by this technique. The initial cost of course preparation is formidable, but it is well within current educational budgets around the world.

But what would be bought with this money would be like no other course taught today. Over the television screen the teacher would not only give some traditional instruction but would even have the children carry out simple laboratory exercises. He could tell the children about the plants in their valley (specific instruction on the local flora can be beamed to each region). The students would be instructed on how to find and collect specimens and on the following days the specimens would be compared with similar examples on the TV screen. They could be told to bring, for example, some rice seed to class the next day, when they would conduct, simultaneously with the instructor, simple germination tests. Student participation and involvement with the teacher is possible with TV instruction when the course is planned for it.

This would be an operative science course, teaching in some ways more material by the time the students complete the sixth grade than would be taught in the United States. It would have to, for most students will not go beyond the sixth grade. Enough instruction must be given to allow them to participate actively in modern agriculture—when that agriculture comes to their valley.

Dr. Gerald Winfield, Chief of the Communications Resources

Division of AID, tells of visiting the International Rice Research Institute at Los Baños, Philippines, a joint project of the Rockefeller and Ford Foundations designed to mount a coordinated attack on rice production problems. Strong evidence was shown to him that within five years the laboratory would have recommendations and rice varieties that would result in 100 per cent to 400 per cent increases in yields in the test plots. But to achieve these yields under actual farming conditions, Dr. Winfield pointed out, the farmer must know "how nature operates." If he is to know this, the elementary grades must teach something about photosynthesis, uptake of minerals by plants, respiration and plant reproduction. And the instruction must be presented with the clear understanding that the information will be *used* by the grown child when, as a farmer, he adapts his government's recommendations to his own local conditions.

In such fashion the successes in the test fields of Los Baños will reach the fields in the far valley.

The Minister of Education must emphasize, beyond any misunderstanding, that each course must be oriented toward: (1) inculcating the students with the importance of resource development; and (2) training them to know how to develop the nation's resources. The course must be designed for students living in a rural economy; it must be adaptable to a country with its own problems of climate and terrain and stage of agricultural development. In no sense of the word is it a course that would be relevant to students in American cities.

In designing this educational system, the overall curriculum is limited by only two things — the number of hours which the television station or stations can broadcast, and the number of hours of televised courses available.

At times a television class will be appropriate for all schoolchildren of a certain advancement; at other hours a vocational type of class will be appropriate only for the children in rice-growing centers, at other hours only in fishery settlements, or in cattle country, or for the city folk, and so forth.

A proof of success of any educational system is its enabling the bright students to rise up to the educational heights for which their abilities qualify them. This is how leaders should ideally come to the fore.

The failure of the present educational systems in the hungry countries is that the leaders evolve almost entirely out of the cities. They are urban products, but the problems of the nation are primarily rural.

In the television system suggested above, the examinations for each course must be organized so that the individual student can have the satisfaction of progressing, of graduating, of advancing up a ladder. This ladder can lead, for the few, to university level work. At the same time, for those with less ability or other interests, this ladder leads to special training, to vocational training, that will enable them later to earn more money than the less favored ones – to make a fishing boat catch more fish, a paddy raise more rice, a flock of sheep produce more wool. For the city students it may take the form of a better mechanic's job or a better office position.

The important point is to have the courses, the ladder, organized and available for the masses across the nation – for the ambitious ones, the interested ones and, I suppose, for the lazy ones whose parents are pushing them forward. Each student should receive a certificate when he passes a course and, it is hoped, is eager to tackle the next one. Yet it is up to the individual to determine how many courses he will take and which ones.

The main thing is to offer each student the training he needs to cope with the environment in which he lives and at the same time to leave open a path which the special cases can use to advance upward at their own speed. This flexibility is a necessity partly because so many students are unable to work full-time at schooling.

In this television system a boy may take twice as long with his schooling as his neighbor, but the ambitious one will end up with just as good an education and without the psychological complex of attending rigid classes with children younger than he.

At the viewing center each student is on his own.

Opinion differs as to whether television can be used to teach young children to read and write without the guidance of a personal teacher. I note, however, that those who say no have generally not worked closely with educational television. On the other hand, I have talked with several persons intimately involved with the development of educational television who feel strongly that children can be taught reading and writing in this fashion from the earliest kindergarten level. Nowhere, unfortunately, has this actually been put to test.

Who says the television screen cannot hold the attention of a young child? How many hours a day will he sit and look at television? In American homes there seems no limit.

Dr. Winfield, referred to earlier, states that techniques of teaching by television could be developed which would allow the very beginning reading, writing and arithmetic courses to be taught better than is now being done by the poorly educated, poorly trained teachers of most of the rural communities and most of the poorer urban districts around the world.

I wonder if the men who hesitate to initiate such courses are not too closely tied to their European/American backgrounds. They have not experienced at first hand the wretchedly primitive schools found in the hungry nations.

It is curious that educational television has so far failed to penetrate the American educational system. My observation is that this is due more to administrative and local political factors than to lack of confidence in the new techniques. Teacher groups look upon the television system as a threat to their positions. School boards fear "outside" control. Superintendents are appalled at the work involved in changing over to such a system.

Yet wherever television education has been tried beyond the level of occasional broadcast lectures, its value has already been demonstrated. Dr. William Brish, Superintendent of the Washington County School System in Maryland (where Hagerstown television education has been functioning since 1956), told me that upon completion of the sixth grade, 40 per cent of the students in the system placed in the eighth grade or better when examined by the Iowa Basic Skills Test in mathematics. The whole county system places above the ninetieth percentile of the United States in mathematics, and three schools in the system place slightly above the ninety-ninth percentile!

Establishing such complete television educational systems nationwide in Europe or the United States would be a disruptive exercise. One forgets, however, how primitive – and new – the educational facilities are elsewhere in the world.

Costa Rica has today one of the best educational systems in Latin America; yet it built its first high school outside the capital city only in 1948. Guatemala, which is vastly more developed than most of the new African nations, had only 115 students graduate from high school in 1949.[15]

It would seem that a well thought out curriculum, dramatically prepared by experienced television laboratories, would be the most exciting and impact-producing innovation any undeveloped country could initiate for catching the imagination of the people and showing them that their leaders are indeed bringing the nation into the twentieth century.

An obvious advantage of the television system is that the mechanical framework is available in the evenings for adult education. A television set with a twenty-three-inch screen can be mounted on a swivel base inside the viewing center, so that the screen can point out into the open air. Because it is nighttime the screen has greater visibility, allowing a hundred or so persons to watch it. The next time you are in San Juan, Puerto Rico, leave the tourist area and visit the square in the old part of the city. There you will see two television sets mounted on poles and visible to hundreds of elderly folk who use the square as a social center. You will probably find *Gunsmoke* on the screen but it could just as easily be a demonstration of canning that season's vegetables.

It is well to recapitulate my brush-stroke ideas about this new type of educational system geared especially for the hungry nations.

These countries have such strong desires for immediate education that the national budgets often are thrown into disorder by the disproportionate percentages spent in this field. Yet the education received by the students is poor and only a fraction of the children receive even this limited education — other than, perhaps, a few early years of reading and writing.

A feasible solution to this problem lies in the use of television combined with correspondence school methods. The *entire* teaching for the rural areas and most of the city schools would come over the television screen. Nowhere has television as yet been given this responsibility. Some American and European schools use educational TV as a teaching tool merely to supplement the classroom teacher. The few undeveloped nations that have tried television have mimicked this same cautious approach.

Accordingly, I advise:

Select the best school now in operation, staff it with the most dramatic teachers available, and use it as the base for televising the entire range of courses offered below the university level. In most nations this would be the first opportunity for students to receive the equivalent of a high school education except by migrating to the cities.

Build no more schoolhouses throughout the nation. Instead, the students can gather in "viewing centers." Here will be merely monitors able to keep discipline and to distribute and collect examination papers.

Each student takes as many of these televised lessons as he wishes — or, rather, as many as the family chores will allow him to attend.

Each student advances at his own speed from one course to the next.

Establish "examination headquarters" where "counselor-correctors" handle via mechanization the papers which the monitors send in each week or oftener for grading and comment. It is likely that one counselor-corrector can handle the papers from several hundred students each week.

Point all courses in the curriculum directly at training the students in resource development and in inculcating in them the realization that such development is vital to the future of both their nation and themselves personally.

The ambitious ones and the bright ones who continue with these courses through the equivalent of high school can be certified as admissible into the national university.

Television is a twentieth-century tool that can make education a reality for all who wish it.

If the material coming over the television is, however, merely of the same education-for-the-sake-of-education culture now being offered in the schools, then all is lost!

More important than the mere use of television is the opportunity now available to rewrite classroom material so as to drive home to each student the need for him to use his education for the development of his nation's resources, to make his forests, his waters and his soil produce more. Television can show him how this can be done and can show him how he personally will gain advancement in the process.

The three R's and all that goes with them must be taught with a purpose that transcends the simple desire to read and write.

A nation's educational system must achieve more than mere literacy. It must produce *educated* citizens, educated in the subjects and techniques that will make the individual more prosperous and his nation less backward.

10

The Fallacy of Higher Education—Ignore the Old, Start the New

LATIN AMERICA is now but a motley crowd of nations with little or no international weight. Few of her men of science reach world renown; few of her men of letters are read; few of her statesmen attain a reputation other than that which courtesy or convenience suggests."[1]

Here Salvador de Madariaga is speaking, a firm supporter of Latins versus the rest of the world. He says this in a context describing the impotence of the universities of Latin America—that is, these institutions are failing in their function of providing effective leaders.

A university controlled by the thought police of a dictator is a tragic straitjacket that will reduce the future usefulness of the half-educated students in the nation's life. The dogmatic fetters of a church unwilling, afraid to allow free and open discussion of all social problems can stunt a university as surely as any dictator.

But equally bad is the school controlled by anarchic students, many of whom are in their forties and "belong to that intermediate territory eternally disputed between loafers and Bohemians."[2]

In other chapters I have used the term "university" in the normal sense in which it is taken for granted in the advanced countries. There, a university is the culmination of a nation's culture. A student is envied, a graduate is respected, a professor is honored. All that is best in the nation is epitomized in university life.

Latin American countries, Asian countries, most Arab countries, many African countries each have an institution that the local people call a university. And the term is, in ignorance, accepted at face value in the committee meetings of aid officials in Washington and the United Nations and even in international educational conferences.

In the majority of these nations, in the great majority of them, the groups of buildings and students and faculty calling themselves a university are in truth only a fatuous parody. The dividing line here is not between hungry and comfortable countries, but something quite different.

The reasons for the impotence of these institutions vary from region to region, but the most disastrous is the lack of discipline among students.

To quote de Madariaga again: "Concerning universities in general in Latin America, a 'student' may fail time and again and still remain a student for as long as he wishes, not only wasting the time of his teachers and the space of his classes, but acquiring the long experience of university life which will enable him to boss its political activity."

He gives this example: "In the Law Faculty of the University of Buenos Aires twenty thousand students are on the registers. Of these, no more than about eight thousand are considered genuine; the remaining twelve thousand are hangers-on who find it in their interest to retain their student status for a variety of reasons, including a fairly high number of cases in order to recruit and organize communist contingents." [3]

Here are quotations from a 1962 review of conditions at the "University" of Caracas.

> The extraordinary privilege [of autonomy] was accorded the universities as a reward for the role played by the student body in the ousting of Dictator General Marcos Perez Jimenez four years ago. Today the Universities are inviolate . . .

In November 1960 [the students] staged a three-day gun battle with police from one of the student residences, blazing away with machine-guns from their own arms cache in the university grounds. In January of this year they shot and killed two soldiers from the sanctuary of the campus and it was touch-and-go whether the enraged army would storm their citadel and put an end to the sacred cow of autonomy once and for all. More recently three irrepressibles squatted on the roof of the nine-floor laboratory building with rifles sharp-shooting at a fire brigade attempting to reach a burning bus slewed across the street from the campus.

One remembers that university education is free, that there is no entrance examination, that the taxpayer contributes $30 million each year to the universities, $18 million of which goes to the Central University of Caracas, that the students arrogantly regard these favors as a right rather than a privilege.[4]

The Venezuelan Government has since curtailed somewhat the autonomy of this university, but the citizens of many other hungry nations will recognize the similarity of these student "activities" to those of their own institutions.

As indicated earlier, the distinction in such a situation is not between the hungry and the comfortable countries, but between the cultured and the not so cultured.

When students take over the administration, the faculty is browbeaten and the level of education generally becomes low indeed. Occasionally, it may be possible to obtain a valid technical training as an engineer or specialized scholar. Occasionally, a professor may gain some international standing through his writing, or a graduate achieve distinction at the United Nations.

In fields of controversy, however, such as the social sciences, the all-powerful student leaders can, depending on their whims of the moment, shout down and terrorize anyone voicing an opinion different from theirs, whether fellow student, faculty member, dean or visiting lecturer.

Active discussion of opposing viewpoints is the life juice of a university. When it is absent, as it usually is in these student-dominated universities, the institution becomes an intellectual nothingness.

The politics of these student juntas is unimportant here. My emphasis is that these "universities" are incapable of giving the hungry nation the trained men and leaders it so desperately needs. The new African nations are each anxious to inaugurate a national university. Some already are established. Let these nations beware of the models they choose to emulate.

> There are no West African universities – yet. There are British and French universities in West Africa but they are importations; they are no more indigenous than the motor cars . . .
>
> Despite minor adjustments in curricula to suit local conditions, the curricula in West African universities are drawn up on the assumption that the African has no indigenous culture worth studying, and no organization of society worth the attention of undergraduates. An African can graduate with a B.A. knowing practically nothing about the intricate political and social structure of his own race . . .
>
> The danger in West Africa is similar to the danger to which India has succumbed: that the inevitable gap between the intellectuals and the mass of the population will widen until in the end even kinship ties and tribal loyalty may be unable to bridge it.[5]

The president of a hungry nation once told me, and he was himself a graduate of the local university, "Going to that school is a waste of time. The only way our university can be improved is to lock and bolt the doors. It would be political suicide for the government to do that, however. The only solution is to start a totally new university a hundred kilometers away so it cannot be contaminated by the old one."

I follow the President's advice.

I propose the national university be left in its undeveloped state to the student shouters and cowed faculty and the training of doctors, lawyers, architects, poetasters and other prestige professions favored by the city-bred with good background.

The Minister of Resources, however, as he conserves educational funds for resource development, will see to it that funds supporting this type of education dwindle. Let the university stay on, but let those who wish to be lawyers, doctors and architects pay their own way. Today the tuition of the universities in these countries is free; the government pays all costs. It is time to charge tuition fees. This will afford the Minister of Resources a means for drying up slowly the imbalance of students going into the prestige professions.

Central America, a purely agricultural area, had 10,546 university students in 1962 — only 187 were studying agriculture.[6]

Most of the money available for higher education must be used to establish and push forward a new institution called College for Resource Development. This new college must be separate geographically, administratively, and financially from the national university. Merely grafting it onto the rotten trunk of the old, decadent university would be, is it not obvious, the kiss of death.

Locate the College for Resource Development away from the capital, preferably not in a provincial city but in a place that can develop into what is known in the United States as a college town. Leave the streets of the capital to the university rioters. If the new college is successfully administered, its students will never be allowed the chance to feel that time exists for such frolicking.

Quite the contrary. The president of the college should be chosen on the basis that he has the drive and capabilities to instill in his student body and faculty the sure belief that they are going to save the nation. They are going to save the nation not by rioting like banshees for that day's political whim, but by learning to turn the key that will unlock the full potential of the nation's future.

For the new college to succeed, prestige must be immediately obtained for its student body. This can be achieved by making the rules for admission stiffer than for a university. Let no one at the university pretend *his* is the better institution. This should not be difficult, because generally the university has no standards of admission. Anyone with a high school diploma can enter.

All important is the caliber of the students selected for the College of Resource Development. *If* those of the right caliber are chosen, *if* its president is dedicated to the college's goals, and *if* he has the backing of his boss (the Minister of Resources), the prestige will be forthcoming.

Often one hears the foreigner say it is impossible for the locals to be good students, that they are innately incapable of sustained study. Obviously, this is nonsense. Students on every continent will rise to the demands made of them by their schools. Since the present schools and universities of most hungry nations do not demand standards of excellence or the study that goes with such standards, the students do not now demonstrate their capabilities.

I refer again to my experience as director of the Panamerican Agricultural School at Zamorano. During five years there I supervised the examination of a total of some ten thousand secondary school students in fourteen Latin American countries for entrance into Zamorano. The education systems from which they came were as diverse as can be imagined, ranging from the comparatively highly developed ones in Chile and Costa Rica to the poor ones in Nicaragua and Bolivia.

Yet by using the same examination procedures – nothing much more than a standard I.Q. test and a personal interview – students of similar caliber from all these countries were selected who were able to handle an intensive, university-level curriculum.

They all had one thing in common, however. This was an aggressive attitude coupled with a high intelligence. The result was that when presented with high standards they met the challenge, regardless of their widely different former training.

They met the challenge of doing the equivalent of four years of university work in three years. They also met the challenge of living in a remote valley with one month's vacation at Christmas as their only time off, except for one Saturday every two months in the capital city. It was a rough schedule, but they met it. Students can meet challenges – when the challenge is there.

The three-year curriculum which Zamorano then had gave more instruction than most Latin universities give in five. In fact, it gave more than most universities in the United States give in four. It did away with summer vacations, for one thing. What was achieved by this was not so much cutting down the time factor as it was instilling in the student (as well as the faculty) the idea that here was a crash program fitted directly to the urgent needs of his own country, and equally important, fitted directly to his own personal needs for achieving success in his future home environment.

From my own experience I thus suggest the College of Resource Development set up its curriculum on a three-year basis and forget about summer vacations.

The hungry nations are in a hurry. They have to be.

As for the curriculum at the College for Resource Development, again only the brush strokes can be suggested.

It should include a school of agriculture out of which will come the agricultural extension agents and the crop and animal research men, as well as modern farmers.

Schools of forestry, fisheries and mines will be needed in line with the nation's range of resources.

The school for land classifiers, which is described later in the section on land reform, should be part of this college.

The number of courses should be kept limited.

To repeat what many others have said, the type of college needed in backward countries is similar to that which the United States evolved when it was backward; namely, the land grant colleges of the last century. At Iowa State College when it was founded, the students studied identical subjects during their first year and a half. They then made a choice of the only two alternative courses offered, "agriculture" and "mechanics." [7]

The miscellany of courses, many in name only, that so many universities offer can only weaken a beginning institution. So keep the College for Resource Development simple. Keep it on the single, narrow track of resource development. And keep it dedicated.

The training of specialists should not be attempted at this College for Resource Development, at least for the first generation. Leave the inauguration of graduate schools to the future to worry about. In a hungry country the lack of native specialists is not a problem it can solve at the beginning. In fact, it would be harmful for a proliferation of specialties, so much a part of modern life, to occur at the college. This training is to be for broad-gauge men. There should not be more than one year of "area concentration" out of the three-year curriculum.

The basic course of general sciences, laced heavily with economics, will be taken by all students. All will take the general courses in agriculture (agronomy, animal husbandry), with strong emphasis on conservation practices – and principles of forestry. Even the last year will not be a year of specialization as we normally think of it. It will simply allow the student to take three or four courses within the field in which he is most interested – not enough to be a specialist, only to have a "speaking acquaintance" – whether poultry production, geology, or fish processing. The graduates must be men who can roll up their sleeves and try to tackle any problem, not men who stand aside and say, "So sorry, this is not my field; you will have to see such and such a man."

Inherent in the instruction at the College for Resource Development must be the belief that the student is receiving the fundamentals on which he can *build* competence through experience within his field of training. Isn't this, after all, what any formal education should be? Who, reading this page, is earning his livelihood based on the isolated knowledge his college courses gave him?

The Instituto Tecnológico y de Estudios Superiores at Monterrey in northern Mexico is one of the very few non-government-controlled universities in Latin America. It was privately founded in 1943 and is continuously and actively supported by all levels of the industrial city of Monterrey. Students number 5000. The institute charges tuition, issues report cards, gives quizzes, holds classes punctually and the professors are full-time (factors that are rare elsewhere in Latin America). For these or other reasons its atmosphere is unique and its academic reputation is high. I noted this comment in a magazine article describing the institute:

> Since the professors devote full time to their classes, the studies are demanding, and the students have no time for the political activities, riots and strikes common at some Latin American univer-

sities. The students are concerned instead with success in the rigid standard courses of Tecnológico, designed to train them for responsible positions that they will meet early in life in Mexico's fast expanding economy.

What the Latins of Monterrey have accomplished, surely the Latins of Mexico City, Caracas, Buenos Aires and elsewhere could also achieve. When that happens the rough criticisms of Salvador de Madariaga, and myself, will thankfully no longer be valid.

11

The Fallacy of Local Graduate Study—It's Inferior, It's Provincial

HERE IS the top of the education ladder, the acme, the ultimate.

Graduate study means specialization in a specific field for two or three years, often longer.

Specialists are indeed vital to the development of the expanding hungry nation. They, when all is said and done, will be the ones to find the new ways to utilize marginal resources, to double the output of resources already in use, to advise legislators on high finance and taxation, to check the contracts and the work of imported foreign technicians, to control the weeds, adapt the fertilizers, breed new rice varieties, conserve irrigation water.

Such specialists cannot receive their training in most home countries. So off go the students. And back come lurid reports of their didoes in night clubs, marriage to alien girls and study of exotic, unrealistic subjects. Worse, an awful lot of them never come home at all.

There has been a great deal of criticism of the students abroad, whether graduate or undergraduate. In the United States today there are tens of thousands of foreign students at all levels of schooling. In Europe there are tens of thousands more. And also in the communist countries. More in Japan, Canada,

Australia. More in the undeveloped countries from the less developed areas, such as in Mexico, Ghana, Egypt, India. In universities in Argentina alone there are six thousand Peruvians studying.[1] It is one of the great migrations of modern times.

And so the family's pride and joy returns homeside with the degree of a foreign university. What happens? The tragedy is that so often nothing at all happens. In fact, the family is lucky if he can get a worthwhile job. It is also lucky if he can relax within the family circle without psychological abrasions or, at the minimum, without white-collar shame at his parents' primitiveness.

Getting on the plane and going forth to conquer knowledge is not enough. The student must learn the right things and learn them in such a way that they are usable in the home environment.

In recent years there has been a trend in the thinking of local officials and foreign aid administrators against the sending of students abroad. Instead, they advise "beefing up" the home universities and, more specifically, establishing local graduate schools.

As a result, graduate schools are now being set up in many odd parts of the world, often schools duplicating the same work in adjacent small countries. The major foundations are playing an important role in financing these new schools. The United States aid missions sign contracts with American universities to "develop" graduate schools in the aid-receiving countries.

It is this activity I now include among my fallacies. The education to be given in these indigenous graduate schools will *not* lead to training adequately the specialists so urgently needed. The trouble is endemic within the new graduate schools themselves.

Basically, the situation boils down to my often expressed dogma: just as there will be more returns from putting money into land *already* developed than into new, hoped-for land, just as there will be more production derived from money invested in resources and operations already in action than in new, hoped-for propositions, so the hungry nations will be ahead of the game if they put their funds into training their specialists abroad where the facilities for this complex form of education are already proven worthwhile than into new, hoped-for graduate schools.

The arguments against sending students abroad for graduate work are many. One Pakistani official said to me, "God knows we have plenty of shyster lawyers who never left the country, but there are no shysters like our shysters who studied law in England." A survey several years ago to find out what seven hundred Bolivians who had studied in the United States were then doing showed that at least two hundred and twenty-five had never returned to Bolivia.[2] Then there are the ones who studied specialties unrelated to their country's needs — like the Korean who became an expert in German history of the *Sturm und Drang* era, the Iranian who became an atomic physicist, the Liberian who aimed only to become a member of the United Nations Secretariat.

But the major objection propounded is that the student cannot obtain in a foreign university the training applicable to the peculiar conditions in his home country. Obviously, if a Filipino studies plant pathology at the University of Wisconsin, the specifics he learns will not be directly applicable to the crops of Luzon or Panay.

These critics, however, miss the point of graduate study, of any form of education, in fact. What the student learns in his courses is the principles of his subject plus the ability to reason out and to cope with the problems he will later face in that field of work. Each student studying plant pathology will have to adapt that knowledge to his own local environment. The student from Florida, as well as the Filipino, must adapt his Wisconsin knowledge. Even, I add, the student from Iowa must adapt his Wisconsin knowledge to the somewhat different conditions across the Mississippi River.

No graduate walks from the commencement platform, diploma in hand, with the complete answers to the problems he will face. He must work out his own answers by applying the principles he has learned in the classroom.

Another objection to graduate study abroad is the delay involved in learning the foreign language. The absolute need to know that language, whether English, French, German or Russian is overlooked here. The specialist *must* know a language in which are found the published material and technical data of his field. He must be able, throughout his professional lifetime, to read the new literature of his field.

It is the rare person who can master a language without living for a while in a country in which it is spoken. In colonial days a small percentage of the boys who had all their primary and secondary education in French or English ended up sometimes with quite good fluency. Even this small percentage, however, stumble and falter when faced with the technical material of university courses. One of the most solid reasons for sending the student to the United States, Britain, Canada, Australia or New Zealand is that he will acquire full use of the English language, today's primary medium for the exchange of ideas and of new technical data.

The student left behind in these new graduate schools in the hungry nations will always be lost from contact with his colleagues. Arabic and Spanish, for instance, are useless as a training medium for graduate students; the necessary professional literature, even basic textbooks, is not translated into those languages except for occasional, happenstance items.

The language barrier is one more handicap which the citizens of the hungry nations must recognize and overcome. This is as true of Argentina and Egypt as it is of Nepal and Burundi.

Another objection given against sending the graduate students abroad is the high cost involved. It is indeed expensive, this traveling to the foreign country and living there for years, even though scholarship funds may alleviate the burden. Nevertheless, the overall cost is less than that involved in constructing new buildings and laboratories and, most expensive of all, assembling and maintaining a qualified staff of professors and other personnel. In discussing this subject of relative costs, the critics usually forget that the graduate education received at Harvard or Iowa State University is paid for in large part by endowment funds or tax appropriations. Even when the foreign student must himself pay the full tuition rates he is getting a bargain.

There is, I admit, the question of native prestige. The citizens of the hungry countries gain an intangible pride when they have something called the School for Advanced Mathematics or the School of Agronomy or the School of Astronomy in their capital city. It sets them apart from the old days. They forget, however, there is no prestige in something that is of low quality, that visiting foreigners regard as no 'count.

A successful institution for the training of professional men amounts to much more than bricks and mortar and personnel. The institution must imbue the student with a sense of inquiry, with a sense of awe towards the potential of his specialty. The student must absorb respect and deep pride in his profession. Dedicated teachers are the channel through which such intangibles are acquired, but the true value of the institution is based on tradition built up over the years it has labored in its field, labored to inculcate these very feelings in successive generations of students.

A tradition of serious endeavor and high accomplishment can only grow out of the nation's educational system as a whole. Unless based on successful elementary and secondary and university standards of excellence, the graduate schools will remain of little value. These schools are the cap to a pyramid and the pyramid must have a solid foundation.

More than any other reason this is why the new graduate institutions now being installed in the hungry countries will exist in failure. They are being imposed artificially on a foundation of sand. Look at the struggling high schools and at the chaotic, often farcical universities, and decide if this is the base on which a graduate school should be built!

Let the hungry nation first tackle the problems within its grasp of ability. Let it first reorganize and establish a sound educational system from the ground up. The graduate schools are far in the future.

In 1950 I had a tour of duty at the headquarters of the Bureau of Reclamation of the U.S. Department of the Interior in Denver. This is the bureau that builds the big dams of the West, designed for irrigation and electricity and, when its officials learned the propaganda value involved, also for recreational purposes.

The bureau had built up the most superb corps of big-dam engineers ever assembled. Unfortunately, it was suddenly noted that, regardless of pressurings for Congressional appropriations, the possible sites for worthwhile big dams in the United States were rapidly being used up. As one means of holding together its team, the bureau offered to loan its engineers as advisers to foreign countries; that is, to determine whether a big dam at a particular site would be physically feasible and economically effective. Sometimes the engineers went under the auspices of the aid programs, more often the foreign governments were glad to hire their services outright. If it was determined that a big dam could be built, and when the money was at hand, then the bureau engineers would often stay on as advisers in letting out the contracts to construction companies and in performing other supervisory functions. This procedure provided an effective and useful form of technical assistance to undeveloped countries.

Another aspect of this same program was for foreign engineering graduate students to come to Denver to be trained in big-dam design and construction. My job was to help the bureau with these students. They normally remained in Denver two years and in most cases their own governments paid all their expenses; aid money was not then involved. They were a remarkably bright group of young men from a dozen countries, both backward ones in Asia and advanced European ones. It was international youth at its best.

And yet, should the ones from the hungry nations have been directed into this rather esoteric, highly specialized field of designing big dams? Regardless of how many such dams might be economically practical in Burma, for instance, should a half-dozen of its extremely limited supply of educated, trained young men be pigeonholed in this work? Burma could better hire from abroad whatever big-dam experts it needs, such as those already available from the Bureau of Reclamation, rather than producing its own coterie. These young men could be better used if trained in, to name one field, irrigation engineering. Constructing a big dam is a one-time project. Utilizing its waters for irrigation is a never-ending problem; only an indigenous engineer dealing directly and sympathetically with the local people can hope to apportion the water equitably.

I offer the following empiricism:

If a hungry nation can hire from abroad trained specialists to do a specific job, then there is no need to spend part of the limited money to educate its citizens for that work, either in locally established institutions or in graduate schools abroad.

If, however, foreigners cannot do the job properly, then by all means educate nationals for it, but do so by sending them abroad to already established, already *good* graduate schools.

Examples of the former, to be hired from abroad, are the engineers to build a bridge or a flood control revetment or a drainage system, or architects to design a laboratory or a processing plant. Why expend money and talented youth on the training of certain types of professional men when such technicians are immediately available from a dozen industrialized countries at a cost far less than that spent on the years educating local boys?

Examples of the latter, to be educated at graduate schools abroad, are financial experts (because these are continuous, never-ending careers deeply involved with the political and cultural emotions of the nationals); agricultural research scientists (because this type of research, to be any good, must last for decades and must be conducted on the spot in valleys far from the comforts so beloved by foreigners in the capital city); and government administration officials (the history of foreign "advisers" so often introduced into government departments of the hungry nations is a long one; usually they do not do much permanent good; always they are too detached from the people, too ignorant of local customs and, above all, too temporary).

It is discouraging to note the percentage of graduate students from the hungry nations who involve themselves in the study of subjects and professions for which there is no need in their home environment. Often, however, the fault lies not with them but with the school they are attending abroad.

Consider first the young undergraduate student. He arrives fresh and green at the foreign school; he is young and he is excited and he knows nothing from nothing. He cannot see beyond the fantastic Act of God that somehow selected him out of all the others to escape the confines of his homeland. No one needs careful counseling so much as he with respect to the courses he is to spend years studying. And what does he get? Indoctrination lectures on how Americans use hot dog drive-ins, how Americans ask girls for dates, why a man bunts to get to first base. In the other receiving countries it is the same, or, if no formal talks are given, the students are left in limbo to find their own sources of information, which, at least in London and Paris until recently, meant that the local communists took over the indoctrination.

Seldom does the new foreign student receive thoughtful advice and guidance as to his courses; he is left, as with the local students, to make his own selections within the rigid framework of "required courses" which that particular school has happened to set up for all its students. The school may make exceptions for the foreign student, but it is on the basis that he is unable, because of incomplete earlier education, to do the required number of years of math or history; the exceptions are seldom made because the required subjects will be of little use to the student in his own environment.

It is left to the student to decide what shall be his field of study; he is mistakenly treated as a mature man of the world who has weighed all factors and carefully chosen his field. If he has not chosen, then the liberal arts department is accepted as the proper location for him until he makes up his mind. This procedure leads to the tragic results of unemployment and misemployment when he returns home.

This sort of vague course selection also applies, in varying degrees, even to the graduate student who arrives at the foreign institution with his field of study already established.

I compliment the U.S. foreign aid program for its long-standing policy of not sending a student to the United States to study unless a specific job using his training will be waiting for him on his return. A broadening of this policy should be the concern of the Minister of Resources whenever government money or limited foreign exchange is involved in study abroad.

The decision as to field of study should be made before the

student ever leaves home. In fact, such a decision should be made even before the scholarship students are selected.

An Asian scholarship student told me, "There is such competition for the few scholarships that all of us are well aware of every detail of what kind of qualifications will win the prize, including the art of smiling at the right people at social functions. It is no trick to adjust our so-called motivations to the prize at hand."

Expressed differently by an American professor: "The trouble with personal interviews and aptitude tests in general is that if the student knows there is a scholarship available for an agriculture college and he is asked, 'Do you want to plow a field or be a movie star?' of course he looks you straight in the eye and breathes sincerity about plowing the Good Earth."

Nevertheless, the only way scholarships and aid funds for foreign students should be handled, especially for graduate students, is for the men in charge, the experienced, worldly men in charge, to decide, even before distributing the forms for applicants to fill out, what courses are to be studied by the scholarship grantees. They should decide what professions are most needed by the nation and in what proportion the scholarships should be prorated among these professions.

The country needs above all else to have its resources developed. Therefore, the scholarship money must be directed into those channels. The hungry, backward, primitive nation needs men who can develop its agriculture, forests, fisheries, mines. It does *not* need lawyers, doctors, architects, engineering specialists and cultured men versed in the arts.

This is heresy, I realize, within the educational and political worlds. For those who disagree I can only suggest they travel out to Nyasaland, to Cambodia, to Korea, to Bolivia and look for themselves.

Here and elsewhere in these chapters I have been making snide allusions to the prestige professions such as lawyers and doctors. Perhaps it is well to point out here the dominant role played by these men, completely untrained in any form of natural resource development, in the governments of most hungry nations.

The presence of lawyers in government is visualized by Americans, but not, probably, that of doctors. In the United States, it is unusual for a doctor to be in public office. Not so in the backward areas.

Recent doctor Presidents in Latin America that come to mind in only this one region are Kubitschek in Brazil, Villeda Morales in Honduras, Arosemena in Ecuador, Siles Zuazo in Bolivia, Illia in Argentina and Duvalier in Haiti. Some have been among their nation's finest executives, such as Villeda Morales and Siles Zuazo. Others have been among the worse. I suppose they average out with the average, but it is an average of their peers, few of whom ever had practical experience out in the fields where hands are dirty. At the 1963 United Nations Conference on Science and Technology for the Benefit of the Less Developed Nations, the two largest delegations from Africa (Nigeria and Tanganyika) and the three largest delegations from Latin America (Argentina, Brazil, Venezuela) were each headed by medical men. The practice of medicine is a limited basis for comprehension of the philosophies and problems of modern technology and science in the development of backward areas. Unfortunately, medical doctors are often the only trained persons a hungry nation has to represent it.

I wish the term "businessman" were not such a forgotten word or, in many areas, such a dirty word. The hungry nations need businessmen; they are an important part of the machinery for the development of a nation's resources. Yet how seldom does one hear a foreign student say he wants to be a businessman. My own suggestion is that all those green undergraduate foreign students who are turned loose on the liberal arts courses to acquire culture should, instead, be placed in business courses, such as bookkeeping and the incidence of taxes. At least those students, when they return home, will not be fish out of water as they go around trying to find a job.

West Africa has a pungent, satirical phrase: "been to." "I have been to Soho." "I have been to the Henley Regatta." "I have been to the Palladium." Anyone who has visited England, or, I suppose, anywhere abroad, is a "been to." The "been to's" of a community naturally gravitate toward each other. It is said a "been to" girl will marry only a "been to" man.

This is of the same ilk, obviously, as the similar boasting of Americans fifty years ago who had been to Paris.

Yet for the returning student the title of "been to" is an evidence of prestige; more important, it is evidence of the *confidence* he has in his own worth. He has been to the outside world.

For many years I was involved in sending students to the United States for graduate study. I watched these same students return to their home countries and have myself hired many of them. Constantly, I have noted that it is this *confidence* which is the greatest asset the student can bring back. Such a man knows his knowledge and skill are worthwhile. People listen to him. It is important they do. Here is a man who has broken out of the local, provincial rut and fared forth into the adventurous world of twentieth-century excitement. His ability and his "attitude" are incomparably superior to men who have not studied abroad, even though, in some cases, the years of study may have been the same.

Establishing local graduate schools costs more money than sending students abroad and the resulting trainees are hopelessly inferior both in education and in that intangible "attitude" and confidence. These hungry countries are intellectual backwaters. So get the graduate students out of these provincial places. Get them out into the world of ideas and action. Give them a language useful in their professional work. When they come home they are indeed worth all the effort – if they have been trained in useful professions.

I am all for the "been to's," but only for those who have been to the right professors to learn the right subjects that will benefit the homeland.

12

The Fallacy of Industrialization—and a Possible Remedy

I SPENT two days in Amman with a young Jordanian businessman. We argued continuously about the future of his country. I stressed that the economic level could not be raised without developing the nation's resources, and the only resources of Jordan are tourists, agriculture and the minerals in the Dead Sea. After two days his repeated reply was still, "Jordan must industrialize. I don't care whether industrialization is bad or good for my country. It is the only way the rest of the world will respect us."

Or as Nehru proclaimed, "Real progress must ultimately depend on industrialization." [1]

Everyone is mesmerized by industrialization.

Today it has become a form of religion with its own dogmas, catechisms, protective saints and supposed miracles. And the unbelievers are cast forth from the sacred temples of the planning committees.

Particularly in the hungry nations. Their reasons for wanting industrialization may be vague and illogical and as varied as the colors on Joseph's coat, but they know they have to have it.

All that the hungry countries dream for their future is epitomized by smoking smokestacks. They know for sure when they get the stacks, prosperity, culture and other trappings of international respectability will somehow come along also.

But industrialization does not reduce hunger or poverty nor does it raise the standard of living except for a few favored circles. Therein lies the fallacy of industrialization.

Up to now the only regions where poverty has been truly mitigated and where comfortable living has been established for nearly everyone are in the agricultural nations like New Zealand, Eire, Denmark and Norway which have a stable population, and in the richer agricultural areas of the United States whose surplus population is drained off to the cities.

I lived for a year in New Zealand. The boast there is that slums have been eliminated, and they have. The boast is also that it is the result of the socialist, womb-to-tomb government. This I doubt. I give credit to stable agriculture combined wih virgin soils and underpopulation.

To industrialize, a nation must have two basic qualifications: (1) a productive, prosperous agriculture able to provide surplus food for the factory workers; and (2) a certain combination of raw materials, primarily, but not necessarily, minerals. Access to the food and the raw materials elsewhere, as in colonies, can be also effective – or the means to pay for importing them with the nation's export of commercial crops or raw ores.

Today's industrialized nations do have these two qualifications. How many of the hungry nations have them? How many of these yearners after industrialization have these two bases for industrialization in even a small way?

All of the industrialized nations are in the temperate zones. Most of the hungry countries lie in the tropics. There are, it is true, raw materials, many industrial agricultural products, various minerals, including iron and coal, scattered throughout the tropical and subtropical zones. Yet it is rare to find a proper combination of them close enough to each other to nourish industrialization. Perhaps in India. Perhaps in Venezuela. Yet neither of these two has an agriculture capable of producing the surplus needed to support a large industrialized labor force.

Changing economic factors, plus research, can alter this curse of deficiency that hangs over the tropics like a miasma. Energy from the sun, from atomic reactors, from undeveloped water courses may some day enable this or that locality to balance out a new agriculture revived by research, and thereby to industrialize naturally — but that is in the next century, if it does happen, not this one.

The industrialization of Great Britain is an often told story, but it is well to summarize it here.

In the seventeenth century the cultivation of legumes in rotation with potatoes and wheat was started, inaugurating a great increase in food production. Prior to then, the English farmers knew little about preserving the fertility of their land.

One theory commonly accepted is that English farmland — and of northern Europe in general — probably would be exhausted today, as it has long been exhausted around the Mediterranean, if it had not been for the black death in the fourteenth century. This plague killed a quarter to a half of the population of most sections of England, France, Germany and Scandinavia; thus the land was preserved until the new legume rotation system taught the people how to replenish the nitrogen in the soil and laid the groundwork for the development of scientific agriculture. For the record, this was the second time the land had been preserved from destruction by historical factors; the first was when the barbarian invasions resulted in the Dark Ages, during which the land of England and particularly of France was able to recover from the bad practices of Roman times.

By 1700 one English farmer was raising enough food to feed three other Englishmen. The farmers were producing a *surplus.* This freed the men needed to mine coal and iron. In fact, a quarter of a century later, by 1725, the Industrial Revolution was under way. Improved agriculture could not, of course, have started the Industrial Revolution by itself. The presence in England of large and rich mineral resources, combined with great deposits of high-grade coal and an excellent water transportation system, was equally vital. No part of England is farther than seventy-five miles from the sea. Construction of canals and use of the rivers supplied cheap transportation directly to the mine centers. Labor-saving devices were generated out of the Industrial Revolution itself as a shortage of workmen developed.

The later agricultural troubles caused by the Enclosure Acts were offset by the cheap food imported from the virgin land areas of the colonies, the United States and Argentina, and paid for by the new industrial products.

Japan is often held forth as the model which the hungry countries should emulate. Here there was a degree of government planning, and so the planners also present Japan's industrialization as a proper model. Up to about 1900 the central government acted as a catalytic agent, shouldering most of the entrepreneurial risks via direct operation or credits and subsidies for iron foundries, shipyards, communication lines, cement factories, etc. Government support of, and control over, the nation's economic life still remains important today and in some fields it is dominant.

Yet planning is not enough. Japan's industrialization could not have been carried forward without certain resources and specific advantages. It did have some coal, a much more vital mineral fifty years ago than today. Also, no section of the country was farther than one hundred miles from a seaport.

Equally important, the government established agricultural experiment stations almost as soon as it began to build factories. In fifty years Japan increased its production of both food and raw materials by 200 per cent.

Yet the agricultural increase was not enough to support the new top-heavy industrial empire. This imbalance has weakened Japan ever since. The nation tried first to rectify this via conquest (although the war lords then in control probably needed no excuse for such adventuring). Since the last war the Japanese have tried to push industrialization ever and ever higher and to push agriculture also to the utmost. The meager farmlands, however, no matter how intensively improved, are not responding in proportion to the industrial expansion. Only the Netherlands uses more chemical fertilizers per acre than does Japan,[2] yet there is a limit to what can be squeezed from the land.

Japan has adopted an active policy of birth control. It now seems the country may establish within a few decades a stable population in line with its true resource and agricultural potential.

Even without such a balance it can today boast of being the fifth industrial nation of the world. Yet have you traveled lately in the backyards of Tokyo and Osaka? Industrialization does not eliminate poverty. Japan may be fifth in industrialization but it ranks twenty-second among the world's nations in per capita national income.[3]

Which comes first, the chicken or the egg?

Industrialization or the agricultural surplus? Which produces the other?

The answer can only be that each successfully industrialized nation had, within its early history, the genes that have permitted its current range of factories. The genes included both mineral resources and fertile land which enabled farmers to produce a surplus that could feed the new industrial workers.

> Since the times of the founders of political economy, and before, industrial development as apart from agriculture has been considered, especially by the Western groups, the goal and often the purpose of good economic policy. Since the industrial group was powerful and since in its power it was prosperous, there were those who reasoned that the artificial generating of such a society would bring with it all the power and wealth of an industrial development . . . Our observations lead us to believe that the industrial phenomenon in any group is the direct, dependent result of the food surplus which a group in a given area is able to produce. Yet even though this surplus is large and constant, little industrial development will occur unless the area also contains, or controls completely, strategically located basic materials from which tools may be fashioned for the necessary and continuous attack upon the agricultural frontier which the area must carry on.
>
> . . . the industrial development will continue until the flow of surplus food is absorbed and often a little longer. That is, until food production upon the margin is reduced by those climatic conditions which labor can not counter.[4]

Will foreign aid gifts or loans used to build factories solve this problem? Whatever might be the short-term results, the final outcome remains the same.

Let the foreign aid be put first into the development of the country's agricultural projects (or fisheries, forests, mines). This is, unfortunately, undramatic and is, therefore, not directly useful to harried politicians currying public favor, but it is the only way to a higher standard of living.

Let not the hungry country compound its troubles by building industries which her assets cannot support. If the new industries could export products that could compete in the world market, the situation might be different, for then she could buy her food and other needed resources. But that prospect is remote.

Daniel Webster said, "When tillage begins, other arts follow."

The trouble with industrialization lies in the harsh fact that factories are economic only in certain geographically limited spots and within shifting periods of time. A textile plant may be all right for one town but not for another, and at this time but not earlier or later. A tractor assembly shop will prosper here but not there. Processing the local raw materials is suitable in one country but not the adjoining one. That sweetheart of the industrialites, that envy of every backward nation, that miraculous Virgin of the new religion, namely the steel mill, is economic only where coal, limestone, iron and easy transportation are found of the right type and in the right juxtaposition and within the right market area.

Why is the United States such an industrial giant today? Orators and editors like to attribute this to American ingenuity and aggressiveness. Is it not, rather, the correct interlocation of coal, iron, limestone and easy transportation, plus all the other minerals, plus all that wonderful virgin farmland of the Middle West?

In discussing industrialization one usually thinks of minerals and the chemicals derived from them. Yet it should be noted that each successful industrial country is itself a heavy consumer of agricultural products.

The 6,000,000 automobiles America produces annually are not made of solid metal. For example, to raise the cotton and other agricultural items going directly into their manufacture 3,600,000 acres of farmland are needed.[5]

And that state-owned factory or smelter or processing plant? The fallacy hidden within the state-owned industry is that *if* its existence had economic justification an entrepreneur already would have started it.

There are, naturally, projects that are so gigantic private capital cannot normally finance them. When such is the case and when the state is sincere in wanting to encourage private enterprise then let it take direct steps to aid a private consortium to raise the necessary capital.

Peru is experimenting with ways to encourage private companies to pioneer in opening up new enterprises in its empty eastern provinces. Most taxes, including income taxes and import-export duties, are exempt for a period of ten years.[6] This would seem to be the right course. If the businessman is unwilling to risk his capital when receiving such an incentive, it is likely that the opportunity for profit in that area is slim.

My point here is that the state must conserve its limited capital (tax money) for use in resource development, rather than wander off into the labyrinth of industrialization. Encourage the entrepreneur with tax privileges, woo him with customs exemptions, praise him with medals of honor, first class, but don't use a *centavo* of government taxes to finance him. Government money is too scarce.

By now, the tribulations and vagaries of modern business life surely have proven empirically that there is nothing, well, almost nothing, that the unfettered capitalist cannot do better in the economic world than the state-owned, bureaucratic installation. Or so say I. Which, alas, will not end the argument of socialism versus capitalism.

But when a plant is operated by a government it ceases to be simply an economic enterprise; it becomes also a political enterprise. In addition to the ups and downs of economic changes it becomes subject to the ins and outs of political maneuverings. It is awfully hard to stay in the black ink in the midst of such four-way buffeting. This is as true in Great Britain as in Ceylon or Egypt or Argentina.

"Do you think Brazil will be the number one power in the hemisphere when the United States declines?" the landlady asked of an American professor visiting in Brazil. It was a rhetorical question inasmuch as she, along with most Brazilians, firmly believes the United States will, not too far in the future, backslide from its present eminence and Brazil will replace it at the summit.

The professor's reaction when he told of this incident at a conference I attended was, "Brazil has been called a sleeping giant for a hundred and fifty years. In my opinion she shows no signs whatever of awakening!" [7]

Both the landlady and the professor are overly credulous. The American does not give enough credit to Brazil for the great things it has accomplished considering the paucity of its mineral resources, the poorness of most of its agricultural land and the burden of that virtually useless Amazon Basin. On the other hand, the Brazilian just plain overestimates her country's resources. Despite its geographical size, Brazil does not have the resources to make it a major power. Research may change this in the next hundred years, for example, by finding out how the Amazon can be properly developed, but as yet the research is not even contemplated.

The glittering facades of Rio and São Paulo to the contrary, Brazil is very likely to remain sleeping as soundly in the next century as it has in this. The slums of Rio and the miseries of the Northeast are the true index of Brazil's poor resources.

In 1961 I visited the site of the new Aswan Dam in Egypt. The estimated cost, with irrigation canals and services, is $1,4000,000,000. It is designed to increase the agricultural production of Egypt by 30 per cent.[8]

The dam is a tremendous undertaking. The difficulties encountered can be appreciated only while visiting it in a temperature of 123°, as when I was there. The Russian machinery was breaking down. Russian tempers were short. And so were the tempers of the Egyptians working with them. Yet these are temporary troubles that will not in themselves balk eventual completion of the project.

In fact, I take for granted the dam will be completed more or less on schedule, unless political factors intervene. However, when completed will it signify the great renaissance of Egypt, as now forecast? This I question.

My Egyptian friends are wildly proud of this gigantic undertaking and claim it will be one of the wonders of this age, which it may well be. They also use the dam as the principal example of how Egypt is progressing under Nasser, how Nasser is bringing modern-day life to the Egyptian people, and how he is leading the country upward to industrial might and power.

One example constantly iterated by them was the manufacture of the new Ramses automobile. The factory is said to be working at full speed, working, I sourly commented, on imported fuel and imported steel and imported everything else. All bolts, grease and paint used in each and every Ramses are paid for out of Egypt's limited supply of foreign exchange.

As I left Egypt the government announced plans to build an airplane — all to show that the Egyptians can "industrialize" as well as the next one.

When the new Aswan Dam is completed it is expected to generate all the electricity needed (and it probably will) for these factories and for an idefinite number of new ones. Unfortunately, cheap electricity is only one item needed in industrial growth. Minerals and food for the workers are also needed.

The only important resource Egypt has is the ability to grow long-staple cotton. It is the finest in the world. But other areas can also raise cotton and can, if stimulated to it, probably equal Egypt's product.

Yet when I was in Egypt I could find only a poorly supported effort to carry forward research on cotton or any other agricultural product. The new dam is designed to increase the country's agricultural production by 30 per cent, but apparently that agriculture will still be carried on by the primitive *fellahin* peasant, toiling and starving about the same as in the days of the Pharaohs. I am sure that applied research, combined with the new irrigation systems, could eventually make the fertile lands of the Nile Valley much more productive. But $1,400,000,000 for the dam and a snippet for research is not the way to achieve this.

The Egyptians naïvely believe that building a big dam and getting cheap electricity is all there is to industrialization and a prosperous agriculture. Reality will be a jolt a few years from now.

Industrialization costs an awful lot of money. The planners in their air-conditioned rooms in each capital city talk brightly of financing industrialization via foreign loans, tax write-offs, special credits, subsidies, protective tariffs, socialistic state control and, of course, more and more gift aid from the United States and other donors.

Except for the free aid, all of this money must come out of, or be repaid out of, the savings of the citizens of the nation. The theory of the planners is that industrialization is going to move ahead so fast that it will generate its own higher incomes that will produce more and more taxes and so everything is automatic and no one will suffer and everyone will prosper and God will at last be in His heaven and all's right with the world.

Prior to World War II, the United States possessed invested capital equal to an average of $2000 per person, including babes in arms. Equate that with the $40 per capita income per year in the undeveloped areas of the world.

> If all underdeveloped areas at their existing population levels were to possess the per capita capital investment enjoyed by the United States immediately prior to World War II, the total investment in those countries would amount to about $3600 billion. It has been estimated that the sum corresponding to about one-seventh of that amount – around $500 billion – would suffice over a fifty-year period to switch about one-fourth of the labor force and their families from agricultural to industrial and commercial occupations. This would give an economic situation similar to that which existed in prewar Japan.[9]

And where was Japan on the economic totem pole before the war? Forty-three countries had a higher standard of living, and almost all of these were predominantly agricultural.[10]

Remember, industrialization does not eliminate poverty.

Some observers are saying that the undeveloped countries are taking second looks at industrialization, that the fashion is waning for mammoth dam projects, steel mills and other spectaculars, that the emphasis is turning toward agriculture and especially to crops for local consumption rather than for cash crops for export.[11]

This may be so. In 1962 an International Economic Association meeting was held in Vienna. For seven days some six hundred economists from industrial nations and from the undeveloped nations, plus a few from the communist bloc, discussed how economic growth could be speeded up. One of the representatives at this meeting reported that "many sensible things were said that might not have been said a few years ago," and a definite change of heart was apparent regarding the merits of agricultural development. Formerly, he said, industrialization was the keynote of thinking in less developed countries. "Agriculture, like international trade, seemed to be regarded as a backward form of economic activity that should be given the lowest priority. As a result, some countries that should have no difficulty feeding themselves have been compelled to spend their scarce international resources on the importation of foodstuffs. This sad experience seems to have driven home the importance of agricultural development." [12]

This shift of emphasis and interest is undoubtedly under way, yet only spottily.

Libya, the newest of the oil-rich countries, has been, perhaps, the most heavily advised, surveyed and aid-propped-up country on the globe. The successive economic surveys have constantly emphasized that agriculture should be the basis of the country's long-range economic development. Yet the government continues breathlessly to give priority to industrial projects.[13]

A friend of mine in an undeveloped country decided to make automobile batteries. At that time all batteries were imported and sold for about $30 each. In the United States a similar battery sells for around $20.

He imported the parts for the battery in a prefabricated form; that is, he imported the cases and the plates and also the acid. His product was a pretty good one, although not as good as the imported ones from Europe and the United States.

He could not assemble his battery, however, for less than $25. He needed a $5 margin to give himself and his retailers a profit. This brought up the price to $30, which was, of course, the price of the imported batteries. No one was going to buy the inferior local battery when the good foreign one cost the same.

The solution to this impasse is trite and commonplace throughout the world today. He got the government to impose an additional $5 duty on the imported batteries, thus making their selling price $35. He now had his price margin of $5 and could meet the competition from the foreign batteries.

Now every battery user either bought the local $30 brand, which was inferior to what he formerly received at that price, or else he paid $35 for the imported. Either way the purchaser had lost the equivalent of $5 out of his personal pocketbook. This meant that he had $5 less to spend in the shops of the merchants located next door to the battery sellers.

To phrase it differently: those merchants were subsidizing their neighbor shopowner and getting nothing in return.

Industrialites will now rush forward and say, "But the laborers at the battery factory would otherwise have been unemployed; their wages are being spent next door with the other merchants. Also, the battery manufacturer is now paying taxes to the government it otherwise would not have received."

This battery "factory" employed nine men. Assembling battery parts is not a particularly skilled job. Their wages were about as low as the other unskilled workmen of the city. And remember our battery manufacturer was spending foreign exchange for all the component parts of his product. No local producer of raw materials was benefiting.

As for the increase of taxes now paid to the government, that is problematical. Whatever the increase amounted to, it is doubtful if it equaled the salary of a single government office worker or matched the duties the government was previously collecting on the imported batteries.

The bouncing ball to keep the eye on is the $5 lost by each individual battery user. His standard of living had been reduced by that sum.

In the backward nations it is generally only through protective tariffs that local industries can compete with products from the already industrialized, already efficient foreign producers.

Are these new, fringe, weak, uneconomic industries really necessary for a nation? In some special cases the answer is probably yes. In 90 per cent of the cases, the answer must be a thundering no.

Unless a nation has a unique resource which will allow a price advantage in the world market, its manufactured product cannot be exported. Research can change this picture, but only for a specific item. Without a chance to enter the world market, the new manufacturer must confine himself to the local national market. If he can stay in business only behind an artificial, protective tariff wall, the country as a whole suffers.

In February 1963 the United Nations sponsored a major conference in Geneva on the uses of science and technology in developing the undeveloped countries.

Russia sent to this conference a delegation of forty-seven men. They expounded at every opportunity to the representatives from the undeveloped nations one basic theme; namely, Russia achieved vast industrialization because of economic planning based on communist dogma; industrialization is simple and inevitable if only the proper (communist) policies are followed. The relation of industrialization to resources was not mentioned.

I was in Vladivostok in 1948. It was a charming city on beautiful hills overlooking the bay. It was the sort of place where tourists would like to wander around taking photographs. The charm was that nothing, but nothing, had changed in the city's architecture and street views since pre-World War I days. The Greek Revival architecture so favored by the Russians of the nineteenth century gave an entrancing unity to the city. As I said, it was a city for tourists with cameras (although I did not take a single snapshot, considering the officials' phobia on the subject). The high standard of living so touted by communist propagandists was nowhere in evidence in this sleepy, poverty-stricken, backwater city.

I traveled by train from Moscow to the Afghan border in 1946. The trip took six days. I had with me a 1914 Russian *Baedeker*. Not once did I see from the train a new construction, a new railroad station. Everything the thirty-year-old guidebook mentioned was still the same. All had been inherited from Czarist days, from Czarist savings.

Russian buildings have a peculiar odor which, once smelled, is never forgotten. It is a compound of moldy plaster, leaky toilets, boiled cabbage and unwashed bodies. Many writers have mentioned this odor. One called it "the smell of poverty."

Russia has industrialized greatly in the last several decades and particularly since those first postwar years when I was there. But is the standard of living appreciably higher for the masses than in 1914? I wonder. The smell of poverty still hangs thick over the steppes.

As several observers have noted concerning this most-written-about country, the present-day economy of Russia is not based on industrialization in the true sense of the word, but is based upon producing a war machine. Factories, communications and other factors of economic life are planned and utilized as part of the war machine. They are not designed to serve the consumption needs of the Russian people, as are the component parts of industrialization in a democracy.

A war machine, even in the modern complex military framework, is a rather simple, coordinated thing relative to the sprawling, diverse industrialization of the United States, Belgium or any democracy.

Russia has always had a phobia about invasion, based on valid historic facts in the Middle Ages. The Russian masses today accept a war machine civilization as the natural appendage of their rulers. Whether these masses will continue to so believe, as year after year their low standards continue hopelessly unchanged, is for the future to learn. Certainly, the news of the vitality and spiraling achievements of the United States and Western Europe will filter through to the Russian masses in the same way that news of Western bourgeois comforts filters to hungry Asians and Africans. The Russians, too, are an integral part of this "age of rising expectations."

Although communism has thus succeeded in achieving an able war machine in Russia, it is doubtful if it can ever succeed in achieving the industrialization it pretends to have; that is, a level of industrialization advertised as rapidly catching up to the American. An examination of Russia's resources shows the nation just does not have the stuff.

Approximately 90 per cent of Russia's territory receives less than twenty inches of rainfall a year. Throughout the world it is the twenty-inch line that normally separates prosperous agriculture from indigence. Russia, in fact, averages less than twelve inches in a fourth of its area,[14] the very rock bottom level for possible annual cultivation.

The peoples of the world are hypnotized by the geographic immensity of Russia. Including its colonies in Central Asia and the Caucasus, it covers one-seventh of the earth's land surface. Yet half of it is too cold for a decent growing season.

The land which grows the food actually consists of only 7 per cent of all Russian territory. This half-million or more square miles is slightly larger than the cultivated area of the United States, but notice that American farmland is far superior to the Russian in quality of soil, amount of soil nutrients and, of course, climate.

Note also that when the census showed 180,000,000 Americans Russia had 220,000,000. This means 40,000,000 more people must get their food supply from an area equal to America's farmland, and from inferior land at that.

> Russia has never been, is not now, and probably never can become a really great and dependable producer of food grains, such as the United States whose corn production alone equals in food value all of the grains produced in the land of the Soviets.[15]

> Experts disagree on the extent to which Khrushchev's present peace offensive is a direct consequence of his colossal agricultural failure, but there is no doubt that the Soviets' inability to feed themselves has had a decisive effect on their foreign policy.[16]

The history of artificial, forced industrialization in various countries is a long one. The record of resulting failures is also long. Yet these are forgotten as everyone contemplates with awe the rapid industrialization of first the United States and then Russia during this century. Surely India and Brazil can attain similar grandeur. Surely Ghana can do likewise on a smaller scale. And Indonesia. Panama. Tahiti. You name it; an industrialization five-year plan is probably under way or is getting set up for action.

The laws of economics are forgotten as the dreams are spun. The specific reasons why the United States and Russia are able to become industrial powers in this particular century – and may or may not become secondary powers in the next – are impatiently shrugged off.

A nation cannot say, "Tomorrow morning at ten o'clock we shall industrialize." The desire to industrialize does not mean it has the *means* to do so. And no amount of money, whether from loans or from aid handouts or from local capital levies, can produce an industrialized state without the proper combination of resources. The fresh money may provide a temporary whiff of smoke, but at the first cutting off of the heat of artificial income, the uneconomic hokum floats sadly away into the empty sky.

Immediately upon independence in 1947 Pakistan formulated ambitious plans for industrialization. Then the Korean war shot up the price of jute and a boom of sorts developed. The government was lenient, indeed it leaned over backward in eagerness to grant import licenses that would enable new industries to start up. The crash came in 1956 with the near collapse of its agricultural markets. Floods, administrative chaos and panic tripled the price of rice. Just to keep the new plants going at capacity would have required an extra $200,000,000 in outside aid for the year 1956. The government and the people of Pakistan had to face reality. The emphasis has since been shifted – to a certain extent – from forcing industrialization to nurturing agriculture. Funds have been diverted into flood and pest control and into fertilizer projects.[17]

Pakistan has received up to now a total of $1,854,000,000 in United States aid, not including the great sums given for military assistance.[18] Yet the nation remains at just about the same level of hunger as when it became independent. Each local and foreign official presents his own reasons for this. At least it is evident that artificially implanted industrialization has dissipated much of the nation's development effort, although I dare say the nearly two billion dollars of imported money assistance has produced *some* results for the propagandists to talk about.

Spain is another example of industrialization misdirected in the belief that this was the quick road to a high standard of living. Inspired by the flow of huge United States aid and military assistance, the country embarked on an overambitious program to become a great industrial power.

> Giant steel plants rose (in nearly inaccessible areas), automobile and truck factories sprang up and scores of new dams were erected to furnish more electricity . . . The sudden boom was accompanied by a runaway inflation that sent the cost of living up 50 per cent. It also nearly bankrupted the economy. By the summer of 1959 Franco's coffers were empty: they contained six million dollars in hard currency, not enough to buy a month's supply of oil.[19]

Spain had to arrange $418,000,000 in loans to stabilize its economy. It has also now made an effort to irrigate the country's parched soils from those dams that were designed not for irrigation purposes but for electrical power. And it is now giving attention to ways to increase food production. Spain is, it is true, more prosperous today than a decade ago. It would seem this is due not to its own activities, but largely to the $1,698,000,000 (up to June 1962) that the United States has introduced into the country via military assistance, economic aid and loans.[20] So much free money swirling around has here produced, as in Pakistan, *some* action.

The economic botchery that Argentina is now experiencing began back in the days of dictator Juan Perón, who commenced a forced-draft program of industrialization at the expense of agriculture. Even after overthrowing Perón, the Argentinians continued to neglect the farmers, with the result that not only wheat but beef, corn, wool and other produce from the fertile pampas went into decline. It was incredible how rapidly this rich goose that had formerly laid all those golden eggs for the Argentinians, making it one of the richest regions in the world, was killed off. New factories were paid for by discriminatory taxes against farmers and ranchers. These same farmers were prohibited from importing cheap, foreign-made tractors. The result was that by

1962 the farmers' purchasing power had declined to 35 per cent less than that of 1939. The effects could be seen in the annual production of wheat, which in 1962 was 50 per cent less than twenty years previously. The sheep herd had dropped 16 per cent in fifteen years and there were 2,500,000 fewer head of cattle. From 1956 to 1962 wheat production dropped from 2,660,000 tons to 1,200,000 tons. "In a nation that depends on agriculture for 95 per cent of its export earnings, such a slump brings disaster." [21]

So much for the sad examples.

Mexico has had a different story – up to a point.

Industrialization there has been rapid and broadly based in the last two decades. Latin American countries look and say, "If Mexico can do it, so can we." They pay no heed to the special circumstances that bolstered Mexico.

Its present progress grew out of a set of fortunate factors which do not today apply elsewhere. During World War II, Mexico, with good highway and railroad connections with the United States, found a ready market for anything and everything it could produce. The United States grabbed at whatever reached the Rio Grande. Yet during these same years there was little for Mexico to buy in return. Thus, a reserve of foreign exchange accumulated.

The Mexicans were forced to *save.*

At any other time, a lively inflation might have developed if the Mexicans had joyfully and carelessly imported refrigerators, radios and fancy California clothes. Instead, in spite of themselves, they were forced to *save.*

As the money piled up, entrepreneurs began to realize there was a ready wartime market within Mexico for goods that could be made in simple factories. So the savings were now invested in these factories. Also, the larger farmers began to use their savings to mechanize their operations and to investigate more scientific methods of production.

Because farm laborers were so scarce in the United States during the war (and afterwards) Mexicans were brought in under contract. When they returned home they carried their dollars with them and also a degree of agricultural know-how that was new in their backward valleys.

In the first postwar years American tourists found war-ravaged Europe unpalatable and turned to the delights of Mexico. The dollars continued to flow in. The Mexicans learned how to cater to tourists, so that today their skill in this field has expanded tourism into the third largest industry of the nation and number one earner of foreign exchange.

More important than any of the foregoing, however, is that Mexico does have a wide range of resources and these are adequately juxtaposed for industrial development. It has coal and iron, not much, but enough, and it has long been an exporter and processor of several important minerals. Also, most of the agriculture is in the temperate zone central plateau, not in the tropical lowlands. The agricultural land is not very good, but it is good enough.

In its own way, the Mexican experience paralleled the economic history of the United States. The Americans at first sold their excess agricultural and raw products to Europe. This excess they for the most part *saved.* It now appears they saved principally because of the stern Calvinist philosophy prevailing in the United States during the last century, not because of outside political events, as was the case with Mexico. These savings were largely reinvested in further agricultural development and eventually in industrial enterprises.

> [Although] industrial growth [in the United States] did not exceed its population growth until about 1890, it had, nevertheless, accumulated a sizeable amount of capital by that time. Following 1890, production increased more rapidly than population, with a consequent further rapid increase and greater general availability of goods. However, if the political and economic conditions had been such that the capital was not accumulated, production would have increased indefinitely at a rate far lower than the rate of population increase. Under these circumstances, the United States might have been destined to be primarily a large, overpopulated, predominantly agricultural country.[22]

The reasoning in the foregoing quotation is valid, but the conclusion seems off center. The fortuitious variety of America's still untouched mineral and agricultural resources, as related to today's economic requirements, must surely have made the United States an industrialized nation, regardless. Yet if it had become overpopulated, today's prosperity might indeed have been an elusive, never-attained plateau. Nevertheless, the threat of oncoming overpopulation hangs ominously over America's good life due to automation, continuing large-scale immigration and blind unawareness of the need for population control.

Mexico, for instance, has nearly doubled its population in the last twenty years. Why has this not led to catastrophe? Instead, the country regards the present time as the most prosperous in its history. Most commentators give the credit to increasing industrialization. Many say it is due to land reform. No one seems to give credit to the increased agricultural production that probably has saved the doubled population from serious famines.

The key group in this increased production was the Rockefeller Foundation. It had first begun work in Mexico in the 1930's, with a small medical public health team, but eventually decided that before much could be done about the health of the Mexicans, the Mexicans would first have to have more food in their stomachs. Eventually this led to the establishment of a team of eighteen agriculturists and one medical man, headed by Dr. George Harrar, now president of the foundation. The results of its years of research have been spectacular. These, combined with the work of other research units in Mexico and of the development efforts by the government plus the increased use of fertilizers and irrigated land, have made a firm impact on agricultural production.

Wheat production has quintupled and

corn harvests are up about 60 per cent, bean production has doubled, broiler production has tripled, and egg supplies have increased two and a half times. Mexico could stop importing wheat in 1956, other harvests balanced for the first time in history, and corn – the basic cereal in the human diet – is no longer in deficit supply. Twenty years ago Mexico's 21 million people averaged 1700 calories a day. Today, a people grown to 37,000,000 average 2700 calories and they have a more varied diet that increasingly includes animal proteins.[23]

Which is not to say hunger has been eliminated in Mexico. All that can be said is that the increased food production, thanks to research, has kept ahead, so far, of the increasing population.

Without this expansion in food production, Mexico's industrialization would not have progressed as it has. The industrialization has been an internal affair; it has not been directed to making and exporting things that can be sold on the international market. One must not ignore, however, the American tourists who leave behind more than $800,000,000 of foreign exchange each year.

Mexico's industrialization should be rated as successful. Note, moreover, that it was not *planned*. It grew out of naturally formed circumstances. Once the entrepreneurs found themselves with accumulated savings to invest they were able — each individual in his own groping, take-a-chance way that is the basis of capitalism — to build factories to take advantage of the nation's resources.

In the last fifteen years Venezuela has had the opportunity to industrialize itself and to raise its economy to, surely, that of present-day Mexico. The oil income has been huge and steady. Iron and other minerals are today commercially exploitable. The agricultural conditions are primitive, but they could be improved if the national energies were applied to this field. Unfortunately, the Venezuelans are not saving, they are not accumulating capital, they are squandering their advantages, which probably will be gone with the wind a few decades from now. Note, for instance, the glittering skyscrapers of Caracas and the fancy officer clubs of the military.

This is the sad story of many postwar national economies.

With the debt burden of the underdeveloped countries reduced (as a result of special economic factors of World War II), and with their accumulation of substantial gold reserves and foreign asset holdings, many of them were favorably placed at the close of the war to embark on development programs. India, Egypt, Mexico and many other countries had sold large quantities of food and raw materials to the Allies at war prices. Where the armies had passed, as in the Philippines, there were large accumulations of dollars from military expenditures. Firm government policies in the immediate postwar period might have restricted imports for consumption and set aside the excess foreign exchange reserves as a capital fund on the basis of which to attract new investment. India, which even before independence had developed a planning system, was able to draw upon its blocked sterling balances and to attract a considerable volume of new investment. Its industrial progress during the 1950's was therefore considerable. In many countries, however, these war gains were dissipated in a brief flurry of luxury imports for consumption by privileged groups, without any permanent enrichment of the economy.[24]

How unfortunate that these few favored, backward nations did not instead pull firmly on their bootstraps and sweat out the rigors of resource development.

Despite my foregoing knocks against smokestacks and gears and such, I do advocate manufacturing – but in the right place and at the right time and within the right scale of size. In fact, I here offer a procedure to enable the small, hungry nation to get started with the type of small industrialization it needs and can handle. This industrialization is directed, but of course, to the production of tools and equipment needed to make the nation's resources more profitable. If these tools can be imported at a fair price and are satisfactory for local conditions, import them and forget about local manufacturing. If, however, the equipment is unsuitable to local conditions, start thinking in terms of producing them yourself.

The easiest way to get the job done is for the government (or independent entrepreneur) to contract with a foreign company.

Such a contracting engineer-design organization is the Business and Industry Development Company (BIDCO) in Washington, D.C., whose name I offer only because I have talked with its president. BIDCO proposes to establish small plants and hand over the keys to fully operating plants oriented to local conditions anywhere in the world. The intent is to spread the design and development costs over a number of similar installations and provide training and management through technical collaboration with small American industries.

Give it $250,000 and it claims it will establish a factory to produce small tractors (plus simple farm implements) suitable for a permanent, nontechnically trained society that will sell for under $500 and allow $60 profit to the owner of the tractor plant. BIDCO says it will build this plant at any geographical site desired and the plant will produce 2000 of these tractors a year plus 6000 implements for use with the tractors or with animals. It will fabricate the tractor frame from five different types of steel bars and plates which can be imported from various industrialized countries. The motor will also be imported (it can be purchased in the United States for $87). The finished tractor can pull a plow and handle a farm with up to forty acres of cultivated land.

This is all, unfortunately, paper talk so far. No one has yet given BIDCO the $250,000 to build the plant for such a tractor. I mention it here only to point out the sort of small-scale industrialization ideas and means that are available to those who seek them out.

I carry the idea of BIDCO's simplified, grass-roots industrialization onward to other fields.

For about $600,000 for machinery and management, the company announces it can establish for a contracting government a so-called small "industrial complex." This complex is not Pittsburgh or the Ruhr. It consists only of a manufacturing job machine shop, a woodworking and pattern shop, a gray iron foundry and limited forging facilities. It is claimed this complex, by assembling and finishing its own manufactures and imported components and steel stock, can produce a wide range of metal and wood machines and tools, adding a value with its own labor and capital equal to 40 per cent to 80 per cent of the wholesale price. The products may include farm machines, implements, tools, towed vehicles, sprayers, pumps, pots and pans, hammers, knives, machetes, doors and windows, millwork, electric motors, etc. Steel stock, rough forgings, and sophisticated components like engines, ball bearings and the like are imported. The fabrication, however, is done largely with local labor and capital; much of it can be farmed out to village industries.

Again, this is paper talk. No one has yet put in an order for this complex. Apparently, it is too small for these officials, both American and foreign, who are conditioned to think big.

In my rounds around Washington bureaucracy I mentioned this BIDCO idea. One AID administrator laughed and said, "A tractor for five hundred dollars! This is impossible. What kind of tractor can be built for that?" I described the tractor in detail, emphasizing the simplicity of its design and fabricated parts and the elimination of all "American extras." His reaction: "Five hundred dollars for a simple thing like that! How can anyone have the gall to charge five hundred dollars for it?" You can't win.

Yet this is the very type of tractor – and "industrial complex" – that the hungry nation should have. They are sized for the markets. They are within reach of accumulations of local capital. Their profit projections are attractive. Big installations, on the other hand, require large amounts of capital, employ fewer people per $100,000 invested, operate at lower capacities and so often operate with little or no profit.

There is a place for industrialization in the hungry nations. But beware of the men with the ideas for big industries. There is not the capital, the skills nor the market to support them.

Beware of those who advocate smokestacks for national prestige.

Beware of those who want to build things and grandly ship them out into the competitive world market.

Beware of the men who claim industrialization is the way to raise the hungry nation's living standards.

13

The Fallacy of Social Reform—Too Much, Too Soon

WE LIVE in an age of social reform. President Kennedy sternly demanded social improvement in Latin America as a condition for Alliance for Progress money. Senator Goldwater and the rightists decry all sorts of things as socialism, yet offer no practical alternative that will insure adequate living for one and all. Former President Eisenhower pontificates about the evils of excessive government spending on social projects, but did nothing effective about the evils when he was in office. It is likely no one can stem the social reform tide either in the United States or in other countries. It is today's wave of life.

Socialism in a nutshell is, I suppose, the collecting of money from all taxpayers and paying it out to the benefit of certain selected citizens in the hope that the welfare of all taypayers will in the long run benefit.

The rich countries like New Zealand, Denmark and the United States can afford to gamble that the hoped-for benefits from socialization will, in fact, accrue. They can afford to subsidize uneconomic businessmen who cannot survive open competition. They can afford to force industries to raise the prices of their products to cover the costs of elaborate social legislation and the costs of the "benefits" each union gets for its own special group.

The rich countries can afford such socialist legislation, but for the poor ones it can be, verily, the death stroke.

Social reform, nevertheless, has become an integral part of planned industrialization. In fact, social legislation is snappily passed in the hungry countries before the first smokestacks are raised. Equal rights for the workers, a fair wage, time off for pregnancies, nurseries, medical care, two-week vacations, one-month vacations, housing, union foremen who do no work, two men for every job, three men for every job, job security, no firings, seniority, retirement at percentage salaries, fifty-two-hour week, forty-hour week.

It is so much a part of our thinking that the American Government sends labor attachés abroad to show foreign labor how to profit from the experiences gained in union negotiations in Detroit, New Haven and Manhattan's Garment District. Some American unions are now pressing for the thirty-three-hour week and one already has a twenty-five-hour week. This automatically becomes the goal of the workers in Panama, Ghana and Burma. Anything less would demonstrate the nation is not "modern," that it is "inferior."

The immediate targets of social legislation and union restrictions in these countries are the big, successful businesses, especially foreign ones.

Few have been so buffeted as the United Fruit Company and the Standard Fruit Company in Central America. They are harangued equally by local officials and by itinerant, impressionable, superficial writers.

An American mass publication in 1962 carried an article on the current troubles of the banana companies in Honduras. It stressed that in their banner year of 1948 they employed forty thousand Hondurans and ran everything in their areas from port facilities to laundries, ice plants, breweries, hospitals and railroads. The writer's conclusion was that "so little trickled over the company fence that, as one Honduran economist put it, 'even our rich are poor.'"[1]

Actually, so much flowed over the company fence that Honduras would have withered without it. United Fruit itself paid out in Honduras $14,000,000 in salaries and taxes in 1948.[2] This was more than one-and-a-half times the *entire* 1948 national budget. Not remotely was there another industry in the nation that approached a tenth of this.

Today there are fifteen thousand Hondurans working for the banana companies, in contrast to the former forty thousand.[3] The 1962 taxes from the companies fell off so drastically that the World Bank and the United States Government had to underwrite the Honduran budget deficit to the tune of $10,000,000.[4]

Banana diseases have made this crop more difficult and expensive to raise in Honduras, but these disease problems could be licked by an all-out research effort. However, such an effort by the banana companies is illogical, because the heavy costs of social legislation have made banana production unprofitable for them.

During the 1950's the Honduras parliament passed a series of social reform laws that together form a model of detailed benefits and protections in behalf of all workers.

The results have been disastrous.

The United Fruit Company is now withdrawing from banana production in Honduras, turning over its lands to workers to farm as individuals. Yet this plantation type of land is unsuitable without heavy capitalization for small-scale farming, except the most abject subsistence type so despairingly evident throughout Central America and elsewhere in the tropical world.

Here and there a few of these individuals may succeed and establish large farms using small-scale plantation methods, and in fact United Fruit is helping to finance these small landowners. However, they will succeed, most probably, because the government will not enforce the social legislation against them, thus bringing their costs of production into alignment with the international market.

The Honduran Government is striving to have the farmers on these newly acquired lands raise bananas in cooperatives, as has proved successful in Ecuador. It is doubtful this will succeed because of the unsolved disease problems.

The government is also desperately inaugurating a program to resettle ten thousand banana workers on undeveloped government land where they will be taught to grow vegetables and cacao. A road is planned to open up this undeveloped land—cost: $10,500,000.[5]

To whom will the vegetables be sold? I do not know. Can the cacao be sold profitably in the very up-and-down, competitive world cacao market? I do not know. Can this heretofore undeveloped land be turned into a prosperous agricultural community? This, as I have already indicated concerning other jungle areas, I doubt.

And so social legislation killed the golden banana goose that provided the taxes and salaries that supported the Government of Honduras. The death blow was the idealistic, too-early social legislation.

I once employed thirty-five women at the Panamerican Agricultural School at Zamorano, Honduras. Thirty of these worked in the hand laundry. For years the school had put off buying washing machines and other laundry equipment in order to keep these women on the payroll, inasmuch as they were a substantial earning force for the adjacent village of Jicarito.

Then Honduras passed a new labor law which, among other provisions, said that every employer of twenty or more women must maintain a maternity ward for expectant mothers. The school had a doctor on its staff and maintained a clinic. Thus, for us to add a maternity ward would have been infinitely easier than for almost any other employer in Honduras. Yet, after investigating the cost of installing and keeping up such a ward, the school had no choice but to purchase the laundry machines and discharge the women.

Of course, it is doubtful this maternity ward law was ever enforced against the struggling Honduran employers. Throughout all hungry nations the successful entrepreneurs, however, immediately become the center of enforcement for each new law. Social legislation thus becomes one more onerous burden they must bear in the fight for survival in the harsh business life of a primitive country.

All of us, of course, want our neighbor to have a living wage. No one wants a laborer to be unjustly fired. Working women must receive special consideration during pregnancy. Job security must prevail against capriciousness. When a man is too old to work he should have enough money, a pension, on which to live. These things all of our fellow human beings should have, must have, if at all possible.

These are not all possible, however, in nations too poor to pay for such social amenities. There they are luxuries, not "necessities" which the lawmakers so foolishly believe they can legislate into existence. Only when the economy is made prosperous can the nation afford the luxury of social legislation.

For a hungry country to impose laws that protect the industrial laborer as idealistically as those of Western Europe and the United States is to shackle its entrepreneurs. Efforts to promote economic enterprises that will employ rather large groups of laborers are hampered and often destroyed.

The reasons for many industrial faults in the United States today, such as protracted unemployment due to labor-saving devices, the reluctance to hire anyone over forty years of age, the shortage of apprentices, are often attributed to social reform factors.

At the moment, the Johnson administration is deep in a campaign "to end poverty" in the United States. It is said that one-fifth of American families have incomes of $3000 or less. One commentator, however, pointed out that federal, state and local welfare programs combined spent $44,000,000,000 in 1962, and that if all this had been divided directly among these one-fifth of American families each would have received $4400 cash, in addition to their other income.[6] It is fortunate the United States is prosperous enough to carry this burden of $44,000,000,000 each year, a large part of which is not, it seems, ending up among the legitimate "poor."

If this level of $44,000,000,000 in welfare expenditures, plus the mass of social legislation and union rules, had prevailed in the United States in 1910 or in 1920, would American industrialization and prosperity have reached its present vastness?

For the hungry nation to install social legislation too early is putting the cart before the horse, and that's no way to get to the top of the hill.

14

The Fallacy of New Roads— Why Bother with Them?

A VARIANT of the fallacy of industrialization is the fallacy of road-building. It is here that everyone goes, according to the old saying, hog wild.

In the developing countries, transport is absorbing 20 to 40 per cent of their public capital allotted for development. During the past decade and a half, 30 per cent of all U.S. economic aid to the developing countries has been for transportation. Approximately the same emphasis has been given to this sector in the program of the World Bank and, in 1960–1961, the Bank's loans for transport increased to 51 per cent of its total transactions.[1]

Time and again in the hungry countries the officials, especially the aid officials, urge in all sincerity the spending of great sums on new roads. And the roads, at least in the eyes of the aid advisers, must be at least two lanes wide, surfaced with an all-weather dustless oil product and contain neither scratch nor wrinkle greater than that which a Detroit ensemble of five inches clearance can skim over without jar or quiver to a visiting VIP's wife's hips.

In contrast, the historical experience of transportation in America is significant. "The mystery — the miracle — of early America is that people went to places before there was any way to get there and took care of their transportation and marketing needs afterwards." [2]

This was not solely a Yankee phenomenon. It was also true of all the New World.

In February 1946 I traveled overland from Moscow to Kabul, Afghanistan, a trip that included train, barge, horse, jeep and truck.

Between Tashkurghan and Khanabad in northern Afghanistan my truck rounded a hill and entered a wide, grass-filled valley that stretched away for a dozen miles between two low ranges of hills. Nowhere was there sign of man except, in the far distance, a caravan of camels marching along single file. The caravan was a long one, perhaps two miles in length.

There, suddenly before me, was the full impact of the eternal, never-changing timelessness of the East. There, with the camels tied nose to tail, one after the other, was the magic of Marco Polo, the fabled Silk Road, the Three Wise Men, Omar the Tentmaker and other half-remembered romances.

The following year, almost to the day, I again happened to come over this same road, around the same hill into the valley. The low ranges of hills were the same and also the clear sky of early spring. This time, however, there was no caravan, only dozens and dozens of pairs of ruts left by trucks. As one trail of ruts had deepened in the soft earth and become impassable another trail had been formed farther away from the valley center. The entire bed of the valley was by now a weaving, crisscross pattern of ruts.

Within a single year trucks had replaced the ancient caravans. Nor did they wait for a proper road to be built, just as our American pioneers did not stand idly around waiting for a road.

Obviously, it was high time to build a road here in this part of Afghanistan, an all-weather road strong enough to carry the traffic of the area's new, postwar trade. I regretted the loss of the beautiful "timeless" caravans, but such nostalgia had nothing to do with the need, the urgent need, of a new road. Yet even here, should it be a question of building an *American* highway of dustless surface, fancy bridges, banked curves and all the rest? The road required was strictly a bed of stone able to withstand truck traffic.

Here is my rule of thumb: when the produce piles up at the trail's end, when it is necessary to reserve your mule train in advance, then it is time to construct a new road or double-lane the one already there.

Here, in contrast, is the rule of thumb of road advocates: after the fine new road is built, transportation costs will become so cheap that trade will bloom into an economic rose.

Their thinking apparently is derived from the afterbirth of the whopping, four-lane, clover-leaf highways connecting American urban centers. These highways, on completion, seem immediately crowded with new traffic and immediately encrusted with gas stations, motels, brutal billboards and like impedimenta. Yet the transportation economics of such urban traffic have not the slightest connection with the *hoped for* "opening up" of a jungle area or isolated mountain valley.

In Peru the rugged, perverse, entangled Andes divide the nation into two separate compartments. The dream of Peru has always been to discover a means of transportation to traverse the Andes and unite the nation. Currently, there are many plans for roads and the aid administrators are anxious to finance any practical project.

At the 1963 meeting in Geneva of the United Nations Conference on the Application of Science and Technology for the Benefit of the Less Developed Areas, there was assembled an outstanding group of scientists, engineers and development planners and administrators. Here were the cream of the world's thinkers in this area of modern endeavor.

Dr. Jack Rigney, head of the agricultural program directed by the University of North Carolina group in Peru, went informally from one cluster of transportation engineers to another. He asked, "What is on the drawing boards, what sort of far-out idea is in the air, that can make transportation cheaper from the eastern slopes of Peru to Lima?" He heard of many new ways of building roads in rough country, but always the answer was, "Disregarding the cost of a new road and not taking that into consideration at all, it will still be 75 per cent cheaper in freight charges afterwards to send cattle by ship from Buenos Aires around the Horn to Peru, as is now done, than overland from the eastern slopes on the new road." [3]

Thus, even if the American taxpayer should give new roads to Peru as an outright gift, the freight charges would remain four times as high as the present supply route.

Among other confusions confusing the local official as he tries so hard to resolve how best to push forward the economy of his country is the barrage of advice from foreign exciters. What's good enough back home in Texas is right away right for you.

President Johnson made a quick trip through the Near East in the name of good will when he was Vice-President. In Beirut his official itinerary included a flash inspection of a highway construction job on the edge of the city. Mr. Johnson stayed long enough to emphasize to the Lebanese Minister of Public Works, "You're going to realize great benefits from work like this. In my country one of the most important steps in our development was getting the farmers out of the mud. In my own state of Texas now, no farmer has to drive more than a mile to get to a paved road." [4]

I shall pass by the obvious comment to this extemporaneous, off-the-cuff remark, especially as mud is the one thing the Lebanese would not mind having in their arid land. But did the Lebanese officials surrounding Johnson know he was failing to equate the resources of Texas with those of Lebanon?

What is right for Texas is *not* necessarily right for Lebanon.

At the optimum the local region of a backward country needs a route capable of supporting merely its rickety trucks held together by baling wire, cannibalization and unbelievable native mechanical creativity, and also the native buses.

In West Africa the latter are called "mammy buses," a wonderfully apt name for the fat, bulging carryalls with the homemade superstructures. The buses waddle along the rough, dusty tracks where no Detroit phaeton would dream of going. Surplus passengers may slip off the roof and axles bend and springs break, but the mammy buses successfully service remote villages which no normal traveler ever sees. This sort of service has long been in operation throughout nearly all areas of the hungry world.

Does such a country really need a more elaborate transportation than the mammy bus?

Foreign aid officials and some pride-conscious native officials with soft bottoms become helpless when unable to proceed into the hinterland in their Detroit fragilities. So they sign reports that the road is "impassable" or the region "inaccessible" and recommend "all-weather farm-to-market" roads.

Should the great sum of money required to build a new highway be spent in behalf of these few, so very few, officials, instead of the many, so very many, alternative things the destitute region desperately needs?

"Inaccessible" is, of course, what you make of it. To replace a mule trail or unimproved old coach road or the mammy bus ruts with a modern highway will cost a varying number of millions of dollars. Someone, foreign or local taxpayer, must produce the cash.

Either group of taxpayers would, I take for granted, be glad to pay for the road if it would, in actual fact, open up a potentially prosperous area. Unfortunately for everyone concerned, the odds are that any area lacking such a road in today's inhabited world does not have the basic resources, the potential production of goods, to warrant building it. As pointed out in an earlier chapter, if the area is economically worth developing, it can be taken for granted this *already* has been attempted and track or trail is already servicing it. Only when the existing track, trail, ruts or road prove to be inadequate for *current* production should expenditure for a more sophisticated road be considered.

The term "jeepable road" was merely a crash term used by the army for a while during the war. It is not heard today in development planning committee rooms.

Highway engineers usually argue that it is cheaper in the long run to put in the complete works of a modern road from the start. They theorize that spending money in the beginning saves money in the end.

Maybe in the urban development of American cities one can forecast scientifically what the trend of use through the years will be for a proposed road and thereby build soundly for the future. In the primitive areas such forecasts are not scientific; they are merely hopes. It is quite impossible to say that so many trucks carrying so many tons of produce will be operating in so many years. It is impossible to forecast whether the new area will, in fact, develop as hoped or merely remain static in present backwardness.

Instead of spending all that money now on the wonderful new road planned by the American-trained, American-blinded road engineers, start small and let the traffic demands set the pace for road expansion.

When the automobile highway system of the United States was first developing and the first routes were being paved, old Highway 69 near my home town area was paved with a one-lane strip. This was a great improvement over the rutted troubles we had had before. Even with the new pavement, however, the ruts and the mudholes and getting struck in them were still a hazard every time we passed another car and each had to drive two wheels off the paved strip. After a few years traffic developed to the point that it became necessary to pave in the parallel second strip. My last time home I noted that plans are now under discussion for a four-lane highway to be built parallel, a mile away, to old 69.

Should 69 have been built as a four-lane highway in 1925? Even the most avid road engineer will say this is a silly question. But this same man will advocate in the hungry country an elaborate, extremely expensive highway with banked curves, culverts, and so forth, in the *hope* that some day future traffic will require it as the undeveloped area develops.

Too often a new highway is considered to be a magic, open sesame stimulus that will by itself start the bloom of development.

A major American aid project in Bolivia has been the construction of a two-hundred-mile highway between Santa Cruz and Cochabamba. A high official of the State Department came to open it with much beating of publicity drums in 1954. The road has been paved for its entire length.

This is a classic example of a road built solely to open up "virgin, undeveloped tropics." It was anticipated that the Santa Cruz district would sprout with new farm colonies upon completion of the road, that the excess farming and mining population of the *altiplano* area of Bolivia would automatically be attracted down from their sterile, high-mountain regions into this new pioneer development.

Here is what actually happened:

> The mechanical engineering involved in building the road was superb. But the human engineering involved was faulty, for the Quechua and Aymara failed to behave like American frontiersmen excited by the prospect of cheap land. They had only recently gained title to the cold, windswept land their ancestors had worked for centuries, and against all "logic" they refused to abandon them for new settlements in the jungle. Only a few thousand natives and some Japanese immigrants had taken advantage of the opportunity to migrate, and many of them left after a year or two, disgusted with the strong-arm rule of Louis Sandoval Morono, MNR boss of the area. Santa Cruz today still has fewer inhabitants than it had in the gaudy days of the pre-World War I rubber boom.[5]

The reference to American frontiersmen is pertinent. At no time did American pioneers wait for a paved highway before going into an empty area. Similarly, the Quechua and Aymara would have gone into the Santa Cruz district long ago if the opportunity for a prosperous livelihood had existed there.

I have been to the four-hundred-year-old town of Santa Cruz. It is not an easy area to farm. Since it once had a larger population than now, it is obvious that efforts must have been made to farm it by local people before they drifted away to what they felt to be a more certain future in the impoverished areas elsewhere in Bolivia.

Santa Cruz may become some day a thriving pastoral district. I doubt this will happen, however, until extensive applied research develops new products or new farming methods, although recent reports indicate success with sugar and rice.

It would have been wiser, say I, to have spent on such research the millions of dollars that the two-hundred-mile paved road cost. Today, a decade later, such research might be about to come up with some solutions.

The road, however, I am willing to bet, has long since gotten potholes in its uneconomic paving.

In 1962 I visited the Chinandega district of Nicaragua. In the last dozen years this has been an authentic boom area. Nicaraguans like to call it the richest district in all Central America and even, some exuberantly boast, in all the world. The principal crop is cotton. Corn is grown but production is low.

I asked many persons there, "Why is the Chinandega area only now developing? If the land is so marvelous, why, after all these centuries of nothing happening, is there prosperity now?" Always the answer was, "Because of our new highway."

About eight years before, the government had built a new highway of asphalt from the capital to Chinandega. Small villages have sprung up alongside it, and even drive-in snack bars. There is considerable wealth, comparatively speaking, in small business ventures now appearing along this highway.

So today the people there give credit for their new prosperity to the new road.

Chinandega is again a case, unfortunately, of everyone looking at results, not causes. The basic, unadorned reason for the new prosperity is that the area shifted over to a new crop, from corn to cotton, a dozen years ago. After the cotton boom was under way the road was built because of pressure resulting from new economic wealth which needed a better transportation outlet.

The reason why this area suddenly began to grow cotton is simple. After World War II the price of cotton rose, along with many other raw commodities. This, combined with the American price support program, led to an expansion of cotton growing in many parts of the world that previously could not raise it profitably. The Chinandega area was lucky enough to get in on the ground floor. Land that had never been profitable before — in fact, land that had never even been farmed regularly before — was now planted to cotton and large profits resulted and the Chinandega district boomed with fresh money.

The new highway was a legitimate part of this boom, but it was not the cause.

New schools of thought for the activation of development work constantly come to the fore. There is nothing static about this "science."

One such school is now strongly and successfully advocating "spontaneous colonization." This new belief holds that it is enough simply to build roads into an uninhabited area and the people will, on their own initiative, materialize along the route, build their huts, and start cultivating the land. There is no need for the government to clear the land in advance, build schools, extend credit, and so forth. Just build the roads. "Spontaneous colonization" (also called "instant civilization") is currently an influential school of thought and one hears the doctrine at many development meetings.

When I was in Brazil in 1963 I met a couple of American aid officials who had just returned from a trip into a "spontaneous colonization" area in the northern, tropical state of Maranhão. They had made a similar trip there three years earlier, shortly after a new road had been extended into the isolated district. They told me how they had then been amazed at the number of families who had already spontaneously emigrated there, built small houses, cleared the ground and planted crops. Most of all, they had been impressed with the enthusiasm and esprit de corps of these new settlers, who acted as if they had discovered true paradise.

Now, three years later, most of the settlers were gone, perhaps back to where they had come from originally. The *ranchitos* were in ruins, the once cultivated fields reverting to bush. The reason for failure was that the land could not support even three years of cultivation.

And the road itself, which three years before had been a fine example of construction work, was now so rutted that at times it was nearly impassable.

Aside from the basic flaw of "spontaneous colonization" – that a road by itself will establish a flourishing community – there is also the trouble that the cost of maintenance of roads in the tropics may soon outstrip the original cost of construction.

At Marcona, an iron region on the southern Peruvian coast, I crossed paths with an American construction engineer. In the conversation he happened to mention Bluefields, Nicaragua, the port on the Caribbean completely isolated from the rest of the country by harsh jungle and mountain terrain.

I asked, "Whatever were you doing there?"

"During the war I built a road from Managua to Bluefields and it was a damn fine road, too."

"But just two years ago friends of mine had to blaze their own trail to get a bulldozer from Managua to their plantation near Bluefields. It took them several weeks of the most awful work."

"Of course. These roads never last long in that sort of country. It is more work to keep them in repair each year than to build them in the first place."

Experienced road technicians, such as are on many American aid missions, today try to get policies adopted by their superiors forbidding the construction of new roads until the local government can afford to maintain the ones already built. From the record, though, their advice is seldom followed.

I can think of no better illustration of the failure of a new road to change harsh economic realities than this story, also about Nicaragua. I give the full background details in order to emphasize how much hard labor and intelligence preceded and followed the building of a new road to replace a mule trail.

My friend Bob Smith arrived in Nicaragua in the early 1950's. He had grown up on a U.S. cattle ranch, graduated from college, worked for a tobacco company and decided the business life was not for him. He loaded a jeep with branding irons, his saddle, a box of veterinary medicines and a box of books and headed south. He had read in the *National Geographic* about a "lot of unused land" in Central America. He checked with the State Department on this and received confirmation, at least regarding Nicaragua. He was young, healthy, energetic and an experienced cattleman.

He spent the first several months in Nicaragua tracking the back country by horse and jeep to locate a piece of cattle land to buy, but found nothing suitable.

He did, however, come across a small area that had been a lake bottom, about twenty-five acres, and decided it would grow tobacco. He bought this land. On the strength of his aggressiveness and obvious farmer know-how, he was able to borrow the necessary money for a tractor, fencing and the gear for getting in a crop. He made $10,000 that year, partly due to the poor tobacco crop elsewhere in the country. The sum, however, was not enough to pay off the cost of the tractor, clearing the ground and other expenses – which, of course, he never expected to do in one year anyway.

Now, the local *políticos* and other fringe natives sort of moved in on the new *gringo* and forced him out – an old, old story around the world. So he left the tobacco-growing business and was by now quite broke. Incidentally, this piece of land is no longer in cultivation. Either the soil had enough nutrients for only a few crops, or maybe bad drainage of this former lake bottom prevented continuous farming. The neighboring farmers followed his lead in growing tobacco, but insects and pests, uncontrolled on a regional basis, caused abandonment of this crop.

Bob's one dividend from this venture was that he had met a Nicaraguan girl who was trying to make a go of a coffee farm which her grandfather had started. This involved riding eight hours twice a week by horse from her home to the farm. She supervised the farmhands, worked like a dog and met the payroll.

They were married and lived on the coffee farm, located, typically, on forty-five-degree hillsides hidden in continuous clouds. The *finca* "mansion" was a dilapidated house with cracks an inch wide and furniture nailed together from boxes. A normal pioneer house, in fact.

Both worked long and hard with their coffee crops, packing their bags to market by muleback, the mules often bogging down to their bellies on the rough muddy trail. The turn upward in their fortunes came only when Bob was able to obtain a loan from the Development Bank in Managua. This allowed him to increase his coffee plantings, clean out the undergrowth and renovate the old *beneficio* operated by a water wheel (to depulp the coffee and prepare it for market).

Yet the couple was not able to succeed financially solely on the basis of their coffee. Bob now began a dairy, using local Holstein cattle. Milk production was not very high, even by Central American standards; actually the vegetation on these hillsides, due to lack of soil nutrients, makes poor forage for dairy cattle. Nevertheless, the milk did provide a cash crop for the family. The milk was sold to local people near the farm who came for it with their own buckets.

There was still no road to the outside world. The mules loaded with coffee bags continued to bog down to their bellies.

Bob and the other farmers kept up a steady agitation over a period of years for the government to help them with a road into their area. And, eventually, the road was built. Everyone staged a big celebration.

Suddenly, Bob's *finca* became a sort of showplace. Officials in Managua, including those of the American Embassy, often brought visiting VIP's here to see Nicaraguan agriculture at its best. It is a pleasant trip on the fine road and the scenery is spectacular.

Only one more detail.

Bob and his family don't live there any more. Although they still operate the *finca,* he could not make enough profit to pay the expenses of educating his children.

The new road, it turned out, failed to provide the extra margin of profit everyone expected. The income from the coffee/milk farm is just as touch-and-go now as it was in the days of the mule trains.

Bob is now a businessman in Managua selling hardware.

15

The Fallacy of Land Reform—and How to Put Common Sense into the Briar Patch

In all these countries the fallacy of land reform is that it is designed and carried out as *social* reform; it is not designed to provide *maximum land utilization.*

Man's memory is a frayed, forgetful thing. Americans have already forgotten the misery and despair of our farmers in the early '30's, especially in the Dust Bowl of the Southwest. We had then the same sort of social and economic decay that today in other nations brings forth the agitation for land reform. American officials in Washington and abroad support this agitation and forget how their own country solved its agricultural troubles.

In 1936 Lee Barnes had a wife and two children, and his small, one-crop cotton farm in Jackson County, Oklahoma, was about to be foreclosed. His farm had, practically speaking, no dollar value.

This was the tag end of the Depression. Thousands and thousands of farmers already had been foreclosed. The majority of the rest were, like Barnes, on the brink.

To meet this crisis the Farm Security Administration (FSA) was started in 1935; it was designed to rehabilitate these farmers through the medium of government loans. The crux of the program was that the loans would be granted only if the farmer followed the advice of his county agent, an official of the Department of Agriculture. The purpose of the regulation was to force the farmer out of his traditional, inefficient methods and into modern agricultural systems.

The job of the county agent was to sit down with the farmer and draw up an individual, especially tailored plan to get him out of debt. This plan might include, for example, ways in which the family could raise its own food, raise feed for the livestock, develop a cash crop.

The plan included soil conservation measures deemed necessary and practical not by the farmer but by the trained government supervisor.

Parallel with the work of the county agent, a home economist gave similar advice and help to the wife, such as insisting that the farm have a milk cow, some chickens, a pressure cooker for canning vegetables for the family food supply.

Money to finance the plan for the Barnes family, as finally drawn up, was granted on the basis of a five-year loan at 5 per cent interest.

The Jackson County agent prepared this plan after several long consultations with Barnes on the farm itself, not at some office in town. The plan spelled out how this one individual farmer could raise all his own livestock feed and his family's food supply and develop a cash crop, or, in other words, how he could pull himself by his own bootstraps out of the mire of his troubles.

The FSA loan helped Barnes to diversify away from his previous one crop, cotton. Within three years he had a milk herd of five cows and a weekly cream check averaging $3.75. This was his cash crop, and it was the only money available for the few groceries and supplies needed from stores. By now, Mrs. Barnes was supplying most of the family food from a one-and-a-half-acre garden. In one year she was able to can six hundred quarts of food. This was enough to carry the family through even the following year, when grasshoppers cleaned out the garden. Within three years, in 1939, Barnes said he would not sell his farm for a thousand dollars (remember, it had had no dollar value in

1936), and he expected to make his final payment on the FSA loan the following year.[1]

Today, in the United States, this story from the Dust Bowl–Okie era seems as remote as the Dark Ages. American agriculture is now rapidly turning into a type of big-scale industry in which small farmers like Barnes have little place.

Barnes epitomizes exactly the type of distressed small farmer – a peasant, to be exact – that every land reform is supposed to help. Therefore, land reform planners of other countries would do well to heed certain factors about this case:

(1) Barnes was already an experienced farmer; he was not someone in a nearby town who wanted a farm.

(2) Barnes was already an experienced farm administrator; that is, he had always managed his own farm. He was not a farmhand or worker on a big estate who had never made decisions, such as when to market and how to plant.

(3) His wife was a true equal in making decisions and helping to pull the family out of their troubles.

(4) Key man in the system was the county agent. Note that he was not a one-time, one-hour thing. He was not a visiting official merely addressing a meeting of local farmers, telling them what they ought to do and then returning to city comforts. He was himself a citizen of Barnes's community and had the same background as the farmers he was visiting and advising. He worked long hours with each farmer, on that man's own farm, drawing up a sound plan specifically for the conditions prevailing there as needed by the size of that family. In the 1930's there was on the average one FSA supervisor for each hundred and fifty farm families, although it was then believed that to be fully effective they should have averaged one for every seventy-five families.[2]

(5) This county agent was backed by trained government technicians, such as the regional home economist, who were available for advice in the state capital or in Washington whenever the agent needed to ask for it. For instance, the regional conservationist already was equipped with aerial photographs of the Barnes's farm.

(6) Incorporated into the plan were conservation practices that would, over a period of time, increase the productivity of Barnes's farm and, incidentally, its real estate market value.

(7) The plan itself was of no value until implemented by a cash loan set with feasible interest rates and terms of repayment. This was no charity gift which taxpayers elsewhere would have to pay.

In the 1930's these FSA supervisors operated pretty much in the same economic environment found in rural areas of the hungry nations that concern us today.

The following summary (covering the short span of 1935-1938) of borrowers of FSA loans before and after "rehabilitation" is pertinent:[3]

	Before	After
Average annual net income per family	$375	$538
Value of home-produced goods per family	$150	$247
Milk produced for family consumption	99 gallons	448 gallons
Fruits and vegetables canned for home use	51 quarts	242 quarts
Meat produced for family consumption	85 pounds	447 pounds
Average number of acres cultivated	107 acres	142 acres

The FSA program, three years after it began operation throughout the United States, included 360,000 families. Within that time their aggregate worth, excluding all debts, increased 26 per cent, with an average net income increase of 43 per cent.[4]

In contrast to this effective work of the county agent system of the United States, I present a story of the way land reform misfires when the goal is social uplift rather than increased agricultural production. I have intentionally avoided using as an illustration the violent seizing of a feudal *hacendado's* land, dividing it up higgledy-piggledy among farmhands and unemployed townfolk, and then leaving them to struggle along as best they may while the officials and do-gooders rush off to save the world some place else.

No, this is about a land reform project that received lavish government assistance at the beginning and has remained under continuing government supervision. Also, I am personally familiar with it, having visited it many times during its formative years, and have kept in touch since.

The Pacific coast of Guatemala is a relatively fertile volcanic ash plain, ten to twenty-five miles wide. The land is flat enough for mechanized equipment.

Six months of the year, in the rainy season, it is a lush, verdant paradise that is everyone's idea of the proliferation of the tropics. The rest of the time it is just swirling dust.

In recent years this area has had a cotton boom, based on the United States price support program that artificially inflates the world price of cotton. The area is sparsely populated, compared to the highlands of Guatemala.

For a number of years I raised corn in small experimental plots in various locations on this coastal strip. My production was always low, about eleven bushels to the acre, and it was hard to get even that. One of these plots was on the edge of the Nueva Concepción holdings of the United Fruit Company. Alongside was a grass airstrip that made it easy for me to fly in on frequent inspections.

Came the days of Arbenz, President of Guatemala who was elected with communist support.

In 1952 he passed a land reform act and his first target was the United Fruit Company. Before positive action could be taken, however, Castillo Armas threw Arbenz out.

Castillo Armas could not repeal this land reform act because it had wide popular support. Also it was not, as such laws go, extreme. In fact, "many impartial observers have since agreed [it] had considerable merit." [5]

The United Fruit Company now gave to the government 100,000 acres at Nueva Concepción (that had yet to be cleared and put into cultivation) on the condition that the squatters who had moved onto all their plantations in Guatemala during Arbenz's time be removed and settled on this donated land. The government, accordingly, initiated a detailed, paper-planned program of rural settlement. American aid personnel participated actively. Fifteen hundred families settled here.

My clearest memory is of the elaborate, intricate plan that was drawn up in the halls of Guatemala City. It demonstrated in precise language that after settlement the net worth of the agricultural production of each family per year was to amount to $15,497 or a total of $23,245,500 for the 1500 families. The net worth of each family, for tax purposes, was to be increased from $125 to $6231, or a total net worth of $9,346,500.[6]

On my inspection trips to my corn plots I would fly over this area and see the progress of the development projects. The first thing done was to build a road into the area (at a cost of $300,000).[7] The next was to bulldoze the jungle. The next was to construct feeder roads.

It was only now that the planners came to the agricultural people, including myself, and asked, "What can they raise at Nueva Concepción?" The answer was that cotton could be grown on a plantation type of holding, but a family-size farm probably would be suitable only for subsistence crops of corn and beans.

"By the way, what size farms will these families have?"

Out of the air the planners pulled the figure of fifty acres — that seemed, offhand, to be an acreage a family ought to be able to handle.[8]

Today 1398 families (many are replacements for original settlers who gave up and left) are living on the land and they are producing, but not profitably. The land is cleared by a tractor pool on a contract basis. This operation is subsidized by the government; that is, paid for by other producers elsewhere in Guatemala. Fertilizer trials (to show how the land can give a sustained yield after the sun has baked the nutrients from this cleared jungle land) were not carried out either before settlement or afterwards.

I recently asked the head of the International Development Services what the overall cost of development of Nueva Concepción has been (this is the private organization under contract to supervise the project). His answer was that it is impossible to present a meaningful figure. It has been, in effect, an open-end program.

Today the critics harangue that the fault at Nueva Concepción is that the government was forced originally to accept second-rate land from the United Fruit Company and to settle on it second-rate farmers (the squatters) in a politically enforced crash program.

That is not, obviously, the fault, nor is it the original poor "planning," if I can use such a formal word for the makeshift unplanning that started the whole thing.

The fault was the attempt to establish family-size farms on land that is suitable only for plantation type agriculture, as evidenced by the successful large-scale production of cotton and bananas on adjacent holdings.

Emotionalism! Thy Name Is Land Reform!

Every facet of the subject is coated with passion. It is hard to carry on a relaxed conversation about it whether with the President of the United States or the head of the newest hungry nation, with the renowned Boston professor or the barefoot teacher under the palm trees, with the journalist who writes about it or the reader in his chair at home.

This dogma of the value of dividing up land has been swallowed hook, line and sinker – insofar, at least, as it concerns someone else's land. I have yet to hear Americans, for instance, argue the need to divide up all land holdings in Kentucky larger than twenty hectares for distribution among the heads of families on the relief rolls of Louisville, Paducah and Appalachia. Yet your Mexican or Pakistani or United Nations advocate of social reform via land redistribution probably would urge exactly that if he were analyzing Kentucky's hillbilly ills so handily near those spacious Lexington area fiefs.

In 1961, a meeting was held in Santiago, Chile, of the country directors for the United States aid programs in Latin America. The discussion revolved around land reform and the means for carrying it out. One of the participants told me that these discussions covered everything from political implications to the cost of placing a family on a farm and making it theoretically self-sufficient. Considerable heat was produced as the pros and cons ranged across the various methods. After two days, an agronomist who was sitting in on the meetings, asked, "And what is to be done about increasing the production of food? During all this time I have not heard this mentioned once." My informer told me that "complete silence reigned." No one of these important officials, arguing and advocating and pushing land reform in these foreign nations on orders from the highest policy level of Washington, had considered this detail until the agronomist injected his pertinent question.

Proponents of communal exploitation, cooperatives, parcellation, state farms, peasant holdings, all besiege the legislators with their separate but equally impassioned arguments.

Colombia currently allots each year, beginning in 1962, $12,000,000 for "land reform." This is 3 per cent of the national budget. The Peruvian "draft law" provides for about the same amount which is about the same proportion of the national budget.[9]

Venezuela has had a parcellation program called the "most expensive 'land reform' ever made in the world." Its four-year program planned to place two hundred thousand peasants on parceled land, but in the first three years (1960–1962) only fifty thousand were actually settled.[10]

Parcellation, for those who are confused, means the government buys private land and then subdivides it and resells it to the landless on installment terms with a fixed term of payment at a low interest rate. Inasmuch as Venezuela has an unusually high cash income from its oil industry, it is able to finance the large amount of capital needed in this system. This plan has the advantage of a peaceable redistribution of land, but it has the disadvantage that the inefficient among the large landowners and those with excess, nonused lands are able to go on keeping their estates intact, the same as ever.

Venezuela has 29,600,000 hectares of land used to raise crops and breed cattle. Before parcellation was started, 22,000,000 hectares were occupied by large estates, over 1000 hectares. Three years later, when the four-year plan is coming to its close, this figure has fallen to only 21,500,000.[11]

Knowledge of the difficulties inherent in both small free holdings and collectives led to a different approach in Puerto Rico when the social changes of the 1940's were put into effect. Several of the largest sugar estates were taken over; but instead of dividing up all the land and handing it over to small farmers, larger units were maintained (though not as large as the original holdings). These were called proportional profit farms; they were to be managed by experienced enterprisers, who were to be free except that the profits were to be divided between them and the workers. The units were large enough to use modern machinery, and it was hoped that a way had been found to effect "reform" without loss of productivity.

The hope was not fulfilled. Productivity did not hold up, and the whole system is in financial difficulty. Puerto Rico has not, for some time, filled its sugar quota, and sugar is still the most important of insular crops. The reason for this failure is that political, not technical, considerations have governed voting supporters of the dominant party and they are over-favored. This has proved to be short-sighted favoritism. By comparison, for instance, with Hawaiian standards, where the old estate management is still maintained, Puerto Rican workers are much less well off – Hawaiian efficiency is superior. Puerto Rico is still so high-cost a producer that only a quota-subsidy arrangement keeps the sugar lands operating at all.[12]

Rural planners often get lost in the forest because of all the tree stumps. The Brazilian Congress in the last ten years has received 208 projects for land reform or related programs. Peru and Ecuador have had much the same experience.[13] However, each year nothing happens, possibly because of this confusion of proposals.

International conferences pass resolutions favoring rural changes, but the terms are vague and no one seems to pay attention after the delegates disband. Examples include the Bogotá Act of 1960 and the Charter of Punta del Este of 1961.[14] There are many others.

I wish that all those who are so busily working for land reform knew something about farming. I wish they had mud on their shoes. Otherwise, the glib assumption that dividing up land will solve all sorts of things would not be heard so often and in such high marble halls.

Perhaps this is the place to mention José Figueres, one of the very few heads of state to have been a hard-working, dirt-covered farmer.

Figueres was the leader who revitalized Costa Rica after World War II and was later President (1954–1958). After studying in American schools, including the Massachusetts Institute of Technology, he returned to Costa Rica in 1928 and bought a "run-down *hacienda* with eroded land and worn-out machinery for processing the hard fibers which had been its principal product." [15] Through the years he developed this into one of the finest farms in Central America.

But the name he gave to his *hacienda* was La Lucha Sin Fin — The Struggle Without End. Any farmer, anywhere, prosperous or indigent, will immediately recognize that there never was a more apt name for any farm. I doubt if there are stars in Figueres's eyes when he talks of land reform.

Established land tenure patterns are often blamed for holding back the progress of a country. The critics generally overlook the basic fact that these land tenure patterns have evolved as a *result,* and are not the cause, of local agricultural conditions.

A report of the United Nations Mission of Technical Assistance to Bolivia states, "The land tenure system almost completely blocks the development of a progressive agriculture." The area under discussion here is the northern *altiplano* part of Bolivia.

To say that land tenure problems are holding back progressive agriculture in this region is simply to disregard the nearly hopeless agricultural conditions there. The hopelessness staggers the imagination. Eighty per cent of the population live over eight thousand feet above sea level and often as high as thirteen thousand feet. Much has less than twenty inches rainfall, the dividing line all over the world between easy and difficult agriculture. Vegetation is scant almost to the point of nonexistence. No matter how the government might try to develop a new land tenure system here, it is difficult to see how, on the basis of *current* knowledge, any sort of "progressive" agriculture can ever come about.

Bolivia has already gone through a land reform program. This has not increased production. It has solved no agricultural problems. All it has done is to lessen social tensions. It has been a *social* reform. The bellies are still empty.

Yet the social reform has been real and I do not belittle it by pointing up the unsuccessful aspects of land utilization.

The past decade [in Bolivia] has brought about greater changes than the preceding four centuries. Almost overnight the Indians were given land, civil liberties, the right to vote, military drill, and rifles. Peasants who formerly did not dare protest to their masters against forced labor of three or four days a week now come to La Paz to explain their problems to the President of the Republic and receive a sympathetic hearing. After interviewing migrant sugar-cane workers in Northern Argentina a few years ago, I was struck by the superior sophistication of the Bolivians, who had formerly been the most backward. Mataco Indians from Argentina and Guaraní from Paraguay generally did not know their ages, what country they came from, or how much they were being paid. But the Toba, who came across the border from Southern Bolivia in the harvest season, were well aware of their salaries, their rights under an Argentine-Bolivian labor compact, and the meaning of inflation and differential exchange rates. The awakening of the Indian population is the principal accomplishment of the MNR, and one which is spreading beyond Bolivia's borders to Argentina, Peru and Ecuador.

The same author also writes:

Now master of his own land and labor, the Indian probably eats a little better and lives more comfortably, but he has neither the ability nor the incentive to produce a surplus for the market. This leaves the urban one-third of Bolivia's population more dependent than ever on imported food.[16]

Bolivia's land reform system was never systematic. The National Revolutionary Movement (MNR) and its leader, Victor Paz Estenssoro, came to power in 1952 by force of arms. Among other social reforms instituted during Estenssoro's first term (1952–1956) was a sweeping away of the old farm-owning class.

Landlords and *mayordomos* were frightened off or driven off, and the Indians seized the land. An Agrarian Reform law issued by presidential decree on August 2, 1953 gave a color of legality to what had already taken place, and promised to pay for expropriated land with 25-year bonds (so far never issued). Although the actual granting of land titles was carried out very slowly (and with considerable violence and bribery of government officials), the number of landholders shot up in a few years from 50,000 to 800,000.[17]

Anyway, Bolivia is the only Latin American nation that has carried out in recent years a peaceful social revolution/land reform such as the present Washington administration so strongly presses for, although, I guess, "peaceful" is an in-and-out word that you use depending on your past experience of the quiet or not-so-quiet life.

Bolivia has had its land reform. The rural regions await, however, their rehabilitation.

Mexico is often held up as a valid example of land reform. I have heard Mexican professors argue that what other Latin American nations need is a revolution like the Mexican one, because out of the turmoil will come true land reform, industrialization and a beautiful flowering of the arts, just as happened in their country.

If nothing else, this demonstrates how the passage of time can gloss over and distort into sweet nothingness the terrors of the Mexican Revolution, say from 1912 to 1922, plus the later horrors of the Cristeros (nearly a million casualties in a population of fifteen million are accredited to the Revolution).[18] This was one of the most terrible periods of barbarism brother has inflicted on brother in this rowdy century. Yet today in this pink cloud of sentimentalization even a Neanderthal like Pancho Villa is turned into a national hero for school children to write themes about.

Cuba is now in the midst of a cruel revolution of the same type, and Mexicans praise it as a fine way to achieve social reform and the redistribution of land.

So let us examine the results of Mexico's land reform.

James Reston wrote in the *New York Times:*

> Some of the land reform in Mexico . . . has been good but in other cases it has been bad. For example, some land that was highly productive in large farms has declined in production when cut up into smaller farms. Many peasants have been given land but are not sure of their titles to it, and others are apparently fearful that if they improve their land, the government will grab it.
>
> This is not to say that there has not been considerable progress.

Irrigation, disease-resistant hybrids, and some effective land reform have made Mexico almost self-sufficient in food over the last twenty years, but the question is whether, under present conditions, Mexico will be able to continue to feed one million new people every year.[19]

The discouraging feature is that the agitation for land, for land reform, continues unabated. The social reformers, politicians, journalists, *et al.*, are worried because there are *still* a million peons "with no land to call their own [and] another million who have land but so little or so poor that it cannot support a crop." [20]

Another reporter summarizes: "The present regime of President Adolfo Lopez Mateos has distributed more land to the landless than any other administration except that of Cárdenas. But Lopez Mateos still has not been able to satisfy all the demands of the peasants because there simply isn't enough arable land to go around." [21]

During the '30's I lived for three years in Mexico, including six months on one of the big old-time *haciendas* during the period the *agraristas* took over much of its land. The only difference here was that the *hacendado* family had maintained a sympathetic understanding with its laborers, which was usually lacking elsewhere in the area. On the neighboring *haciendas* tensions were so high that owners could not safely visit their properties. If they did, they might be shot. There were instances of bullets crashing through lighted windows at night and other unrulinesses of a disturbed countryside.

On the *hacienda* where I lived, however, the family and the workers strove hard to maintain civilized relationships, although each side fought out the land distribution vigorously through all the legal and governmental channels available. This situation of "armed amity" was aided because the *hacienda* fortunately did not abut on any villages. In the Mexican land reform scheme villagers also had rights to receive land from adjoining *haciendas* because the ancient village communal lands had often been seized in previous generations.

Thus, at this particular *hacienda* both the *hacendado* and the farm workers were not inflamed, "egged on" is the exact phrase, by local *políticos* and by hungry villagers inexperienced in farming but anxious to get in on the new deal.

In the end, the land was divided. Each head of a family among the workers received, generally speaking, an adequately sized piece sufficient for peasant agriculture. This was possible because no villagers had to be accommodated; the population of the *hacienda* area was kept in balance with the amount of land under cultivation. Furthermore, these were workers experienced in farming this land; they were not imported from somewhere else. The *hacendado* was allowed to keep his house and an adequate amount of surrounding acreage for effective farming on a sort of large scale. Thus, he continued to retain a section of the land Charles V of Spain deeded his family and also his fortress-like house, dating from the end of the seventeenth century.

This one incident, this example of the one *hacienda,* can accordingly be held up to show how a land reform program was carried out efficiently and humanely, and also as legally as was then possible in the Mexican political climate.

Was *social* reform or was *economic* reform the result of this forced land redistribution?

The valley has, as a matter of fact, merely continued at about the same level of agricultural production as before, in contrast to many other areas where such redistribution has often drastically curtailed output. The standard of living among the workers, never, in truth, very high, is still about the same now that they are independent farmers. Thus, there has been no economic improvement. However, a framework of contentment and private initiative has been established that can be a firm base for whatever agricultural development may eventually be provided by research. Thus, there has been a decided social improvement.

The one definite change has been for the *hacendado.* Because of activities he took up in Mexico City he acquired the funds for building a dam to irrigate his restricted acreage. This is now a prosperous farm, because of the outside capital he brought in. There is even, which is beyond my comprehension from the old days, a swimming pool in the patio, protected within the high, thick walls and gun turrets that staved off many a wandering band of *revolucionarios* and *bandidos* through the centuries. The swimming pool means, I guess, that electricity has now replaced the candles and lamps, but whether the power lines have yet reached the adobe huts of the peon farmers I do not know.

I suppose the reformers will be disturbed because the swimming pool is not a community affair for everyone, rather than the private property of one family. Before those persons, who are almost always, it seems, city folk, cast that verbal stone, they ought to level down their own capitalistic urban life from where some suburbanites have private swimming pools and a lot do not; some have the big cigar, some do not. A factor of land reform agitation is that so many of the agitators strive for a levelized, socialized living in the countryside that would horrify them if applied to themselves in the city.

It is for this reason that the results, as in the case of this Mexican *hacienda,* are social, not economic, improvement.

At a conference I attended in Washington I was intrigued by a comment by Professor John J. Johnson of Stanford University. He said he had talked to two hundred army officers throughout Latin America in 1960, asking each one, "What is your country's number one problem?" Not one answered "Land reform."

This is an amazing fact in view of the constant propaganda on the subject throughout each Latin American country, plus the continuous barrage of free-wheeling advice on the subject by almost all *Yanqui* journalists, aid officials and successive "personal" representatives of successive U.S. Presidents.

Professor Johnson gave the following as his explanation for the apparent lack of interest of these army officers in land reform. The officers when young are stationed in the provinces. There they get married, typically to girls from landholding families. In the course of time many of these inherit all or part of the property. Whether or not they then leave the army, they have a continuing interest in the operation of the family farm. Certainly, they are not advocating its being divided up and given away to others for free. Hence, he says, the lack of interest of the military in land reform problems.[22]

Although I find this original thought interesting, my own reaction is that quite likely the need for land reform, in its brutal subdividing aspects, is *not* the prime problem, as so often claimed in Latin America. The younger military officers, who are often close in feeling and understanding to the true sentiments and anxieties of the back-country masses, sense this. The much publicized propaganda of social reformers, politicians and foreigners has often, in my opinion, created an artificial demand for land reform *in the capital city* that does not always hold true in the provinces.

Proper legal titles to farms are so taken for granted in the comfortable countries that it is difficult to comprehend the confusion resulting from insecure titles elsewhere. It is often a major factor crippling and defeating attempts at rural rehabilitation.

For instance:

As an outcome of a centuries-old history of land-grabbing and semi-nomadic land-squatting no one knows who owns much of the land of Brazil, including much of that now occupied and in cultivation. According to the 1950 census, in some states more than half of the farm establishments were occupied by persons without legal title to the land. The howl of alarm provoked by a recent reform bill providing for an examination of the legitimacy of land titles for all rural establishments of more than 500 hectares as well as any others of doubtful legality is thus understandable . . . The long-established pattern of squatting and nomadism has made a climate of violence and insecurity a commonplace aspect of rural life in Brazil. The *Associacões de Lavradores*, rapidly growing up in Rio and adjacent states, are primarily defensive organizations against the arbitrariness of landowners and the rural judicial and police officials whom the landowners often control and against the destructiveness of the hired and independent thugs who roam the countryside.[23]

Brazil is an extreme case, but many other countries also suffer from lack of sound legal titles. Whatever may be the historical reason, it is obvious that in one way or another the problem must be resolved, and resolved before the initiation of development projects.

The peaceable way would seem to be to train a special corps of title experts, give them the legal status of judges, have them hold proper court, and then enforce their decisions.

The alternative would be to cut the Gordian knot with a sword, to empty the can of worms by seizing all lands to which two or more persons claim title, disavow all such titles, and distribute the land among the best qualified farmers available, whether among the claimants or not.

The humane will advocate the former method; the communists and other social totalitarians will exhort for the latter as a jumping-off point for further wholesale seizures.

Without a firm title no farmer is going to spend his capital on improving his land, initiating conservation measures, making long-range plans. Until the title mess is cleared up all effort at rural rehabilitation is talk into a hot wind.

Everyone, including the *latino* himself, is so busy criticizing land tenure in Latin America that it is easy to overlook examples of good agricultural patterns.

Honduras, for instance, has a long record of excellently devised laws regulating the holding and sale of land. The first land law was promulgated as early as 1829. Thereon, about every decade, other pertinent laws have been passed. The holding of land has thus been continuously examined and regulated by the government. Many of the features, even of the early laws, are what social reformers today advocate as part of land reforms in other countries.[24]

Honduras is, and always has been, a country of small farmers. Since the country has never been overpopulated, until the present explosion, each citizen in the past generally has been able to own land.

One discouraging point, however: despite the lack of *haciendas,* and even of a class of *kulaks* (prosperous farmers, to use the Russian epithet), the shout for land reform is today as loud in Honduras as elsewhere. I leave to others to explain this emotional paradox.

The foregoing on the Honduran land laws is limited to affairs in the country's heartland.

Land tenure on the banana coastland is another matter. The laws that allowed the big American companies to obtain huge blocks of jungle land there must have been wise, because otherwise the area would never have been developed. Similarly, the current laws must *per se* be wrong, because they, plus the unrealistic social legislation, have led to the decay of the area.

All this is another way of emphasizing that the law of nature will in the end prevail regardless of wise laws and poor laws. *Haciendas* never developed in the central regions of Honduras because the topography and soil made them unprofitable; the wise laws did, however, preclude the rise of social tensions. On the jungle coastland, however, small farming is difficult. Here only large plantation agriculture is economically feasible, at least until research develops new techniques and crops for family-size farms. Hence, the current unwise laws hampering the large plantations have been a major factor in causing social tensions and the fervent cry for land reform.

Hereafter I am through scolding the use of the land reform movement as a social crusade for uplifting the morale of farmhands, for leveling all people into hoped-for equality and for doctoring all those ailments of mankind beyond the city sidewalks.

Since the term "land reform" has been so twisted and abused by the impassioned ones, I can only suggest it be abandoned and a more exact phrase substituted, such as "rural rehabilitation" or "agrarian development."

Fortunately, this change in emphasis is already apparent among those who have had direct contact with the subject, rather than just talking about it; the trend is already under way to concentrate not merely on dividing up the land but on *developing* it.

So I concern myself from now on strictly with the job at hand: how to increase the production from a hungry country's agricultural resources.

I repeat my oft-emphasized ABC's:

(A) The quantity of land available for production is, for all intents and purposes, fixed. New lands, undeveloped jungle, the valley over there, will all cost more to bring into an uncertain production than it will cost to increase the output of an equivalent amount of land already in use.

(B) To increase production from land now in use it is necessary to: (1) utilize research to provide better technology; and (2) train the farmer and his family in better farm management.

(C) The farmer must have a *farmable* piece of land before his training and the results of research can be of any good to anyone, especially himself.

The traditional non-Marxist land reform schemes have been based on the technical thesis, after social reform aspects are stripped away, that one-family agriculture produces more than does estate agriculture. It is claimed that an independent farmer, farming his own land, is a more efficient unit than a large estate manned by indifferent employees.

Depending on the crop being produced, I go along with this as a generally valid thesis, although on tropical land this will seldom be true. I disagree, however, that brutal government-controlled land redistribution results in efficient one-family units. The empirical record in those countries that have tried it surely disproves that credo.

As a substitute, therefore, I here offer a program or agenda that should lead *peaceably* to the redistribution of land holdings into their most efficient units.

If in a certain area the one-family unit of the right size and the right soil components and the right transportation advantages is the most efficient unit, then, I claim, my agenda will result in such units. If in that same valley the large estate, properly administered, is the most efficient unit, then such a grouping will automatically evolve.

It is usually asserted in countries which have large estates that they ripened and grew fat under the aegis of special police protection, special tax advantages, hijacking of communal lands, and so forth. Where this has been true, my program will force these artificial estates to disappear as surely as any government-sponsored harsh redistribution system.

Everything must have a name.

Let's call this Paddock's Peaceable Progression Plan for Permanent Pastoral Patrimonies, or, in short, the Progression Plan.

One step progresses automatically and peaceably from the one before it.

Alas, it is not a simple, one-syllable agenda that the Minister of Resources can absorb, propagandize and put into action before the next elections. Implementation of the Progression Plan must extend over several years. But when it is finished, land productivity throughout the nation should begin to approach its maximum — which, of course, ought to be the objective of every rural rehabilitation program.

Taxation is the machine which is to drive the Progression Plan along the road.

Land classification is the oil that will lubricate the machine.

Education is the syndrome from which flows the oil.

Without a proper classifying of all farmland the machine will not run. On the other hand, the most exact classification will be of little use unless fed into a properly functioning bureaucratic taxation machine.

Every nation produces many agricultural items. The variety will increase as research expands. The variability of the land must be adapted to the range of available uses — grain crops, cattle, sheep, vegetable produce, fiber crops, forest products, specialty export crops like citronella. Old-fashioned land reform systems ride roughshod over these variables like bulldozers.

Land classification will determine the most advantageous use of all land, not just a regional area, but each individual piece, whether now under cultivation or not. This will require, obviously, a large team of governmental personnel and they must be *trained* technicians. Determining the best use for lands that change character perhaps every few miles is not for amateurs.

In the hungry nation it is, everyone will agree, impractical to wait the several years needed for such a professional team of experts to be trained. The public wants action right now. Agitators for land reform are pounding at the door.

Therefore, under the Progression Plan, we do a couple of other things first in order to get the show on the road. Let us turn to taxation.

Item 1 on the agenda. So, leaders of the hungry country, whatever may be your tax system, the first item in the Progression Plan is to *double* the present rate of taxation on land that is *not* in use. (If there is no such tax, levy a light one.) "Not in use" means, simply, neither the owner nor anyone else is using it. Lying fallow in a rotation system is not in use. One cow every mile is not in use. However, such worries as to what is and is not in use are not important at this point.

This tax doubling is, as a matter of fact, merely a propaganda device, as it is doubtful any sizable increase of tax income will materialize. Its purpose is twofold: (1) to alert owners of land not in use that they are going to face difficulties later on; and (2) to satisfy the general public that something is being done in the field of rural rehabilitation. The wealthy landowners who, so everyone says, are not farming all the land to which they have title are unlikely to oppose the government violently, inasmuch as the new tax, even though double the old one, will probably not be large.

It should be incorporated in the law and stressed in newspapers that utilization of the land does not mean simply clearing it of the jungle cover and forgetting about it. In most cases forested land should be left forested and thus be considered utilized land. In Costa Rica there has been the unfortunate situation that the government taxes unused land and regards land as "improved" if it has been cleared of trees to make charcoal. The horrible result is that it pays a man to cut off the trees, make the charcoal and let the rains erode away the topsoil without further utilization. Such action is clearly visible in Ancaicayan, Colombia, where today a $400,000 dredge works day and night just to keep up with the silt coming off the cleared land.[25]

No trained personnel or special surveys are needed at this time to enforce this doubling of the tax. Just accept whatever classification the owner offers to the tax rolls.

Landowners, big and little, will, however, take a hard look at their pieces of unused land. A few who are especially enterprising will begin to search the money market for capital with which to convert the unused lands into production units. Others, especially those who have held land merely as a sort of family trust inherited through the generations, may start to sell the less valuable parts. Most, of course, will simply sit tight and do nothing.

Meanwhile, the government has a breathing period to organize other aspects of the Progression Plan.

Item 2. Simultaneously with Item 1, the government must begin the training of a corps of men capable of classifying agricultural land thoroughly and correctly.

This training program should be conducted with great fanfare and drum beating. This is to stir up the landowners. When they see the government is indeed beginning to take steps to carry out a program that eventually will lead to accurate taxation, they will realize they must prepare to protect themselves or pay the consequences.

The training school must produce an elite corps. If, later, its members fail at their job of land classification or if they succumb to bribes and political pressures, the economy of the country will suffer in direct proportion to their ineffectiveness.

If a country is so low in morale — and in morals — that it is incapable of producing an elite corps, then don't start the Progression Plan in the first place — or at least not until the leaders can drum up a conviction among the citizens that such a group is indeed a feasible and honorable goal of the nation.

The first group of land classifiers from this training school should be ready for graduation in about three years, with additional classes graduating each year thereafter.

Item 3. Simultaneously with Items 1 and 2, the owners of unused land should be encouraged to give these areas to the government in lieu of taxes — not just this new tax, but any other taxes they are paying. The government must set up a workable procedure for receiving this land via the tax system.

All government land, both already owned and to be received from private holdings, will eventually become the nuclei of national forests, watershed protection areas, and conservation districts. As a matter of long-range policy, the government should make strong, continuing efforts to acquire the maximum amount of nonagricultural land.

Item 4. The country must be mapped by a detailed aerial survey, or at least the cultivated areas should be mapped. A cadastral survey is the goal which will be the basis for establishing legal title to all farms and which will assist in conservation measures.

Mapping companies can be easily hired to do this job on contract; several are available in the United States and Europe. Or get this mapping done as part of foreign aid or military assistance. Precedence for this is already on record, establishing that American air force personnel are eager to do the job. (I daresay the Russian air force would be equally joyful to do it.) The nice thing about this mapping is that it can be done openly in the name of science and the advancement of terrestrial knowledge without reference to queasy military tie-ins.

Item 5. Two years after the first tax and one year before the first land classifiers graduate, the government again doubles the tax rate on unused land.

The tax on this land is now rather high. Before the Progression Plan the tax may have been only a dollar on each unused acre. This has now been doubled twice, so the tax is now four dollars. Since no way to enforce it has been established, the tax is still not producing much money for the treasury, but the landowners are again warned they must eventually act concerning their farm property. If a piece of land is suitable for use, then the owner must soon be prepared to put it into cultivation. If he does not have the capital for this, he must borrow it. If he cannot borrow it, he must at some time in the future sell the land. If the land cannot be sold – that is, if the land cannot be farmed profitably – then the owner can give it to the government in lieu of taxes.

Most, however, will still continue to sit tight and do nothing.

Item 6. Simultaneously with this second doubling of the tax, the government hires two or three world-famous land classifiers. They lecture at the school for three months and then take the senior class into the field on test cases. There is a need for test cases to be brought before the courts or tax bureaus. It is the most effective means of warning all landowners of unused land that they must soon come to a decision.

Test cases can be selected from those landowners who have registered their land for tax purposes under obviously wrong classifications. The purpose of having prominent, internationally known scientists at hand to testify is to start off the legal work of land redistribution at the highest possible plane of prestige and completely free of suspicion of government (political) bias. The students will benefit from working in the field with the international leaders of their profession.

Item 7. We are now approaching the end of the third year of the Progression Plan. By now, land should begin to come on the market in ever greater quantities. This is the unused land which the owners prefer to sell rather than try to cultivate. It is, naturally, the poorest grade of land. Nevertheless, it is land, of a sort, for the landless. Also, it ought to be cheap. Government or commercial credit facilities can backstop the buyer. Actually, however, it is questionable whether this poor land makes a good credit risk; perhaps none of the landless should be encouraged to buy it. They probably can make just as poor a living in the city slums. The produce from such sad land is not going to help the nation's economy.

Item 8. The fourth year. The tax rate on unused land remains unchanged. However, a nominal tax is levied on *used* land that is not meeting production standards equal to 25 per cent of the average for similar farmland in the same district, as determined by the government. This tax rise is also primarily a propaganda device, because the government actually has no idea what 25 per cent of the production standards of a district is. So no attempt should be made to enforce the tax. It will be noted that this tax is not aimed at the farmer with, presumably, too much land; i.e., unused land. This tax is aimed at the inefficient farmer, whether he is peasant or landed aristocrat.

Item 9. The first group of land classifiers have now graduated. They are trained to judge effectively the way in which a piece of agricultural land can be used most profitably. They know how to compile agricultural production statistics. They know how to establish norms of production which all similar farms in an area ought to achieve if farmed efficiently. They are an elite corps, proud of their profession.

Since the group is limited in number, they should not be scattered thinly over the country but should be concentrated in one district. Therefore, a district should be carefully selected that can be used as a training model. In theory, it seems best to have it in the heart of the best agricultural land.

During this year this group compiles data and classifies the land of the district so that all necessary information is at hand.

Item 10. The fifth year. All taxes remain unchanged. However, now the taxes are strictly enforced in this one district. The classifiers, plus this year's new graduating class, move on to other districts adjacent to the one that has already been classified. As soon as a district is classified the taxes are enforced.

Item 11. Classifying a district is not, unfortunately, a one-time thing. One or more classifiers must remain in the district permanently, partly to determine the annual 25 per cent norm and partly to update land classification by taking into consideration new marketing fluctuations, new research developments, catastrophes such as floods, and all the other things that bedevil a farmer year in and year out.

Item 12. As soon as it is feasible after the classifiers have firmly launched their program in successive districts, the boom is really lowered on inefficiency and misuse of land.

Morally, this should not be done until all farmland in the country has been classified, so that all farmers can be treated equally under the law. Practically, this may not be possible. For one thing, too many years of waiting may be involved. More important, it is preferable to have land redistribution come about gradually, rather than in one big hullabaloo.

Lowering the boom means doubling the tax rates again, both the one on unused land and the one on land which is not producing at a rate equal to the 25 per cent average of the region.

Basing the tax rate on the original dollar per acre, the present tax rate on unused land has risen to eight dollars an acre, that on land which is not meeting the 25 per cent has risen to four dollars.

Note that the efficient farmer who is achieving the 25 per cent is still paying taxes at the *same* old rate that perhaps has been in existence since his father's and grandfather's time. Note also that the large estate farmer may achieve 25 per cent on part of his land and pay the old rate on it, but on other parts he may have to pay the new rates.

These taxes are now being collected. There is the group of classifiers going around the countryside who are capable of determining if land is in use or not and comparing correctly a farmer's productivity, his efficiency, on a piece of land in relation to that of his neighbors.

Item 13. When taxes are doubled in the preceding step, it can be assumed considerable land will be put on the market by those who are unable, or unwilling, to farm it properly. The market price of land should drop, and drop radically.

There is now a need for credit facilities to be available to the buyers, plus additional credit to purchase seed, tools, fertilizer, and so forth. The wise government should earmark a portion of its tax revenues to provide these credits. If this is not enough, there may be additional funds available within the framework of current aid programs. As a matter of fact, the international world is overflowing with credit money, both the kind that is granted only to sound credit risks and the kind that is handed out free and easy under political colorations. I doubt if money for the new farmers will be a problem. I hope, just the same, the money is loaned as a commercial bank would do and that repayment will be required — it is not only better in the long run for the nation's moral fiber, but it will be insurance that each farmer will keep up his production.

The wise government should also insist that the land sellers be required to keep their money within the nation, rather than sending it off to Switzerland. The nation needs to have these men invest their capital in the various forms of resource development, such as the right kind of small industries.

I refer back to my story of Oklahoma farmer Lee Barnes in the dark days of American agriculture of the Depression.

He gained solvency and his land gained productivity directly through the aid of adequate credit and through the aid of expert government men working personally with him. Success was won only over a period of years of hard work and rigid saving by himself and his family.

Agriculture is a difficult, complex business. Rural rehabilitation and maximum land utilization cannot be achieved if left only in the hands of sociologists and demagogues. Only advisers who are skilled agriculturists, guided and supported by a firm government program, can win this battle. These advisers, I trust, are now forthcoming from the new College for Resource Development that I proposed in an earlier chapter.

Nevertheless, this corps of advisers, usually called extension agents, is only as good as the information they have available to extend to the farmers. And, as Jefferson said, "It takes time to persuade men to do even what is for their own good." [26]

Fundamental to any land program must be the realization by one and all that *new* agricultural knowledge must be found. Tax incentives and other government benefits are not enough to produce adequate agricultural increases for the expanding population. New varieties of seeds, new methods of sowing, harrowing, weeding, harvesting and marketing must be developed.

This means research.

The Hand of God has dealt harshly with these backward, hungry countries. It has granted them only marginal resources and in so doing has tied them to the miserable life which places them outside the pale of the twentieth century.

Man must alter the Hand of God.

I take up this most important of all subjects after a detour into the un-Godlike ruckus of foreign aid.

16

The Two Fallacies of Foreign Aid—The Yo-Yo and the No Know-How

I HAVE TRIED to think back and remember at which point in my succession of Foreign Service posts I first came into contact with foreign aid in action. I believe it was in 1951 when I was traveling through Paris as a member of the Canadian National Defence College. During our briefing it was mentioned there were then four American ambassadors stationed in Paris. The Canadian colonel next to me turned and said, "My, my, how bustling you Americans have become! Are you really sure it takes four Americans to do one man's work now?"

To a diplomatic officer four ambassadors at a post are as incongruous as four Presidents in Washington. The extra three men in Paris were, it turned out, involved in military matters and economic and financial aid in relation to the reconstruction of Europe. Already the postwar proliferation of titles and offices and the revolving door of personnel were in action in our foreign affairs – and especially in the administration of foreign aid.

In the receiving countries, foreign aid becomes quite a different sort of synthesis than the development of a nation by its own citizens out of its own resources. The thinking is different, the goals are different, the time element is out of another calendar.

Throughout these chapters I have tried to fix attention on those problems which each small, isolated, hungry nation must tackle to develop whatever resources it may have. I tried to steer clear of the Kilkenny cats fighting and arguing specific procedures of foreign aid. Those programs are, from the viewpoint of most receiving nations, not the major element in their overall efforts to conquer their range of problems. Foreign aid is expected to supplement the development of a nation; it should not control and color and tamper with a nation's own efforts.

But the balky bulldozer does just that in too many instances.

Also, in the aid-giving countries and in the world press as a whole, foreign aid unfortunately has come to be synonymous with any and every kind of economic and sociological activity out over the horizon.

Many nations give funds in the name of foreign aid and several claim to give more per capita than the United States. Eleven countries (Belgium, Canada, Denmark, France, Germany, Italy, Japan, Netherlands, Norway, Portugal, United Kingdom) have been giving a significantly greater percentage of their gross national product in foreign aid since 1956 than has the United States.[1] And there are also those aid-receiving countries which themselves give aid to other nations, which must surely be the height of budgetry sleight-of-hand. However, here I limit myself to the aid process of the United States.

American foreign aid contains, embedded within itself, not one but two fallacies that foredoom the program from its announced goal of development of the undeveloped nations. Individual projects may accomplish their objectives, but the foreign aid program as a whole will always fail to *develop* soundly and permanently, whether on a continental basis or on an individual country basis. The two fallacies do not derive from humans, neither foreign receiving officials nor Americans, nor from a lack of imaginative ideas or a lack of dedication, nor, most obviously by now, from any lack of money.

The proof of failure should be self-evident from the annual troubles of the foreign aid budget in the Congress. A smooth, successful operation winning its victories would be the darling of congressmen. Instead, "there is no function of government that has been so studied and reorganized. It has passed through seven structural changes and no fewer than eight Presidential committees."[2]

"A special chamber of torture is reserved in the capital for the man who runs foreign aid, and yesterday it received its twelfth victim in fourteen years [David E. Bell]."[3]

In the end, the passing of the foreign aid bill becomes, almost every year, a matter of the personal prestige of the President of the United States. I can think of no other sector of American life that must annually receive this extreme, personal intervention by the Most High. It is a self-evidence of failure. Which is not to belittle the gallant, far-striving goals the aid officials set for their work.

To get at the marrow of what the term "foreign aid" is in practice, in contrast to what is said in public statements, and to understand the dividing line between the two self-defeating fallacies, it is important to segregate into two blocks the mass of projects lumped together under the catchall term "foreign aid." Often one hears the recommendation that the program should be divided into military items (to be turned over to the Department of Defense) and the economic items (to be retained in the present AID).

I suggest, instead, they be divided into *political* and *apolitical* items.

"Political" includes all forms of military assistance. It includes the crash economic programs rushed in to bolster a weak ally or to give token faith in a new regime. It also includes those aid allotments that are little more than bribes to a government or a ruling clique to keep them kindly disposed toward us in Cold War altercations.

"Apolitical" includes projects designed for the long-range resource development of backward countries.

This distinction is, I hazard, seldom drawn or clearly understood even at the higher policy levels. After all, was there ever a more euphonious alias for a bribe than a "foreign aid" allotment? Even military assistance, at least many forms of it, or at least announcement of its wide extent, is often more palatable to the receiving nation if labeled "foreign aid."

FALLACY NUMBER ONE

Yo-Yo Politics Lead to Yo-Yo Instability.

The political items contained within the term "foreign aid" are by their very nature short-term, because who can foretell the international politics of next year or next week. Thus, it is legitimate for them to be governed by annually altered budgets and by improvised policies and shifting personnel. In fact, "foreign aid" is not a bad name for these funds; it is quite accurate.

When this political block of items in former foreign aid programs is analyzed, with hindsight allowance for all the muddling and bungling involved in international tomfoolery, one can argue an excellent case that such money has been wisely spent, that full value has been received by the American taxpayer, and that the White House, the Congress and the aid officials have been intelligent and imaginative in manipulating these funds to American advantage. In the great game of international power politics there is no need for Americans to take a back seat behind the "more experienced" Europeans or the "wily" Orientals. The evidence to date is that we hold our own very nicely. And this block of political foreign aid activity has been a major tool in American success.

This is nothing new in our government's life. As Hans Morgenthau has pointed out, "The first Appropriation Act adopted by the First Congress of the United States in 1789 included a modest contingent fund for such purposes"; that is, international influencing.[4]

Just the same, this political activity has for certain been a drag weight around the bundle of money intended by the Congress for economic development activity. Making use of so-called "development" programs as a facade behind which to carry on political matters has, it must now be apparent, merely ended in the canceling out of true development. Always the political factor dominates the decisions as to which projects to initiate. The overall foreign aid policies are both laid down in Washington and implemented in the field by politically motivated officials for their political objectives of the moment. Hence, the emphasis on "propaganda" projects that can be *seen* within a couple of years, even in countries that are removed from international disputes, as Uruguay.

The Washington columnist Arthur Krock said:

> The controversy this year [over the 1964 foreign aid budget] is not over military foreign aid . . . The issue in Congress, as for the previous nine years, is over economic foreign assistance, its administration and the soundness of its concept. This concept is that the world Communist movement would have captured the new, uncommitted and undeveloped nations without the steady inflow of dollars – moreover, with no strings attached.[5]

He added that the drastic House action in cutting the budget "registered a national disenchantment, of which only the executive seems unaware, with foreign economic assistance and its administration."

The "disenchantment" is indeed at hand, but mostly because the "concept" of economic foreign assistance does not clearly draw the line either in Washington or in the public mind between the Cold War aspects and the *development* aspects.

The public does not understand what it is supposed to be supporting. The Congress is perplexed as to what these demands for money are all about. We do not grasp the *why*.

In contrast, look at Sweden. The Swedes are now spending 1 per cent of their gross national product on foreign aid, twice the rate of the Americans. Yet the chief objection within Sweden to the foreign aid seems to be on the part of those who believe the government should be spending more, not less.[6] Sweden has limited its foreign aid primarily to a single, concrete field, that of population control, and its personnel are technicians in that subject, not political theorists or moneylenders. The Swedes accept and understand this work as a worthwhile, important program that will directly benefit the struggling, backward nations, and they are willing to pay a healthy part of their national income thus to help the needy ones.

The American aid program, on the contrary, has never been reduced to a philosophy, to clear objectives, that the public can grasp. On the one hand, the program is criticized as a diffuse, every-which-way, buckshot affair, but the public is not instructed that this sort of program is necessary to implement complex Cold War actions (from which, incidentally, Sweden withdraws its skirts in ladylike neutrality). On the other hand, the *development* goal, which everyone so carefully tells the Americans is the real purpose of their aid program, is a goal that, it is plain for everyone to see, is not being attained. No wonder Americans are confused and disenchanted.

Instability, the feature of our foreign aid that is most familiar to the public both in the United States and abroad, stems from today's international spasms, all those crazy speedboat crises rushing out of nowhere and splashing everyone, especially the foreign aid personnel.

In 1963 military coups d'etat overthrew the properly elected Presidents of Honduras and the Dominican Republic. As a sign of disfavor for this undemocratic procedure, President Kennedy canceled the American aid programs in both countries and withdrew aid personnel (sixty employees plus families).[7] Ninety days later Kennedy changed his mind and reinstated the aid programs (even though there was no change in the local Honduran or Dominican governments). The original AID personnel, however, had been scattered. So new teams were sent in and everything had to be started up again – with different people and different guidelines – almost as if all the earlier millions of dollars and great efforts had never existed. All for a political three-month policy.

Critics mourn, from their vantage point outside the cockpit of action, the absence of firm, reasoned and constant American policies with respect to this or that area, such as Latin America or Southeast Asia. Such firm policies would be fine to have, and would certainly be profitable, but it is not in the nature of the beast. Beyond the three-mile limit, government activity of all types, and definitely not just foreign aid, becomes flotsam shifting with every political wave. It is impossible to make long-range plans for anything affected by, or endangered by, the succession of international crises or by our own domestic politics as related to them. Even our affairs with a stable nation like Tunisia are tensed and changed by the crises elsewhere in the area.

Before the days of transoceanic telephone and jet planes, before Washington became important enough to be involved with each daily crisis around the equator, our representatives abroad could relax and lead snug lives. Not today. Our international world is too tempestuous, too wobbly, too close at hand. Our personnel and the guidelines and the policies and the reorganizations flit by like fireflies.

Americans so often look down primly on other peoples for their coups d'etat, their bowling alley cabinets and the other evidences of quicksilver troubles. Americans fail to realize how unstable their own government is in its operations abroad. The experienced foreign official learns the hard way how little faith he can place in the words of the American representative across the desk from him; the American will be gone in a year or so and the Washington policies he sincerely expounds will be just as temporary.

All this instability comes most clearly into focus with our foreign aid because it is so exposed out there on the battlefront. The aid official at his desk in Conakry, Recife or Dacca never knows what new policy, new budgetary cutback or new superior officer the next Washington telegram will announce.

This is why the aid programs at their various levels always seem to be under the direction of just-arrived amateurs, why the projects in all programs have, for the most part, been reduced to things that can be put up and *seen* within two years. That is all the leeway of continuity and stability the new foreign aid official has within which to operate. True resource development is hopelessly outside this narrow time limit of aid personnel.

It is wrong to point the finger at any person, such as Eisenhower or Kennedy or Johnson or any of the AID directors, and blame him for the instability. It is, I now accept, endemic. I also accept it cannot be changed with respect to the handling of any fluid political matter abroad, not just the foreign aid work.

I know of no way now available by which long-time aid programs and long-time budgets can be adopted and adhered to in Washington over a period of ten or twenty years and the aid personnel kept at a mission for, surely, a minimum of four years. This is a situation the American public and the Congress must face up to and accept as unalterable in relation to the foreign aid programs as now organized.

"We are asked to use five-year plans to cope with twenty-year problems using two-year personnel and one-year money." [8]

This is instability. It is also politics. It is the ebb and flow of international affairs. When our government officials are successful in this turmoil of international complications, as I consider they mostly have been since the war, then the instability in foreign aid is a minor price to pay as part of that success.

Thus, United States foreign aid has a sufficiently successful political aspect and it has an unsuccessful apolitical development aspect. And I can see no hope for the development aspect ever to succeed as long as it is amalgamated with the political.

Yet it would be a tragedy just to stop this development aspect of foreign aid and say it cannnot be done. The American public may be "disenchanted," but, so far as I can judge, it is still willing to pay out great sums to help backward nations; it is willing to do this not only because of the underlying humane reasons, but also because of the realization that America's own well-being will be buttressed if today's hungry nations can develop into relatively prosperous and stable entities. Even those senators and representatives who are most reluctant to vote the annual aid budgets seem, as I read their criticisms, not to be against the principle of aid to *develop* these nations; they are merely irritated by, and rightly suspicious of, the protestations of the White House that *all* these budget items are going to bring about development when the evidence to date is quite the contrary.

The political and apolitical development aspects of foreign aid must, in some manner, be separated into two quite independent organizations. Each must be given the opportunity to argue its case before the Congress for its annual appropriations. If either one cannot make a good case for the need for its funds, it does not deserve the appropriation. Today, by having all items folded into a single agency, when the case for one aspect is not well presented and substantiated, the Congress smites everything.

Give the name Foreign Aid to that organization that will include all those political and military items now found in AID: urban development, military assistance, hospitals, roads, new colonization projects – everything the propaganda machine can play up so colorfully. And include those crash programs that bolster tottering currencies and tottering regimes and the yachts for heads of state and the surplus food for the 100,000,000 mouths.

To the other organization give the name Foreign Resource Development and assign to it those projects of a long-term nature, the projects intended truly to *develop.*

So here is the place for me to cut away from the political Foreign Aid organization. Let it go its own way. Let us concentrate on this other, apolitical, Foreign Resource Development organization.

Fallacy Number Two

No Know-How.

This fallacy goes back to President Truman in his 1949 inaugural address that started the whole thing with Point Four, and has been reiterated constantly since then by about everyone else.

Point Four contains the key sentence: "Our aim should be to help the free peoples of the world, through their own efforts, to produce more food, more clothing, more materials for housing, and more mechanical power to lighten their burdens." [9]

All very well, but Truman also said: "For the first time in history, humanity possesses the knowledge and the skill to relieve the suffering of these [hungry] people. . . . Our imponderable resources in technical knowledge are constantly growing and are inexhaustible .... We should make available to peace-loving peoples the benefits of our store of technical knowledge in order to help them realize their aspirations for a better life." [10]

"Know-how" has been a litany ever since, up to and beyond President Kennedy in 1963 when he spoke to the Third World Food Congress and said, "We have the ability, as members of the human race, we have the means, we have the capacity to eliminate hunger from the face of the earth in our lifetime. We need only the will." [11]

The sad, tragic fact of life is that we do *not* have the know-how. We do have vast stores of knowledge which we have been able to utilize within the United States under the specific conditions of our own climate and geography to bring huge increase in our productivity. Unfortunately, how we do it in Kansas, California and Florida must be readapted, relearned in the alien environments abroad. This is true whether in agriculture or education or labor union elections.

This quotation from Milton J. Esman is perhaps the best illustration of what I mean.

> No sane person would attempt to put a space ship in orbit without elaborate supporting educational and research activities. Yet this is precisely what we have attempted in the more subtle and complex areas of overseas operations . . . There is no professional enterprise on which individuals can embark at this epoch of history fraught with more complexity, more untested problems, and more costly consequence of error than operations with the revolutionary changes now under way in the newly independent and emerging countries.[12]

Know-how is a tricky thing. We know how to increase the sorghum production in Illinois; we do not know how to do it in Pakistan. We know how to build highways in South Carolina; we do not know how to build them in Cambodia without constant, too costly maintenance. We know how to build low-rent apartment houses anywhere; we do not know how to wipe away the slums around them. We know how to grant loans to farmers in Colorado; we do not know how the same type of loans will affect the farmers of Iran. We know how to teach biology to Oregon school children; we do not know how to teach the same data in Gabon. We know how to levy taxes in Boston; we do not know what taxes should be levied in Saigon.

Know-how! Thou art a fickle goddess!

Fickle because sometimes American techniques can indeed be transplanted with little adaptation and without delay. For instance, American hybrid corns were rather easily introduced into Yugoslavia. This is often used as an illustration in support of big-scale "know-how" programs elsewhere. Note, unfortunately, that Yugoslavia is in the temperate zone at the same latitude as Iowa and that its climate and soils are not too different from sections of the United States. The success in Yugoslavia has little relation to the problems confronting our officials in the hungry belt around the equator.

Know-how! Thou art also a false goddess!

A Suggested Solution

The separation of Foreign Aid projects from Foreign Resource Development projects should lead to a new bureau charged with the handling of the latter. The backbone of its work will be in the area of agriculture, forests, mines and fisheries, and these can generally be developed only by *first* finding and then adapting locally the "know-how" Washington so fervently believes it already has.

None of the projects within the Bureau of Foreign Resource Development would or could be razzle-dazzle, because they would be under the direct supervision of scientists who would possess the necesssary feeling of timeless continuity so vital to the program. Also, there should be no political necessity for flamboyant press releases.

Nor would they be expensive, as aid items go. The entire annual budget of such a bureau probably need not be more than $200,000,000. This should be enough for a major, massive attack to learn how the principal resource problems of the undeveloped regions probably, but only probably, can be overcome.

Let this bureau set up research stations or institutes in the several regions of the hungry belt around the world – regionally, not one for each country. These stations would be charged with carrying forward twenty-year research programs in the same fashion as the government has long conducted research projects within the United States.

Research is an old, well-tested and successful function of our government. Today it is spending $15,000,000,000 a year on research – for everything from finding out how to sterilize insects to sending a man to the moon. To a lesser degree this has been going on for a hundred years. The Hatch Act of 1887 systematized the government's agricultural research; the Bankhead-Jones Act of 1937 so strengthened it that the subject is now seldom a matter of controversy. American universities, using government one-year funds, regularly make ten-year staff research appointments. Surely this framework of continuity can be expanded to include this critical research-development work abroad.

To achieve continuity would require that personnel remain at their regional stations for a minimum of four years, not the two years which is so much the rule with our people abroad now. Before World War II it was understood that an ambassador or consul general remained at his post for four years; junior officers stayed for at least three. It is a good rule. In resource development activity such a rule is vital.

The authorizing bill must stipulate that the director of this bureau and all ranking aides both in Washington and in the field be *technicians,* not lawyers or bankers or accountants. They must be trained in the specific disciplines of resource development. After all, remember that President Truman's original Point Four proposal emphasized *technical* assistance. Only in later reshufflings, as the competition with Russian activity grew, was this technical viewpoint lost sight of and the emphasis shifted to social, political programs. This shift is so great that today European aid-giving countries utilize fourteen times more technicians in the field than does the United States![13]

The type of applied research projects and the process of putting them into motion I take up in the following chapter in relation to the efforts of the hungry nations themselves to initiate their own research programs.

It is necessary to answer here, however, one domestic American group that may doubt the advisability of our doing this research abroad; that is, research which may enable the foreign nations to compete against American producers. Such a doubt shows ignorance of the fallout of international research.

The Rockefeller Foundation has conducted research for many years in Mexico. This has resulted in major breakthroughs in the control there of the potato late blight and wheat rust diseases. Potatoes are now becoming an important crop in Mexico and wheat production has greatly increased.

At the same time, American potato and wheat farmers will benefit, because these same discoveries will be adapted by research in the United States to improve our own varieties of these crops. Yet the discoveries could not have been made in the United States; it was the unique climate and other conditions prevailing in Mexico with respect to these two plant diseases that were the key factors.

The principal economic activity in the Sudan is cotton production. If an American cotton research station were to be established in that region two benefits would accrue, assuming that the research work evolved successfully: (1) The Sudanese cotton growers would benefit and also the Sudan economy; *national development* would come about, as a result of the regional station's efforts, in the way that current foreign aid programs yearn to achieve. (2) The American cotton growers probably would benefit because of the new knowledge gained about the cotton plant in the Sudan. American cotton men may worry, at the time of the initiation of the American research station for the Sudan region, that American funds are going merely to help Sudanese growers compete against Americans. They should understand, however, that it is likely they will themselves gain from this research just as surely as the foreigners.

Nevertheless, if American cotton growers fail to think this through, if their congressmen prevent work on cotton abroad at these new research stations, omit that work. Let the station do work on something else such as rinderpest disease of livestock or on kenaf, a fiber plant the United States might profitably import. Leave it to the Sudanese to do their own cotton research. The purpose of this discussion on research and development is to clarify thinking on American efforts to help the hungry nations. It is not intended to argue with Washington lobbyists.

Research abroad under the auspices of the United States Government is, however, already a well-established activity, based on the realization that certain problems can be investigated to greater advantage there than at home. The clearest example concerns the Bureau of Mines and the Geological Survey of the Department of the Interior, which have long sent out their own geologists both to assess the value of foreign ore deposits and to train local geologists (an obvious activity, as the United States consumes at least a third of the world's mineral output).[14]

Other areas for the Foreign Research Development bureau would be the development of methods for mass, elementary education and cheaper methods of using local materials for road and housing construction so that the hungry nations can spend less of their national income for these needs.

None of this is possible unless the United States has a bureau especially geared for long-range development work in the hungry nations. The bureau will need four props: (1) stable technical personnel; (2) noninterference by the White House executive branch as the political winds come and go; (3) overall control and protection by the State Department, the same that it gives to other government activities abroad; (4) steady congressional backing.

As I see it, the most stable element in the American Government, except for such as the Civil Service, is the seniority system in committees of the Senate and the House of Representatives. This has played a major role in the steady continuity of many domestic programs, especially of domestic research. The directors of most of these programs, such as in agriculture, appear at the budget hearings not to press and fight for appropriations but to discuss and explain their work and their plans for growth over an indefinite number of years. The budgets remain "annual," but the plans may stretch for a decade or more.

The Dean of Agriculture of the University of Wisconsin, Dr. Ira Baldwin, told me that when he once appeared before the Finance Committee of the Wisconsin State Legislature to explain a dairy cattle breeding research program the University wanted to initiate, the legislators asked him, "When can we expect to see results?" He said, "Don't even ask for any for twenty years. We'll be lucky even then to have some results." And the legislators accepted this as a satisfactory answer.

The same understanding can prevail in the Congress with regard to foreign resource development in the hungry nations.

The Congress in successive Foreign Assistance Acts has consistently included directives such as this one in the act of December 1963: "It is the sense of Congress that, in the administration of programs of assistance . . . every possible precaution should be taken to assure that such assistance is not diverted to short-term emergency purposes (such as budgetary purposes, balance-of-payments purposes, or military purposes) or any other purpose not essential to the long-range economic development of recipient countries." [15]

Congressmen say this but they do not get it. The fault lies in the Congress not defining, or perhaps not understanding, clearly what it means by "long-range economic development." So the members of Congress should not be too surprised, as they recently were, to learn that $800,000 labeled "technical assistance" actually went to buy road construction equipment. I was in the Senate gallery as this was discussed; one senator, an outspoken critic of foreign aid, rapped his desk as he stated, "That's capital investment. If this money were really for technical assistance, I would support it."

Would the Congress favor the establishment of a separate, politically neutral Foreign Resource Development Bureau? I believe so. The 1964 Foreign Aid Bill took pains to stipulate that "no provision of this Act shall be construed to prohibit assistance to any country pursuant to the Peace Corps Act . . . the Mutual Educational and Cultural Exchange Act . . . or famine or disaster relief." [16] These were acknowledged as nonpolitical activities.

The so-called Humphrey Amendment to the last two Foreign Assistance Acts provides that "the facilities and resources of other Federal agencies shall be utilized when such facilities are particularly or uniquely suitable for technical assistance." [17] Little has been done to implement this clause. The fault seems to lie with the officials of AID, or rather with the atmosphere within which they now operate. When "technical assistance" is used as a synonym for all the political miscellany of the present foreign aid program, the officials are bound to lack the imagination (or need) to see how the facilities of other federal agencies can be utilized. The great resources and decades of experience which are built into the Departments of Agriculture, Interior and Commerce, which are available to AID officials, remain, for the most part, outside their range of thinking.

This situation forms the background of the comment a traveling professor made to me as he leafed through the program book (list of aid projects) of one mission abroad. "This reads like a sociology textbook! There isn't a nickel here that will be spent to produce an extra sack of rice or open a new mine."

A nonpolitically established Foreign Resource Development Bureau could concentrate single-mindedly on its one objective: to prepare and maintain long-term *development* plans for the hungry nations. Its work would not be a new, untried exercise. The full spectrum of help and experience of the other federal agencies would be behind it and also the guidance of the Congress, resulting from its long support of research and other forms of domestic, decade-long development work.

"After all, no one expects general and complete disarmament tomorrow, yet we direct immense effort toward it. Why shouldn't we start planning now for a general and complete world agricultural program?" [18] Or fishery program. Or mining program. Or forestry program.

Today our corps of American ambassadors in Latin America is probably the most able ever assembled. Yet even they usually do not understand the nature of resource development as distinguished from politically oriented aid. One of the best of these ambassadors said to me that the most effective development program in his country was a combined group of American Peace Corps personnel and local young people also organized as a form of native peace corps. These were working jointly on a community development project in order to arouse the people and stimulate the spirit of the area. The ambassador emphasized the good will and respect between the two groups of corpsmen and also the awakened "drive" within the community itself. When I pointed out that although he was calling this a development project it was, in fact, merely an illustration of successful public relations, he did not understand. To him it was enough that at least in this one instance the specific objective of an "aid" project was being achieved harmoniously. Considering how seldom this occurs, the ambassador was right in being proud of this success within his jurisdiction, but, again, it was not *development*.

Half of Latin America is forested. Yet not one of our aid personnel is currently working there as a forestry technician. There is no qualified person even to write up a forestry idea or project for inclusion in the aid program in these countries.

Hundreds to wipe the noses of the unhappy; only a few to put shoes on the weary feet.

Part IV

17

How to Alter the Hand of God: Research

I ONCE spent two weeks trying to make an American corn picker work on the south coast of Guatemala.

A corn picker, for those who have not been down on the farm lately, picks and husks ears of corn. As modern farm machinery goes, it is not too complex.

This area of Central America is where the corn plant originated. It should produce some of the world's highest-yielding corn. It doesn't. In places like Iowa, the corn has had to be transplanted and adapted to alien climates and soils. Nevertheless, the yields in Guatemala are only about a seventh of those in Iowa. In the markets of Guatemala City I have seen corn selling for five times the price quoted on the Chicago market.

One reason for the high cost is the amount of hand labor required. Hence, my desire to try out the corn picker.

The representative of the American company personally delivered the corn picker, a brand-new one fresh off the boat. We were to try it out on the most progressive farm in this region where some new corn hybrids were being raised, hybrids that I had myself been involved in developing and recommending for use here.

It was a beautiful field, level, just like Iowa. The tropical sun was broiling hot as we labored, but not as hot as the Iowa sun in July.

Together with the owner of the farm we sweated and grubbed and toiled to make that corn picker work—and failed. We adjusted the rollers. We brought in new rollers. We practically rebuilt the machine.

After two weeks the corn could not wait longer to be picked. The farmer rushed out to hire a crew of Indians, who did the job as expensively as they had been doing it for the past half-century.

A few years later, at the Panamerican Agricultural School in central Honduras, I tried again. The school bought a corn picker of another American brand (no reason for the change; we happened to get a better price).

Our field was also a beautiful stand of corn. It was level and the professor in charge had done an excellent job of preparing it properly and keeping the weeds out. The corn was a different variety than the one in Guatemala, but I again had been involved in developing it and was thus familiar with its characteristics. Here, too, should have been the ideal place for a corn picker to do its picking.

After literally weeks of work we did get the machine to pick the field, but not to husk it. Every conceivable adjustment was made to have it operate the way it does so smoothly in the United States, but it never did.

Next year, we tried again and failed. Perhaps too many weeds. Perhaps the weeds were too fibrous for the cutter bars designed for Iowa farms. Perhaps the husks were too dry or too tough. Perhaps the corn ears were at the wrong height on the stock. Always there was something. When each factor was corrected, something else went wrong.

The moral of the story is not that the American corn pickers are not good machines. The moral of the story is that if Central America wants a corn picker to pick its corn it must develop a machine especially for its own fields. Nor is it a question that agricultural engineers cannot develop such a corn picker. They probably can do so with ease. As yet, they have not been given the task.

Unfortunately, the corn picker developed for the south coast of Guatemala probably will not work in central Honduras.

The moral of the moral of the story is that each hungry nation must itself develop the research that will develop its resources. Each nation must itself take the initiative. It cannot directly transfer to its own problems the techniques and solutions developed in other areas of the world.

Local research must be done on the spot to find out how to apply those foreign techniques.

A lot of big names in the world leadership have the conviction that science already has the answers needed for the ample life in the hungry nation, that it is just a question of getting that knowledge into the thick skulls of the unlearned, that solving the hunger of the world is merely a matter of logistics. Successive American Presidents speak brightly of sharing American know-how, as I stressed in the preceding chapter on foreign aid.

President Kennedy suffered from this blind spot. I repeat here his statement to the Third World Food Congress in June 1963 that I quoted earlier in part. "We have the ability, as members of the human race, we have the means, we have the capacity to eliminate hunger from the face of the earth in our lifetime. We need only the will . . . For the first time in the history of the world we do know how to produce enough food now to feed every man, woman and child in the world, enough to eliminate all hunger completely." [1]

Pope Paul also has this blind spot. In his 1963 Christmas message he stated, "Instead of increasing the supply of bread on the dining table of this hunger-ridden world, as modern techniques of production can do today, some are thinking in terms of diminishing, by illicit means, the number of those who eat with them. This is unworthy of civilization." [2] This reiteration of the Catholic ban against population control is couched in moving language, but the "modern techniques of production" are, unfortunately, not at hand, either today or in the foreseeable future, in the "hunger-ridden" nations.

At the 1963 World Food Congress this theme, that science already has the answers, was repeated over and over again. Alas, the delegates who make up these international discussion forums, as well as the members of the Vatican Curia, are seldom people who have actually worked in the fields and tried to apply the scientific knowledge they are talking about. Else they would not speak so glibly that the answers are at hand eager and ready for use.

Even the scientists themselves must learn this diabolical fact the hard way. When I first arrived in Guatemala as a plant pathologist fresh from graduate school plus a couple of years of teaching, I knew I had one of the finest educations in my field. So when I saw the poor Indians on their eroded hillsides following their ancient ways of planting and cultivating, I was positive all I had to do was to show them the twentieth century, and, like the thirsty desert rose, the corn would forthwith shoot to the sun and blossom in the fullness thereof. So I planted my experimental plots and used all the cunning of my education, and what did I get? I got the same low yields as my Indian neighbors. My North American knowledge was impractical until I learned to adapt it to Central American conditions.

My friend John Niederhauser arrived in Mexico in the late 1940's to join the Rockefeller Foundation staff. He had his Ph.D. in plant pathology, plus several years' experience working on potato problems in upstate New York. In Mexico he found the potato crops suffering the same trouble as back home, a universal disease called late blight. He *knew* that all he had to do was to import blight-resistant potatoes from New York. So he imported them and he planted them, assuring the skeptical Mexican farmers of the beautiful results to come. What happened was that the potatoes blighted as they came out of the ground, and he got no crop at all. The potatoes were resistant to New York blight, but were not, in spite of then held theories, resistant to Mexican blight. Niederhauser resorted to spraying, in the conventional way he had learned in the United States, but he was unprepared for the violence of the blight attack in Mexico. He tried all the gimmicks he had ever heard of. In his desperation he even, and this he knew was the ultimate of uselessness, hired small boys to pick off the blight-infected leaves. A decade later, and with the resources of the Rockefeller Foundation backing a research program on late blight, Niederhauser and his fellow workers finally produced a potato that was blight-resistant in *Mexican* fields. Only *then* were they able to provide the country with a revolutionary new food crop. Mexico is now a world center for late blight research.

No matter how the famous of the world may assure you that science already knows the answers and thus it is just a simple little thing of umpteen million dollars to get that knowledge quickly into full fruition in the primitive regions, listen ye not. They know not of what they prate. All that science does know is the theories that might work, because, based on a century of investigation, they do work back home. But to transfer these theories into usable technologies elsewhere requires *local* adaptation.

Research, unfortunately, is the most undramatic of projects. It takes a long time. It is carried on out of sight. It is expensive.

The outsiders do not understand it. They consider the research worker to be a theorist removed from the practicalities of the world as he mumbles on in terms of years and seems so indifferent to the rioting around the corner.

And they are right. Research will not solve the problems of the present. All that can be hoped for in most cases is that the problems of the next generation will be alleviated – if the research does, in fact, succeed in finding the hoped-for solutions, and this is not at all certain.

Yet the value of technological progress resulting from research is apparent for all to see.

To produce twenty bushels of wheat (on one acre) in 1820 in the United States, fifty to sixty man-hours of labor were required. This involved plowing with a horse pulling the plow, harrowing with a bundle of brush, sowing the seed by hand, harvesting by sickle, threshing by flail. By 1890, eight to ten man-hours were required to produce the twenty bushels (on less ground). The tools were a gangplow, a seeder, a harrower, a binder, a thresher, all drawn by horses. By 1930, three to four man-hours were needed. The tools now were a three-bottom gangplow, a tandem disk, a harrow, a twelve-foot combine, all drawn by tractor or powered by their own engines.[3] By 1962 the figure was 2.4 man-hours via combines refined with such nice features as air conditioners and transistor radios.[4]

The factor that seems to have set off this train of progress was that, beginning around 1800, there developed a nationwide interest in improving agricultural education, tools and techniques. This culminated, in 1862, in the Morrill Land Grant College Act. In relation to America's present prosperity there is probably no more important date.

The state agricultural schools that resulted from this act had vigorous research programs under way by 1875–1880. The original aim of these programs was merely to improve local farming methods. They resulted, however, in the creation of the science of modern-day agriculture.

The Hatch Experiment Station Act of 1887 formalized and inspired greater and greater agricultural research throughout all parts of the country.

The expansion, the explosion, of American agricultural production is evident for all to see. The advantage of virgin lands waiting to be tilled played its role. Yet without this scientific activity, it is possible that American farmers would merely have moved onto these lands after the Indians were gone and proceeded to produce, as in the past, their twenty bushels to the acre with their one horse, bundle of brush, seedbag, sickle and flail, and would not have been able to take advantage of the Industrial Revolution. The new lands would have been settled and farmed, but the way of life probably would have remained the same as in the days of President Monroe, a pleasant, bucolic Era of Good Feeling.

Agricultural research in Western Europe followed, largely, that in the United States and in many fields has now surpassed it. Research stations have been for seventy-five years an integral part of government and university activity on that continent also. Today the results are everywhere in sight. Parts of Western Europe, such as France, are also now worrying about their surplus agricultural production.

In contrast, cast your eye on the hungry regions. Food production has remained as constant and as low in per capita yields as a thousand years ago. Research has rarely been initiated except with respect to certain export crops in foreign colonies. "Outside the advanced industrial countries, most people are still busy at the tasks invented by neolithic men." [5]

So now the sovereign new governments want to expand their agricultural production. It is urgent that they do so. It is vital they do so if they are to remain viable nations.

One can only be dismayed at the long road ahead. In most of these nations there is not even one effective experiment station in operation, or even planned on paper. Seventy-five years ago each of our states had at least one experiment station in full operation.

American and European research principles already developed can help a new nation, of course, by showing the way. They remain, however, only an aid, nothing more. The hard, tedious, trial-and-error research needed to turn these principles into applied technology can only be conducted on the spot. In some areas, because of these already proven techniques, the breakthrough in increased production may come quickly; elsewhere it may take the full seventy-five years, or maybe never at all, at all.

Is research too luxurious for the emaciated hungry nations? The complex techniques and the long years build up to a big pot of money. Can the frail frame of a primitive country support this weight?

The answer is simple. If the country does not carry out research, regardless of cost and years involved, it will always be hungry and frail.

Fortunately, the overall evidence is that research does pay for itself. The dividends of research in general are enormous, although specific projects fail and taper off into nothingness, and individual companies may get disgusted with their own research programs and curtail them.

It is estimated that for every dollar invested in agricultural research in Iowa, $300 has been returned to Iowa farmers.[6] I dare say this probably is considerably underestimated. Data now being verified indicate that the United States receives *yearly* 100 per cent return on all money spent on agricultural research since 1930. Is there a better investment anywhere?

Yet the research is not enough. The results of the research must be made known and utilized. In agriculture this usually takes the form of extension work. The extension corps (of whom the county agents are the best known, although they are only a small percentage of the total number of personnel involved) has the job of persuading the farmers to give up their present habits of cultivation and turn to the new. And farmers, like everyone else, cannot afford to try out the new until convinced it will pay a higher profit than the present.

What makes agricultural research different from other forms of research?

As in other facets of agriculture, research is harder, longer, more vulnerable and more gosh-awful ornery than the parallel processes in industry.

The techniques of trial and error, drudgery of detail and lucky intuitions of trained minds are the same. The extra factor, however, is the inordinate number of years involved in even the simplest research. This is because there is no way to speed up the growth of plants and animals. In the industrial research laboratory it is often possible to jazz things up with various catalysts. Out in the open air, however, one has to wait for the ever variable seasons to come full, leisurely cycle. And it takes just so long, and nothing shorter, for the calf to get born and the corn stalk to mature. At least, we can be thankful that farm animals do not have the two-and-a-half-year gestation period of elephants.

In the well-equipped laboratories and experimental plots in the United States, staffed with trained scientists and with precise records going back many years, it is considered that twenty years elapse between the time a plant scientist finds in a farmer's field a single bigger ear of corn, a stronger stock of wheat, or a redder tomato and is able to return to that farmer the resulting seed, which can be used to grow without chance of failure an entire field of the bigger-eared corn or the stiffer-stocked wheat or the redder tomatoes.

These twenty years are used in testing and retesting the plant, crossing it back with standard varieties to maintain all the good qualities of the old and to introduce, in a dependable way, the new characteristic and to make certain the new combination can withstand the vagaries of climate, of insects, and of fungi.

There are few shortcuts in agricultural research.

For one thing, it cannot be handled by the average college graduate, but requires scientists trained in the philosophies and techniques of research. Such training is acquired through graduate study and apprenticeship. Agricultural research is not for the novice.

It is a distressingly complex field for the undeveloped nation to enter.

Tanganyika, for instance, may decide to establish a research program to develop the knowledge needed to increase livestock production. What does all this involve? It does not mean, you may as well know right away, simply hiring from abroad a couple of research men trained in livestock production and telling them to go to work. It involves much, much more.

First, you send taxonomists throughout the country to look for promising high-yielding, disease-resistant grasses and legumes that may already exist in the area. Agronomists must then test the potential of these plants. These or other agronomists must have the knowledge that will enable them to import from other parts of the world grasses and legumes which, because of similar climate and other factors, might conceivably flourish in Tanganyika. Plant pathologists must investigate the resistance of both the imported and the domestic grasses and legumes to the diseases known to be prevalent in Tanganyika. Entomologists must make similar tests as to the susceptibility to local insects. Soil scientists must determine which soils are most useful for increased production of livestock feed and the fertilizers to be used. Plant breeders and geneticists must select plants suitable for those soils. Then come the problems of crop rotation, use of green manure, time of year for planting, when to harvest, feed value, etc., etc., etc. All this I have labeled "first."

Second, but simultaneously, it must be decided what breeds of livestock are to be used. Can the local variety be improved without importing breeds of unknown adaptability? Will the temperatures of Tanganyika permit the fast-growing Hereford type from the United States, or must the slower-growing Brahma type be used? Perhaps the Santa Gertrudis? How susceptible are both the native breeds and the imported ones to the local internal parasites, ticks and flies? What feeds must they have in the rainy season? In the dry?

Third, how do you market the final product? Will it be suitable only for the local market? Should the extra effort be made to raise livestock that can compete in the international market? How and where should storage facilities be developed? Should these facilities be designed to compensate for poor transportation systems or to compensate for seasonal gluts on the market? What type of farmers' organization should be developed to transport and market the product – cooperatives, private companies, government agencies?

Fourth, after the researchers have found their improvements it is then necessary to get that information into the heads of the individual farmers. It is a long process, and a time-consuming one, to get farmers anywhere, be it in Iowa or in Tanganyika, to change their old methods for the uncertainties of the new. They must be *convinced* it is to their advantage to make the change. Telling them is not enough. They must see the results of this research demonstrated before their eyes in their own valley.

Are you, Tanganyikans, appalled at the tortuous road ahead of you? Worse, remember that beef cattle and dairy cattle require two quite different research programs. Worse yet, what is found to work well in one part of the nation probably must be entirely adapted by further research for another province.

The flesh recoils at the years of effort ahead, yet the mind knows there is no alternative. So get started.

Although all of the foregoing must be done, you are lucky because others in Europe and the United States now know that all of this is necessary and have already developed the techniques for accomplishing it. Others have tried to take shortcuts and ended in failure.

When you understand that the research project will take twenty or forty years to accomplish, you are better off than if you had planned to rush ahead on a useless five-year plan. For therein was concealed the major reason for the failure of so many of those quick agricultural plans started so carelessly with pompous fanfare.

Research requires years. It also requires stability.

Political steadiness is the best kind, but there are others that can act as a substitute. This is fortunate, because up-and-down politics seem to be a part of the scenery in most new and not-so-new undeveloped nations. There is economic stability such as France has had throughout a century of political brouhaha. There is financial stability like Portugal's. There is social stability as in Costa Rica.

Once a research project, any research project, is begun, it must be isolated from outside upheavals. To cease for even a year – or at least this is so in agricultural research – is in all likelihood to lose all the ground gained.

Research stability is achieved by steady financial income and by a steady administrative director who will fight to maintain work on a specific project once it is under way, who will not be drawn into pleasant side paths of "pure" research or of some new fashionable project of the moment, and, most important, who will not waver before public opinion and head-of-state "advice" to change goals and shift the projects onto some new political tangent.

Stability is so important in agricultural research because if the vital breeding stocks and their records are lost, it is as if the project had been dumped down the drain. Plants and animals must have constant care.

This lack of constant care can occur so easily, for instance, where there is a change of government and the budget of the research institution is curtailed. In a revolution the national treasury may become bankrupt. In the politics of the moment it is easy to cut off the research money in favor of some pressing political expedient, or to replace the director with a political party man who has to be paid off with a sinecure.

In 1959 the President of Guatemala appointed as Minister of Agriculture the publisher of a leading newspaper which constantly and viciously attacked the American aid work. The appointment was made, as the President later stated, to honor a political commitment. The new minister continued the attacks in his newspaper and otherwise made difficulties for the U.S. aid personnel. Therefore, the American authorities decided to terminate their $800,000 a year support of various agricultural programs. One was a promising corn research program that had been in operation for thirteen years, begun at an experiment station set up by Iowa State University and then continued by the aid organization in cooperation with the Guatemalan Government. Now this and all other research efforts receiving financial and personnel support from the American Government were abandoned.

A few months later the minister was gone (due to Guatemalan politics, not the aid fracas). American support of agriculture was resumed.

"Resume" is not the right word. Some former projects were reactivated. Generally, an entirely new set of projects was initiated as new technicians with new specialties and new ideas came in.

The corn research program was a very dead casualty. Even the lapse of a few months was enough to lose the continuity of the breeding stocks and records. The hope of expanding Guatemala's principal food crop by research was destroyed as thoroughly as if Genghis Khan had ridden past. If the program had been maintained there would by now have been twenty years of steady work. It is possible a significant breakthrough in the increase in production of this food crop could have resulted.

It is true the Guatemalan Government has been carrying on a research program of its own in this field. However, it is conducted at the level of about $8000 a year, which is far too meager to produce significant results; the former program, operated and financed jointly by Americans and Guatemalans, had involved more than $100,000 a year.

One can only mourn the President who appointed, merely to fulfill a political commitment, a Minister of Agriculture known to be antagonistic to the aid projects which were the bulwark of that department's work, and also mourn the American authorities who canceled out their program largely out of irritation and pique, when even a slight acquaintance with Guatemalan politics would have indicated the new minister would not remain long in office (he was in office less than a year).

Anyway, the corn research was away with the wind – and also the early prospect of more corn in Guatemalan stomachs.

In 1954 I was offered a job that attracted me very much, to head the research program at a new tropical agricultural station being set up by Point Four (the original AID organization) at Pichilingue, Ecuador. The head of the agricultural aid group for Ecuador was Norman Ward, a dynamic and imaginative executive. The prospect of working with him and bringing to fruition the well-laid plans being drawn up for the station was tempting, but my then job had not reached the point where I could leave it, and so I had to turn down the offer.

The Pichilingue station grew until at one time it had a technical staff of twenty Americans and Ecuadorians. It became the most promising tropical station in the Americas, with more than two thousand acres and large experimental plots of cacao, coffee and other crops.

It was always hard to get the necessary appropriations each year from the limited American funds, but the station survived and the work progressed.

In 1964 I visited Pichilingue for the first time. It was a discouraging experience. The buildings were in disrepair, the jungle was nibbling at the edge of the plots and financial starvation was everywhere in evidence.

When the Kennedy administration and the new Alliance for Progress were inaugurated, there also came into force new ideas, new theories, the new broom. One order was to cancel out American support for the Servicios. These had been organized in the late '40's as cooperative efforts between the aid program and the individual Latin American governments in the fields of public health, education, agriculture, and so on. American financial support amounted to a half or a third or two-thirds of the total, and American and local personnel worked jointly together; the major specific requirement was that an American aid technician had to be in charge. Generally speaking, most aid work in Latin America was carried on within the framework of these cooperative Servicios. Now, suddenly, Washington stopped all this. Pichilingue, to use only one example, was cast adrift to float or sink according to the ability of the Ecuadorians to support it. Although they are making strong efforts to keep it going, the finances are just not available. Hence, the steady deterioration.

Chief catastrophe was that the American personnel were withdrawn so precipitately that the planting diagrams for the research plots were lost or taken away, thus destroying the value of many of the records.

The irony, of course, is that this happened at the very time when the American Government was allocating unprecedented funds for the Alliance for Progress. By comparison with the old days unlimited funds were now available, but the new officials in Washington, competent professionals in their own fields but amateurs in foreign aid development, were themselves the destructive force.

For me personally the visit to Pichilingue was saddening. Having nearly gone there ten years earlier, I could only wander about this formerly fine institution and imagine the dedicated effort and long hours and hard work that American and Ecuadorian personnel had exerted here, and contemplate my feelings of frustration if this had been my own years of work that had been swept away to no purpose.

In some types of industrial research it is possible to "set aside" the work and come back to it a couple of years later. This cannot be done when plants and animals are involved.

"It is much easier for a poor country to acquire a steel mill than a modern agriculture."[7]

Up to now this has been a doleful, woeful account of everything that makes research difficult.

It is time to let in a few rays of sunshine.

The bottleneck of any research program – in Europe, the United States and everywhere else – is to find qualified men to carry on the work of each specialized, subdivided field.

Fortunately, there is today a procedure available that produces quicker and more certain results than for a government to go out and try to import the right men or to send its own students to foreign universities for training. Importing men is a gamble that you have hired the right ones and in the right combination of specializations; sending nationals abroad to be trained takes too many preliminary years before the first test tube is filled, and it, too, is a gamble that you have put together the right team.

The most efficient method for getting the research under way *now* is to sign a contract to have it done by an established research institution. This is a common practice among industrial companies, and the facilities are similarly available for agricultural, fisheries, forestry and mineral research. These institutions are mostly in Europe and the United States, but there are now a few in the tropics. There is, of course, no substitute for having your own institution, staffed with dedicated nationals all with their Ph.D.'s and long professional experience. If you have all this, yours is not a hungry nation!

But if you do not have it, don't wait until you do. Your population will soon engulf and swallow up your resources. You may begin to build up your own institution, but in the meantime, go out and buy your research.

Take Yemen as a hypothetical exercise. I choose Yemen only because it is so far away and sounds exotic and I know nothing about it.

If the Yemen Government wants to obtain an improved variety of corn (and I do not even know if corn is raised there), it should sign a ten-year contract with a research institution. This will not see the job completed in any sense of the word, but it will get the research under way and, most important, insure ten years of initial stability. The full research program on this corn project should be planned, certainly, on a twenty-year basis. Nevertheless, tangible results will be achieved within ten years so the powers that be can see before their eyes what is happening and can appreciate the value of protecting and continuing this research project.

When drawing up the contract the Yemen Government should specify the goals that the research institution must meet. Often a scientist will say, "You can't predict the results of research." This is indeed true of "pure" research. However, I am here talking of *applied* research. This is research that will adapt to local conditions the basic scientific principles already discovered and developed in the United States and Europe. I have seen enough research of this nature to know that results can be predicted – provided enough money and enough qualified men are put to work on the job. This is, in fact, what happens when a commercial research institution signs a contract with an industrial firm; spurred on by a large enough fee, it guarantees to meet the goals specified.

The Yemen Government thus stipulates that one goal is to develop a corn that will produce an average of 20 per cent more corn than the variety now in use. If the institution does not give evidence of leading the way to this goal within the time specified, the contract will provide that it will not receive the full fee. The institution can be located in Oxfordshire, California or The Hague. No matter. The preliminary work may be done anywhere (and the administrative control), but on-the-ground testing will have to be performed in Yemen.

The research institution will require, probably, the deposit in a foreign, non-Yemen bank of a sum of two million dollars to be paid at intervals to cover the ten years' work. At least, it is foolish if it does not require this, considering the political uncertainties, and the budget vagaries, of most governments.

The greatest value of this advance deposit, however, accrues to the country itself. Such a deposit is the only guarantee of stability for the research project. If funds are left to the whims of annual budgets and to the convolutions of local politics, stability vanishes and so does hope for the planned results.

This procedure also allows the far-seeing leader currently in power to guarantee that his research projects will be carried on even if he is forced out. Every month the world's newspapers have their quota of headlines about overthrown governments, revolutions, and coups d'etat. Most are in the hungry nations. Each new administration seems always to rush to toss out the window everything identified with its predecessor (a procedure not unknown in Washington). A signed research contract financed with funds in a foreign bank rides safely above the upheavals of politics.

I remember reading that when the Trujillo regime was finally overthrown in the Dominican Republic, the new chief of state, Juan Bosch, found chests full of gold coins hidden here and there in the presidential palace. Too bad the sincere, dedicated Bosch did not deposit a couple of these chests in a foreign bank to cover the cost of a few research projects to increase his country's corn production. A military junta overthrew him in seven months. If the chests of gold had been given to finance such projects, then, no matter how many more Dominican juntas come and go, at least this research would have continued and, a couple of decades from now, the citizenry probably would be raising statues in honor of Bosch and the increased food production and prosperity his foresight had provided. However, Bosch is gone, no research is under way, and probably the story of the hidden chests of gold was apocryphal anyway. But you get my point.

A couple of details more about the contract with the research institution: it should specify such things as waiving visa work-permit restrictions, waiving customs duties on laboratory equipment and restrictions on its being removed from the country and waiving taxes on research operations. I mention this because it is surprising how often a government may be eager to spend $100,000 a year on such a project, but will drag its feet and suborn a contract when it comes to making essential tax and visa concessions.

There is also the touchy matter of foreign research men placed in charge of local nationals. The contract should go into detail concerning the hiring and training of local citizens as assistants to the research men. A corps of dedicated assistants is a bulwark of continuity in the work and of continuity of government support. Yet the disadvantage is that nationalistic naïveté so often raises its ugly head among the semitrained. They believe they have learned it all and ought to be getting the fine salaries and fine housing of the foreigners. They become ripe for the preachings of the nationalistic press and demogogues of which every nation has its claque.

Some men of experience in these things advise that the contract should specify that no local citizens at all be hired as assistants. Otherwise, the nationalist urge may result in their demanding to be put in charge of the project long before they are capable. If there are indeed nationals qualified for such work, that's great. Put them to work on another project somewhere else.

Yet it is vital that nationals be trained in research work, and the best way is as assistants to the foreign specialists. A corps of such trained nationals is itself a national resource. So my own advice is to work out a compromise on this touchy, emotional point, but to get it all down in black and white in the contract.

Another matter (I apologize for these details, but we are breaking new ground here as I have seen none of this published elsewhere): foreign aid officials have shown themselves to be unwilling, or unable, to give money for either short-range or long-range research projects; nevertheless, if the receiving government insists that aid money be applied to these projects it is likely the aid people will go along and provide the funds. However, thereupon they then may want to give the money to the local university to conduct the research. They call this "beefing up local institutions."

These do, indeed, need a dose of vitamins, but my advice is to go about it some other way, such as starting them off at the bottom by financing elementary research training exercises that will teach the techniques and philosophy of research.

Our goal is to increase the output of all resources. This job is too vital to the nation to be turned over to a university or other institution that does not take the work seriously or that will collapse with the next revolution or budgetary crisis.

Giving research projects to the weak merely means loading the odds against success.

Assign these *applied* research projects not to the amateurs but to the professionals, who will uncover the answers to how production can be increased. Draw up the contracts, put the required funds into a foreign bank, and turn your attention to other things while these professionals, removed from local instabilities, do what they have contracted to do.

Science up to now has concentrated on the problems of the fertile areas of the temperate zones. Consider these fields of activity that have had almost no benefit of research:

(1) How to make the soils of the hot, humid tropics produce.

(2) How to make the tropical forests pay off.

(3) How to overcome the curse of the arid lands.

(4) How to develop marine resources.

(5) How to utilize marginal mineral resources hindered by difficult transportation.

(6) How to improve the quality and lower the cost of production of tropical export crops so they can meet the competition of constantly improved synthetics and substitutes.

Before the full potential of the resources of all those hungry nations in tropical and semitropical areas can be unlocked to produce a *surplus* for their citizens, the above problems must be solved, solved by research.

My own wish is that each of the major foundations would take upon itself the task of supporting and guiding a program of concentrated research in one of these areas. They are geared to provide the stability so greatly needed.

Note that the president of the World Bank reported that of $6.8 billion dollars it has granted in development loans, only $500 million have gone into agriculture.[8]

The Soils of the Humid Tropics

The tropics are a fascination to the traveling northerner, but a curse to the man who must live in them.

The visitor sees the poverty of the people but he romanticizes with a variety of reasons why they "refuse" to work, such as lassitude from the heat, no need to labor when a man can reach for a banana, and the others you have all heard.

The visitor sees the lush greenery (during certain months) and believes the land is lushly fertile. Actually, it might be considered as virtually sterile. The soils are almost devoid of nutrients. I have seen ponds of standing water remain free of algae even after several weeks. So little nitrogen drains off the slopes that the water does not contain enough of this chemical to support algal growth. In contrast, a month-old pond in Iowa can be so thick with scum you hesitate to wade in it.

The two problems that must be overcome in the tropics before the land can be cultivated as intensively as in the temperate zones are: (a) the economic use of fertilizer; and (b) the control of weeds.

The dozens of other problems that require attention, such as disease and insect control, conservation, marketing, the need to evolve higher-yielding varieties, are secondary to these two major targets.

A difference to be understood between tropical and temperate growth is that in the tropics nearly all the plant food is stored within the living plants, not within the soil. In summary, this is because all plant wastes (branches, fruit, sap, leaves) are immediately attacked by insects, fungi and bacteria when they fall to the ground. The nearby plants and trees quickly reabsorb this waste through their shallow root systems. So when the land is cut over and formal cultivation started, there is no cover to protect the soil and no root system to reabsorb the nutrients; these are immediately washed away or leached by the heavy rains. My own worry is that future research will never find a way to use these soils for full-scale food crops except by the heavy use of fertilizers. If so, the problem must be to find a cheap, economically usable fertilizer. Fortunately, the soil texture in the tropics is usually good; this means it will respond easily to fertilizer treatment.

There are exceptions. I lived in Java for three years before the war. Here is indeed the fertile lushness expected in the romantic tropics, combined with spectacular scenery — the island is surely one of the most beautiful places in all the world. The answer is that Java is a volcanic area. The Dutch colonials built an elaborate system of irrigation works. This led to the constant refertilization of the soil by depositing the silt of the rich volcanic ash. Also, the Dutch did considerable research on tropical products. It is likely that when research now begins on tropical agriculture it will have to begin where the Dutch stopped at the outbreak of the war. Note, however, that the rest of the East Indies, except for Bali, which is also volcanic, remained thoroughly primitive and undeveloped. Even the Hollanders could not succeed. In Sumatra a costly plantation type of agriculture did grow up but only in certain items, such as rubber and teak forests. The Hollanders spent large sums of money trying to resettle villagers from overpopulated Java on the other islands, but these efforts were nullified by the typical poor tropical soil conditions. It is no accident that Indonesia today, without the firm hand of the Hollanders in control of the complex agriculture, is in economic trouble.

As I write this, I note that Khrushchev is now rushing to set up a $42,000,000,000 expansion of the chemical industry directed primarily to the expansion of fertilizer production. Also I note a new American book on the development of agriculture which says, in essence, that all it takes to end the world's hunger is more money. If only this were true!

Japan uses a hundred times more fertilizer per acre than the farmers of India. Yet can one simply tell the Indian farmer to go ahead and use more fertilizer? Unfortunately, no. In India it takes more than twice as much wheat to buy a pound of nitrogenous fertilizer as it does in Japan.[9] "In the case of rice the differences in prices are even larger. Farmers in India pay between three and four times as much for this fertilizer as farmers in Japan in terms of the price that they receive for rice, while the farmers in Thailand pay more than five times as much. Little wonder then that farmers in India and Thailand find fertilizer unprofitable." [10]

How can nitrogen fertilizer be made as profitable in these countries as it is in Japan? Construction of nitrogen manufacturing plants as in Russia is part of the answer, but research on the economical use of fertilizer is of equal importance – and this does not seem to be included in Khrushchev's crash program.

Let us shift to the subject of weed control.

Rice yields more food per unit of land than any other grain. It is the staple in large areas of the tropics.

Although weeds are the affliction of the tropics, flooded rice paddies overcome the problem. The flooding holds back the broad-leaf weeds while the rice, which is a fast-growing grass, survives.

In other tropical agriculture the farmer plants his seed alongside the weed seeds and all of them spring up together. The farmer simply does not have enough hands to beat down and control the weeds that are competing with his crop by choking it to death.

In temperate zone agriculture, in contrast, the cool spring forces the seeds to germinate slowly and allows the farmer enough time to hoe out the weeds. Also, the cold winter has reduced the fungi and insects that lie in ambush to attack all crops. The winter climate of upstate New York is indeed vicious, but the farmer, with his one crop a year out of a growing season of only four to five months, produces far more and has, by comparison, an easier time doing it than his tropical counterpart, who may raise two or three crops a year but has a truly backbreaking job getting enough food for his one family.

Today the temperate zone farmer has a variety of chemical weed killers available to him because of scientific research. They are extraordinary things to watch in action as they kill off the unwanted weeds but leave the crops unaffected. Unfortunately, they cannot economically be utilized directly in the tropics without further research.

A concentrated attack on weed control by a hungry, tropical nation ought to pay off as fast and as profitably as the fertilizer program. On a list of priorities, I would certainly place weed control ahead of research in crop diseases and insect control. All of these other problems must be tackled, but if money is limited, hit the weeds and fertilizer first. I say this despite the astronomical losses everywhere from crop and livestock pests. In the United States, "for every dollar the consumer pays for food, approximately 33 cents is tax paid to the realm of man's competitors" [11] – that is, parasites and kindred harpies that attack our food plants and animals. The typical hungry farmer in the typical hungry nation ruefully admits, "I grow one row of grain for myself and one row for the birds."

Nevertheless, the problems of weed control and lack of fertilizers are even greater. The humid tropics force a different kind of thinking and a different kind of action schedule than would make sense in the lush, the really lush, temperate zones.

The dancing, sarong-clad, reaching-for-a-banana natives of romantic movies are, oh sad moment of truth, few and far between around the equator.

The Tropical Forests

I had had my pilot's license only a couple of months when I was flying my single-engine plane at high noon in bright sunshine a couple of thousand feet above the floor of Guatemala's Montagua Valley. The motor purred beautifully, everything was great. I had a visiting United Nations official as passenger and we were in the middle of a lively conversation.

I noticed the haze ahead but did not think much about it. This was the dry season and thus there was no danger of rain squalls or dangerous cloud formations.

Then, without warning, the plane was blanketed and all landmarks were lost in the thickness. It was my first time flying blind and I remembered all the warnings about how easy it is to spin out of control in a cloud. I also remembered all the mountain ridges around me.

The smell of woodsmoke was acrid and I realized the smoke was from the forests below that the Indians were burning. And I remembered the stories of how small planes can become lost in clouds of this smoke. Even ships out of sight of land have become engulfed in it.

Throughout much of the tropical world, forest burning has

been the annual dry season custom ever since, apparently, the first Neolithic agriculture. In theory, only the space to be cultivated for the next few years is burned (after which the weeds take over and a new space is fired). Actually, not much effort is made to control the fires and they are left to burn themselves out.

As for my plane, I managed to hold it steady and to rise above the level of the nearest mountain ridges. I swung over to the next valley, which had a less dangerous smoke haze.

My rather green-faced passenger, partly in emotional relief, let loose a diatribe against the "stupid Indians, so stupid they burn their rich forests, so damn stupid they don't even know that burning is the worst possible way to treat land."

This same denunciation is heard from all visitors and also from most of the educated local people. Governments pass laws and inflict penalties in efforts to stop this annual conflagration.

The world's feeling towards forests has been dominated by the attitude of the Central Europeans. There they have created almost a religion in the painstaking care and worship of their forests. This attitude has now become prevalent in the United States, and it is about time.

Nevertheless, what is good for the temperate zone forests is not necessarily right for the tropical stands. They are two completely different organisms.

Burning these hardwood forests to make space for subsistence agriculture is, as a matter of fact, a pretty good system. The fires are not the raging holocausts that the temperate zone so often experiences. Anybody's hut in the area is usually protected. Nor is this the destructive fire used to destroy forests for the sake of charcoal. This fire kills weed seeds and insects and fungi, but small game move on ahead. The hot flames split open rocks and thus release chemical nutrients to be absorbed into the soil. The one bad feature is that serious erosion often occurs during the beginning of the rainy season before the ground cover has a chance to grow again.

Anyway, there is no other system available to these farmers for clearing their land. Besides, the fires are not really destroying anything of value, except, at times, the pine and dry xerophytic forests.

Economic planners, both local and foreign aid officials, call the tropical forests "great resources" awaiting development. As a matter of fact, their only real value is strictly as a form of conservation to protect watersheds, retain water, keep rivers from silting, and so on.

As standing timber awaiting conversion into dollars, tropical forests have little value. Like the worn-out soils of the hungry nation, like remote mineral resources, they are not a form of wealth. They are composed of a great variety of species. Many are heavier than water and will not float; many split, warp or decay rapidly if sawn into lumber; most are worthless. A square mile can contain, literally, hundreds of kinds of trees. In contrast, the temperate zone forest may have only a half dozen, or even be solid with a single species. This is why it is economical to harvest mile after mile of forests in the temperate zones. This is why, in the tropical forests, the lumber business consists of cruising across the land picking out a tree here and there, cutting it down, and then going on to the next tree, which may be hundreds of yards, perhaps more than a mile, away. This kind of selective lumbering, known in the industry as "creaming" or "high-grading," is commercially feasible for certain expensive cabinet woods such as mahogany, but it is not economically feasible for the run-of-the-mill building lumber.

Venezuela has 120,000,000 acres of forest land, yet forest products are one of its major imports.[12] In the ports of West Africa one often sees imported lumber stacked high, and yet the tropical forests are almost within sight. The usual local reason to explain such imports is that there are no sawmills or plane mills or wood finishing plants that will prepare wood in the proper sizes. Thus, the consumer, such as a house builder, prefers to import wood already prepared for use rather than take the time and pay the expense for cutting local trees. This is not, however, the true reason, which is that the lumbering of temperate zone forests is so mechanized and efficient that it is cheaper to import such products than to "high-grade" the local forest.

As of today, these tropical forests have no value except for the rare cabinet woods. Nevertheless, they do have certain unique factors that proper research surely ought to be able to turn into commercial profits.

The forests grow in poor soil, and it is doubtful they can ever be turned into areas of intensive agriculture. Therefore, full attention should be given to the task of utilizing them as forests. Note that 50 per cent of Latin America is forested. Even Asia and Africa with their vast deserts are 20 and 28 per cent forested, respectively.[13] These are the areas, I repeat, where hungry nations are located.

Tropical forest research, so far, is almost nonexistent. Nevertheless, we do know it takes tropical conifers seven to fifteen years to grow to the size attained by similar trees in northern Scandinavia in seventy to one hundred years.[14] It is also known that tropical forests lend themselves to management practices and some successful research has been done on plantation growing of teak, mahogany, cedar and eucalyptus. But the job is hardly begun. For instance, in Central America "teak is the only tree that has shown any promise as a plantation timber," but virtually none has been planted.[15]

A task for research must be to find a way in which stands of usable trees can be grown without all those hundreds of other species getting mixed in. Research can show how to control weed trees and work out the economics that will make this profitable. In the United States the seeding of forests by air has become a highly developed science. For instance, the seed is coated with an insecticide and a fungicide, plus a compound to make the mice feel sick if they eat it, plus aluminum to disguise the seeds from the birds. Can such a technique be transferred to the tropics? Nobody knows.

Another factor. The exuberant growth in tropical forests is truly formidable. Nearly all the herbaceous plants known in the temperate zones are found in a woody condition in the tropics. Milkworts are stout, woody twiners; periwinkles are represented by handsome trees exuding milk; even violets are found the size of apple trees.[16]

Something should be done with all this. But what? I wonder

if a machine could not be invented to plow through the tropical forest, cutting and chewing everything in its path at one end and at the other spewing out a form of pulp that could be converted into newsprint or compressed fiberboard. As research projects go, such a machine ought not to be beyond development, although today we do not know how to make pulp from these woods without spiking it with long-fiber pine. Anyway, the machine should pay for the cost of clearing the jungle. Once it is cleared (without burning), I am told by experienced foresters, the area can be planted or seeded with three or four species only, instead of the hundreds now there. It would be a difficult job, they say, but the end results would be highly profitable. But who will know if a tropical forest can be managed as a crop until research shows the way? Alas, no government has yet shown interest.

Jay Hardee, the forester with the most experience I know of in tramping the bush of the tropics, says:

> It is ridiculous for man to be content with the forests as they occur in nature. He has not been content with harvesting the wild animals that happened to occur on the earth; he has improved the animals and learned to manage and domesticate them. Neither has he been content to harvest fruits, berries and seeds that the Creator put on the earth. Even the grasses have been selected, improved and managed.
>
> Not many decades from now wood and wood products will be produced near population centers and transportation arteries very much as agricultural crops are today. Selected species will be planted on prepared soils, they will be fertilized, cultivated, protected from diseases and insects, and mechanically harvested much as corn is today. Considerable progress has been made in this direction in the past two or three decades in certain temperate countries. But virtually nothing has been done in the vast tropical regions of the world – the very area where there is the greatest need and probably the greatest hope for a radical production revolution through such research.[17]

Teak has long been raised in plantation operations in many parts of the tropics. Within fifteen years many such stands become marketable. Often a plantation becomes self-supporting within five years by selling the trees that must be thinned out. Yet I know of no noncolonial government that has actively backstopped such big-scale operations. Quite the contrary. The small governments of small nations are usually frightened (or greedy) of anything big, and the plantation owners often lead a hazardous political life. For instance, they have almost no protection against squatters or against the petty "pirates" who cut and steal individual trees.

The Nicaraguan Government recently published a handbook for potential investors. It lists twenty-five "possibilities for investment" in Nicaragua. Oil, natural gas, molybdenum, lead, fisheries, coffee, cotton, cattle, hotels and handicrafts, but not a word about forests. Yet 60 per cent of Nicaragua's land is covered by forests! [18]

The Arid Lands

In Australia during the war I traveled with an Australian army truck convoy from Alice Springs to Darwin, right straight up half the continent. The trip of eight hundred miles took three days. Until then only a single telegraph wire had connected these two places. However, the military had just rushed to completion this dirt track, and our convoy of some thirty truckloads of troops was the first overland reinforcement of Darwin, which the Japanese had bombed a couple of months earlier.

Alice Springs is, or was at that time, the only village of consequence in the entire interior of the continent. Darwin was the only port of consequence for a couple of thousand miles in both directions of vacant coastline. Here was true pioneer territory.

All of the interior of Australia is usually referred to as a desert. Actually, only certain sections are desert; the rest is arid.

One cannot draw the line clearly between "desert" and "arid," but in my mind there is a vast difference; it is the difference between death and life, even though the life in the arid regions is not twitching very much.

On this ride from Alice Springs to Darwin we saw considerable animal life, and always there was ground cover. I rode with the colonel in the lead car and had an exciting view of kangaroos, wallabies, emus and flocks of macaws before the trucks behind us scared them away. I felt as if I were re-experiencing the pioneer days my grandparents had told me about when they went in a covered wagon through Omaha, then with only two hundred inhabitants, on out into the wilds of Nebraska to settle.

In those days Nebraska was also called a desert. Look up the old grade-school geography books published before 1880, and even later, and you will note that everything between the Missouri River and California was labeled "The Great American Desert." As it turned out, only a few patches of it were true desert; the region was merely arid.

A significant line in American geography is the hundredth meridian as it runs down the center of the Dakotas, Nebraska, Kansas and Oklahoma. To the east of it there are twenty inches or more of rainfall; to the west there is less. To the east there is fertile, *normal* agriculture; to the west is dry land farming. West of the hundredth meridian the United States is arid.

All of Australia except parts of the fringe coastal areas is also arid. One-third of Latin America is arid and half of Africa. Worse, large areas not classified as arid suffer from disastrous dry seasons. And when the rains do come, they are often at the wrong time for effective agriculture.

The term "arid" has not been precisely defined by geographers, but the following summarizes my point: "Areas of meager and undependable rainfall and of sparse vegetation commonly called 'arid' account for roughly one-third of the land surface of the globe.[19]

That's a lot of land. Something ought to be done about it. Research holds out the only hope to the hungry nations for developing profitable enterprises in their arid regions.

So far, except in Israel and Australia, this research has hardly begun. Here and there, nevertheless, interesting projects are under way. One that may lead to worthwhile results is the research, as in Libya and Texas, of spraying shifting desert sands with a petroleum compound to bind the surface against the wind, thus allowing ground cover to be sown.[20] A similar technique has been developed by Standard Oil of New Jersey to cut down evaporation between rows of cultivated plants; it is claimed the water thus saved has increased yields substantially.

Recently Dr. Ralph Slaytor of the Australian Government's Division of Land Research and Regional Survey reported additional ways to save water. One involved spraying plants with a waxy chemical, partially closing the leaf stomates and reducing water loss by 50 per cent. However, growth was reduced by 25 per cent. But he noted that if transpiration (water loss from a plant) is reduced by half, "it is tantamount to doubling rainfall." [21]

Another project which may result in significant water conservation in pools, lakes and reservoirs involves covering them with a layer one molecule thick of an impermeable liquid that significantly reduces evaporation. Two drawbacks must be worked out, however: (1) waves can break the protective layer; and (2) only about half the surface of the water can be treated, the rest must be left open or the water will "decompose" from a disruption of plant and animal life in the water.[22]

In the United States the big money has gone into dams for irrigation, but that is not the type of arid land development I mean. About the only major impact research in America has been in the form of dry wheat farming, and this seems to be the case also in Russia.

Research into arid areas should take two forms: (1) improving cultivation methods of the food crops grown on the arid fringes, such as wheat, millet, barley, dates, and also improving the varieties used; and (2) discovering and breeding plants that show industrial possibilities. Every plant that grows naturally in the arid lands should be investigated to determine if it has some quality that, with breeding and selection, would make it suitable for a food or commercial crop. An advantage here is that arid plants can survive under conditions of extreme water stress and, therefore, can grow under a much wider range of conditions than can the plants of "normal" areas. Their usefulness thus can be extended beyond the arid region. Also needed are methods for reseeding pastures and planting new cattle forage, as well as methods for eradication of poisonous plants, which are a feature of arid flora.

Grain sorghums do well under arid conditions. They are a major food crop in India, China and parts of Africa. In the United States they form the third largest grain crop, after wheat and corn, although here sorghums are used for industrial purposes, such as adhesives and sizing for paper and fabrics, and also as an important feed for poultry, cattle, sheep and swine. American research on grain sorghums began fifty years ago. It took forty years of work to develop varieties that could be harvested by machine. Today the hybrid varieties are so fully under research control that the scientist could probably deliver on order to you whatever type of sorghum plant you want, full of starch or not, full of oil or not, full of sugar or not, and more or less in any combination of amounts of these you desire. He can also put the kernel on any size stalk you want, tall, medium or short. Or if you don't like the looks of the sorghum plant (why, I cannot imagine) he can make it look like wheat. The goal of current research is to develop grain sorghums with any proportion of protein and carbohydrate so they can be fed directly to cattle in the appropriate ration form. All this is available to the temperate zone farmer. It is time to get to work orienting the research on this versatile, easily managed plant for the other zones.

The hungry nation looking for exportable crops should search for fibers, medicinal alkaloids, essential oils and gums in the plants of their arid regions. Guayule, if the research begun on it during World War II were resurrected, might still become a profitable source for rubber; canaigre for tannin; istle for fiber.

The only organization I know that has accepted a sort of responsibility in this field of arid lands research is the United Nations Educational, Scientific and Cultural Organization (UNESCO), and surely that attenuated body is the least likely ever to achieve results in a serious, prolonged program. What is needed is the major effort of one of the major foundations, or a mass attack by some of our seven thousand full-time research men in the United States Department of Agriculture.[23]

Also needed is an awareness in each hungry nation that it must do its own research in its own arid lands. One such program is the Agricultural College of the Monterrey Institute of Technology in northern Mexico, most definitely an arid region.

Abuse and drought have spoiled the land around Monterrey for anything but goat raising, but Tec hopes to restore it for cattle. Buffel grass from Australia and Sudan grass from Africa are being tested at Tec's experimental farm, and recommended for fodder is a native bush, "herb of the wild horse," which grows six feet tall in two years under the most adverse conditions. Since water is a major problem in the area, students are investigating the minimum water requirements of important plants.[24]

Ideally, one wishes that several nations located in the same arid ecological area, such as those in North Africa or the Near East or the Andes, would combine their financial resources into one major regional research center.

Actually, there are today so few trained men in all the world in this field of arid areas that it is doubtful if all of them combined would form a large-scale research institution. Or so the experts tell me.

In the arid lands the world does indeed begin from rock bottom. However, in 1965, there will begin a worldwide International Hydrological Decade which, hopefully, will draw attention to the problems of these lands and unloose the purse strings to support the needed research.

Fisheries

Here, in contrast to the lonely arid lands, everyone is avid with interest. Everyone who has been out in a boat is an expert. Sunday supplements and magazines carry stories about the "inexhaustible" riches of the seven seas. The wildest sorts of development ideas are reported in the press. Fisheries officials are attached to aid missions. Prestige research institutions are already in operation.

The paradox is that although the experts are by now well aware of the limited possibilities of expanding the world's fisheries, the general public does not yet realize this unhappy fact. However, the wonderful thing about research is that it is never possible to forecast what the future may develop. Based on today's knowledge the future of fisheries is limited, but on tomorrow's knowledge . . .

"Although man has not yet fully exploited the marine fish resources, they are not so vast as some have been led to believe. Pending the development of totally new fishing gear and feasible marine pisciculture techniques, such as control of species composition, management of harvest, and fertilization to raise the standing crops," it is not likely the world can expect to do anything more than, at best, double its current fish production.[25]

Here, again, the hungry nations of the tropics and semi-tropics are at a disadvantage. Just because a country has ocean front property does not mean it can expect to have a profitable fishing industry. Again, it is a question of nutrients.

Fishing is good where you get nutrients, either lost through erosion, such as at the mouths of rivers, or from upwelling of water from the bottom of the ocean. Just as a crop of corn requires nitrogen, phosphorus and potassium, a crop of plankton, the basic food of fish, needs the same chemicals. Few waters have these nutrients in abundance.

One of my more exotic weekends was with a group of friends on the island of Guanaja off the Caribbean coast of Honduras. The only village was built on stilts away from the shore to escape sand flies. We went swimming with aqualungs. Never, anywhere, have I seen such wondrously clear, iridescent, crystalline water. Fish surrounded us in the thousands. For dinner we had huge lobsters. Never was there more luscious lobster. It is said that the greatest variety of marine life in the world is along this coast.

The village had had a small fish cannery, but it was long closed down. Why? What had gone wrong in this sea of fish? The local people said there were not enough fish to keep the plant operating!

A few months later I met up with the fisheries expert of an aid mission. He explained, "When you find crystal-blue water, perfect for skin diving, you know automatically that marine life is scarce. Only when the water is murky is there enough plankton to support enough marine life for commercial fishing. The cannery was closed because it had fished out these waters in a couple of seasons. You saw so much fish when you were swimming only because no one had been fishing in these waters for some time.

The local people there are Seventh-Day Adventists who do not eat seafood. So no one at all was doing any fishing. Reopen the cannery, however, and in a couple of years the waters will be empty."

The problem for research is not only to find the fish. The problem is to develop them as a regular crop. Here again nearly all marine research is organized for temperate zones. How different is the marine life of the tropical waters? This is still unknown.

Before embarking on ambitious commercial fishing and cannery development, the hungry nation should think twice. Make sure the fish will be around after a couple of seasons. Make sure a resource worthy of development is really there. If it is, find out how to protect and nurture it so it will give a *sustained* yield year in and year out.

The California and Norwegian fishermen during the last ten years have sadly learned their seas are not inexhaustible.

Along the coast of Peru today a fantastic fishing boom is under way. A Klondike gold rush fever has gripped the area. Small coves are choked with fishing boats. Streets and vacant lots in the ports are lined with hulls being rushed to completion. In the last five years Peru has suddenly become the world's greatest fishing nation.

How long will the boom last? That is left to the gods. Man himself is doing little to protect and *sustain* this resource. No one knows the habits or life cycle of the anchoveta, the fish they are all after, and the few who are trying to find out do not have, apparently, adequate facilities to answer the question within the allowable time limit. Already, the men must get up earlier and the boats go out farther in order to get their hauls.

What is needed is a tax or percentage donation from each man's catch to pay the world's best fishery scientists to come to Peru and find out the fish facts of life and to devise effective control regulations.

Or the black day may come when the thousands of fishing boats are out in full spate but the little anchovetas just aren't there at all, not anywhere at all.

Mineral Deposits

Ever since I visited a coal mine in England and crawled on hands and knees through tunnels to the final ratholes where the men were hacking away at the black stuff, I have known that no wage is high enough to pay miners. No matter what peculiar new labor gimmick their union leaders demand this week, give it to them. Without doubt, they have the most horrible jobs Satan ever devised for the human race. I visited a mercury mine in Mexico. The deposit was in the form of a ball and the mining operations had hollowed out deep within the ground a huge global cavern big enough, it seemed, to scatter skyscrapers around in. Flickers of light came through the blackness from where the men were working up and down and all over the walls. I have never seen such a symbol of the loneliness of men cut off from all things good.

Labor problems in mines are like none other. Mining laws are like none other. Government and private feverishness for ore profits is like none other. I suppose this is why so many nations, especially the weak, vulnerable ones, go haywire with nationalism, against all rules of common sense, at the first rumble of dynamite.

There is a lot of mineral around the world. Nearly all nations, including the hungry ones, have ore deposits. Whether or not they are presently marketable is another matter. Each nation is anxious, so very anxious, to get the mining started. Yet an executive of one of the big international mining companies told me recently there are only six undeveloped nations where he would today risk his money in view of the antiforeign, nationalistic climate so rampant around the world. His six were Costa Rica, Iran, Pakistan, Peru, the Philippines, and Thailand. Even a couple of these, as of this moment of writing, would seem to underline the *risk* rather heavily.

If nothing else, this should illustrate that the hungry nation which wants to get its ores developed can attract considerable attention when it becomes so unique as to establish a proper investment climate for the international risk men. The big mining companies are accustomed to gambling millions on ore veins and market prices. They are also willing to spend freely on research to determine whether an ore deposit is, or could be made to become, commercially profitable. But only if the local government is friendly to foreign investment, has sensible mining laws and sane labor legislation.

Mineral research takes two forms: exploration to find the deposits and methods to turn the ore into a commercially profitable product.

One authority states that a main drawback to the effective application of scientific research to ore exploration lies in "the infancy of the basic science itself." He points out there has not yet been a stimulus of necessity to push forward minerals research, such as has advanced other sciences.[26]

This is quite a contrast to the popular view that bearded, grubby prospectors and clean-cut geology teams of mining syndicates have already examined and reexamined every corner of the globe.

Since World War II a whole new range of instruments has been developed to aid man in the search for minerals. These can be adapted to "the use of radioactive tracers to solve problems in extraction and detection; automation and instrumentation that increases tremendously the amount of data available; computers to handle the increased amounts of data to provide accurate and fast inventory of reserves; to calculate efficient research patterns the way reserves increase as grade decreases."[27]

Yet none of this really takes the place of the field geologist out tramping the rough terrain. According to Dr. William D. Johnston, chief of the Foreign Geology Branch in the Department of the Interior, none of these "glitter-puss, glamorous" tools is a substitute for field geologists. He has told me a country can make a contract for photogeologists and geophysicists to scan its entire area and the results don't mean a thing except the nation gets a million-dollar bill. However, when the photogeologists and geophysicists work hand in hand with field geologists, the results can be spectacular. He points out that the big problem in exploring for new deposits is "to control the glitter" of the new instruments.

Thus, the obvious advice to the nation anxious to get into the mining world is to make as complete a geological survey as possible of the country, using the latest instrumentation combined with a full-scale force of trained geologists. Here again this work can be contracted for with existing institutions in the United States and Europe. The goal here is not petroleum, which has its own techniques of exploration, or gold, which always captures the public's fancy, or iron and limestone for that dreamed-about steel mill. The goal is to see if any one of the entire spectrum of minerals is present in quantity sufficient to warrant mining operations.

Between the two wars thirty-four "new" minerals became well established in commercial and technical use.[28] The headlong rush of today's technological progress is constantly creating demand for hitherto useless minerals or is suddenly making profitable hitherto marginal deposits.

It is up to the hungry nation to find out if it has the ore resources to warrant it a seat on this bandwagon. The ticket giving it the seat, however, is kindness-to-foreign-investment. If a country has the capital and the trained men to go its own nationalistic way in the development of its own mineral resources, all well and good. However, I know of no hungry nation that is in the position to do this on its own.

It *must* seek foreign help.

Mexico, despite its years of experience as a major mineral producer, is a current case to note. In 1961 it passed a law designed to force all foreign-owned mining companies to sell out to Mexicans and to prevent the issuance of new concessions to interests not predominantly Mexican. Although high Mexican mining taxes and the fall of international ore prices have played their part, this new law has had drastic adverse effects.

> [The mining industry] has suffered from government attempts to transfer control of the industry from foreigners who are able and willing to spend what it takes to find and exploit mineral deposits to Mexicans who are not. . . . When the law was passed, U.S. mining executives predicted Mexican interests would be hard put to find the $125,000,000 they estimated it would take to buy up the majority stock in the foreign companies. This is proving to be true.[29]

One stopgap measure has been the granting by the government of extra tax benefits to the Mexican mining companies and prospectors.

The "tax benefits" mean, obviously, that other Mexican taxpayers are now forced to pay from their pockets the subsidies to these firms.

Worse is the fact that Mexico has arbitrarily cut itself off from the world flow of new mining knowledge and of risk capital. The prospect for many new development projects in Mexico's ingrown, cut-off mining centers is now doubtful.

Yet the nation, despite this carefree squandering of the $125,000,000 and of, most likely, the efficiency of its mining industry as a whole, continues to be a hungry, backward, undeveloped area notwithstanding the patina of skyscrapers, tourist hotels and scattered factories. Much of the population continues undernourished and officials seek more and more free *norteamericano* food for hungry children.

So to the hungry nations, I can only advise: Make certain you get the maximum price from the foreigners for your mining concessions. Make certain the export tax on the ore is the maximum the market will permit. Make certain the labor legislation is reasonable. Then leave it to the foreigners to solve the research problems involved in mining, transporting and marketing the ore. You have enough other problems to worry about. When there is someone around to pay you money to solve your mining aspirations for you, go ahead and let them do it while you turn your attention to other things.

"Undeveloped mineral resources, unlike money in the bank, earn no interest." [30]

Export Crops

In a speech at the United Nations, Adlai E. Stevenson said, "Exports must provide the major part of the foreign exchange required by developing countries." [31] While this applies to all exports the major problems revolve around special crops. One ever increasing problem is how to improve the quality and how to lower the cost of production of tropical export crops so they can meet the competition of the constantly improved synthetic and substitute products. The sort of crops I mean include cacao, coffee, tea, sisal, rubber, peanut oil, palm oil. Not all of these are yet threatened, but it is likely the competition will be forthcoming whenever entrepreneurs decide profits can be made. In today's technological world an adequate substitute for almost any agricultural product probably could be synthesized if a big-scale research effort were made to do so.

The nations whose economies are unduly dependent on a single export crop must in self-defense carry forward research to improve its cultivation, processing and marketing and thus lower the production costs.

The story of synthetic rubber is well known. Unpublicized, however, is the successful fight of the rubber producers of Malaya, through research, to lower their costs of production to meet the competition of the synthetic product. The Malayan growers themselves financed the research by a tax on their product. In 1940 Malaya produced three to four hundred pounds of rubber per acre. Today, the average is over a thousand pounds and it is still going up.[32] Malaya now claims that no matter what the price of synthetic rubber may be in the future, it can always produce natural rubber at a price that will meet the competition.

Cacao is particularly vulnerable to its synthetic counterpart, which is already in wide use. The slightest rise in the international price of cacao butter is immediately absorbed by the expansion in the use of the synthetic product. At least one "chocolate" candy bar without any chocolate at all in it was introduced in the United States during such a price rise; it continues to be successfully marketed even though the price has fallen back to normal. American food and drug laws prevent its being labeled as chocolate, but the public does not notice or care. And few countries have stringent labeling laws. Yet the cacao-producing nations are spending virtually nothing on research to improve the marketing of their product, whether for industrial use or as a food. In the United States when you order a cup of hot chocolate, what do you get? A spoonful of instant powder tossed into a cup of hot water. If, instead, the consumer received the sort of real hot chocolate still served in Vienna, American sales might be higher. Twenty years ago in Mexico (which was the original home of the cacao plant) chocolate was prepared in the traditional Aztec fashion, twirled into a delicious froth by a wooden stick with rings. Today what do you get? Powder tossed into hot water.

From such are the needs of marketing research.

Yet even out in the fields the cacao plant is a strangely unknown item. Man still knows almost nothing about how the flower of the tree is pollinated. In Africa a large number of the cacao pods wilt at times and drop off (Cherelle wilt), but this is less of a problem in Latin America. No one knows why. No one knows how many pods a tree can, or should, carry – production figures range from two hundred pounds per acre of cacao beans in Ghana to two thousand in Tabasco, Mexico. There are reports of three thousand pounds elsewhere.[33] This is a mighty big variable. For every pound of cacao beans produced, two pounds of pod are thrown away. Yet it is known that the pods, when properly processed, can be used as cattle feed. Relatives of the cacao tree produce pharmaceutical gums, but can the cacao tree itself? No one knows. Only research can answer these questions.

I use cacao only as an illustration. The same situation prevails in other important tropical export crops – sisal, pepper, peanuts, palm kernels, copra, carabao hides, and all the rest. The little research under way is being done by the marketing companies in the United States and Europe, or, occasionally, by the universities. The University of Wisconsin has had a research team on cacao in Central America for the last four years, for instance.

The United Fruit Company has long had an elaborate research program on bananas (and other tropical agricultural products). It is now beginning to withdraw from the production end of the business. I daresay the so-called "banana republics" would be truly shocked if anyone suggested the novel idea that they should contribute money to the company's research program.

As for coffee, I do not know of a synthetic substitute for it yet. Nevertheless, it ought to be rather easy to develop one. Coffee has been reduced also to a spoonful of powder in a cup of hot water. The taste is still there, but the delightful aroma is gone. Since coffee has no food value or special fat qualities, today's technology should have little trouble putting a pseudo taste of coffee into a pile of powdered something or other (and maybe adding the aroma, too) whenever it is determined profits can be made. What will this do to the economies of a dozen coffee dependent nations is anybody's guess, but it will be sad.

All this is to emphasize how vulnerable most of the export crops of the hungry nations are – or, to say it differently, how vulnerable is the already low income of these nations.

It is universally recognized that a basic fault in the economies of many of these nations is the dependence of their export trade on a single item; note the percentages in the table on page 322.[34]

Although the goal of a sound economy is diversification, it is foolish to idle around waiting for that fine day. Until then each nation should concentrate a major part of its research effort on improving its most important product. This involves the bettering of each step of agricultural cultivation and of the processing and marketing that follow, so that when competition arises the end product can be sold more cheaply and still produce a profit.

Ideally, it also means that those countries producing the same export crop band together their research facilities to expand consumption abroad and to meet the competition of synthetic and other substitute products. The coffee countries, for instance, are already joined together in an international association, but most of its time and effort is spent in setting up quotas and rigging artificial prices; research plays only a minor role.

> Way down among Brazilians,
> Coffee beans grow by the billions,
> So they've got to find those extra cups to fill,
> They've got an awful lot of coffee in Brazil . . .[35]

"Serious food shortages and even famines will appear before 1980" unless all the world's resources are used to the maximum, says B.R. Sen, Director General of the United Nations Food and Agricultural Organization. He adds that even if birth-control

COUNTRIES DEPENDENT ON A SINGLE EXPORT COMMODITY

Country	*Crop*	*Approximate per cent of Exports 1957 – 1960*
Nigeria	Peanuts	87%
Senegal	Peanuts	85
Chad	Cotton	76
Cuba	Sugar	76
Colombia	Coffee	75
Burma	Rice	71
Guatemala	Coffee	69
El Salvador	Coffee	67
Panama	Bananas	66
Dahomey	Palm Kernels	66
Yemen	Coffee	65
Haiti	Coffee	64
Ceylon	Tea	62
Ecuador	Bananas	60
South Vietnam	Rubber	60
Somalia	Bananas	60
Ghana	Cacao	59
Pakistan	Jute	58
Brazil	Coffee	56
Sudan	Cotton	56
Costa Rica	Coffee	56
Ethiopia	Coffee	54
Uruguay	Wool	54
Algeria	Wine	53
Ivory Coast	Coffee	52

measures are adopted on a wide scale, population will still increase substantially because of the large number of children who will be forming their own families ten, twenty and thirty years from now, that already "the small gains achieved in food production in many developing countries have been wiped out by population growth." [36]

Shipping out $1,500,000,000 a year of so-called "surplus food" by the United States,[37] or trying to expand this already uncontrolled program, merely befuddles the issue. The starvers do not want just a sort of handout a day to keep them breathing. They want three square meals that will make them healthy.

To attain these square meals is a job for leadership. The leaders of each hungry nation must themselves assume their share of this responsibility. They must face squarely the tragic fact that the Hand of God has not favored their land with the resources of the rich countries. They must then proceed to generate the ingenuity that will make their arid regions bloom, their fishing nets bulge, and their national economy produce the surplus that will raise the people to comfort and into the modern world.

Always, and especially in our century, a Fifth Horseman has ridden alongside the terrible Four: War, Famine, Pestilence and Death. This Fifth scourge of mankind is Paucity of Resources. He has ridden undetected in the shadow of the other Four, cloaked in ignorance and credulity. The ignorance came from the buffeted populace of a nation blaming their miseries on exterior things, like bad government, evil enemies, illiteracy, selfish and irresponsible leaders. The credulity came, at least in our day and age, from the weekend experts on their flying weekend trips listening to natives who boast of "undeveloped" resources, swallowing whole the myth and coming away to write gullible reports and recommend faulty development projects.

Yet now humanity may be on the threshold of unhorsing these scourges. Research can loosen the cold grip of Paucity of Resources and thereby, if combined with population control, also do away with Famine. Pestilence is already in subjection. War, at the atomic brink of total destruction, may draw back and subside. Death is a matter for a man's religion to make meaningful.

The twentieth century has not been a happy time for most of the world's population. Rather, it has been ill-fated, heart-stricken and wretched for the great majority of the human race.

If the twenty-first is to achieve the Golden Age we ourselves have missed, it will be won only if today's research programs have set in motion an adequate food supply, not only for a few corners of the temperate zones blessed with good soils and rainfall, but for the farthest reaches of all continents.

Conclusion

THE TROUBLE with Guatemalans is they have too much Spanish blood; they can't have a stable government because they are too passionate – or so said Miguel Ydigoras Fuentes concerning the time the military deposed him from the presidency of the country.[1]

"I'm trying to make a first-class nation out of second-class people," is the exact statement that the President of one country made to me.

Foreign visitors, aid officials and writers toss off their criticisms. But the worst critics of conditions in the hungry nations are the local leaders and the local elite.

Nevertheless, as a matter of honest-to-God fact, when all is said and done and you get away from the frustrated leaders and the introverted intelligentsia and get down to the grass roots, you will find that the people of these nations have already done an extraordinary job of development.

Here they are, with almost no education, certainly without the right kind of education, no tools to speak of, certainly not the tools of twentieth-century technology, no money in the bank or even in a sock under the mattress. Yet they survive, or nearly all do. They have established sovereign nations and the nations keep on going, in spite of everything.

To raise corn on a steep, eroded hillside takes a lot of skill, intelligence and guts. The fact that the farmer ought not to be on that hillside, that he is there only because of the pressure of overpopulation, should not becloud one's fullest admiration for the man himself.

The human race is a fantastic organism. There are no second-class people anywhere, and that is the glory of the human race.

All this lamenting over the "underdeveloped" nations implies that the citizens are sitting on a gold mine but are too lazy or lack the imagination to get out the gold. Quite the contrary. They are *not* sitting on a gold mine. It is just an outcropping of barren rock.

The citizens have done a fine job of surviving despite the paltry resources around them. It is this lack of resources that has placed them so low, not lack of hard work or imagination or intelligence. Any group from any area of Africa, Asia or Latin America, if placed a hundred years ago on the virgin lands of Iowa, would today be living a comfortable life.

We know, in retrospect, that a major intangible strength of the Americans of the last century was their Calvinist belief that it was sinful to squander, it was righteous to save. This was an important factor in producing the savings, the capital, that have today led to the present outpouring of American riches. Other races, nevertheless, also have their intangible strengths. The pragmatic tribal traditions of Negro Africans, the humane Confucian philosophy of the Chinese at least until today's communist orgy, the idealistic brotherhood of the Buddhists, and the stern moral code of the Moslems in the rural areas of the Middle East have been such intangible strengths.

Any "underdeveloped" people who have managed to make a nation out of their exhausted soil and limited resources are fully capable of raising it to comfortable estate – when blessed with wise leadership.

So far, they have been thwarted because their leaders have too often gone off down the primrose path of unwise projects. Weak leaders have squandered the national income on easy, flashy things like hospitals, apartment house centers, smokestacks, presidential palaces, paved roads, public buildings, unneeded, inefficient armies and other devices that can be *seen*. The fact that foreign aid officials in their ignorance and in their political maneuverings have abetted this waste of the nation's circumscribed resources does not relieve the leaders of the primary fault.

All the modern technology of resource development is today

available to the leaders of these hungry nations. The pattern of aid assistance and good will from the more fortunate nations is in active operation to help these leaders.

Accordingly, it is up to the leaders to act on the basis of their native common sense in winnowing the chaff from conflicting advice and to act in the cold realization that national prosperity cannot be attained via short-term construction of easy, physical things. It is attained only via the long, difficult saving out of whatever surplus the resources can be made to produce (plus whatever the leaders can beg, borrow or steal from the aid-givers), and then plowing that saving back to make the resources produce still more surpluses.

References

CHAPTER 1

[1] Peter Arnott, AP dispatch, *Philadelphia Inquirer,* Jan. 21, 1963.

[2] Octavio Paz, "The Mexican Revolution Today," *Dissent,* Vol. IX, No. 4 (Autumn 1962), p. 324.

[3] *Newsweek,* Oct. 8, 1962, p. 31.

CHAPTER 2

[1] J. B. Condliffe, "Foreign Aid Re-examined," *SRI Journal* (Menlo Park: Stanford Research Institute), Vol. VII, No. 1 (1963), p. 194.

[2] R. G. Hainsworth, "How Many People Can the Earth Feed?" *Foreign Agriculture* (Office of Foreign Agricultural Relations, U.S. Department of Agriculture, Washington, D.C.), Vol. XVII, No. 2 (Feb. 1953), p. 24.

[3] Frank A. Pearson and Floyd A. Harper, *The World's Hunger* (Ithaca: Cornell University Press, 1945), p. 27.

[4] Hainsworth, p. 27.

[5] Pearson and Harper, p. 49.

[6] Robert L. Pendleton, "Agricultural and Forestry Potentials of the Tropics," *Agronomy Journal,* Vol. LXII (1950), p. 114.

[7] Sylvanus Griswold Morley, *The Ancient Maya* (Stanford: Stanford University Press, 1947), p. 316.

[8] Pan American Union, Statistics Section, Washington, D.C.

[9] Charles S. Simmons, Soils Scientist in U.N. Food and Agricultural Organization, in letter to William C. Paddock, Feb. 12, 1963.

[10] Morley, p. 34.

[11] Information Service, Population Reference Bureau, Washington, D.C. Untitled publication dated Sep. 1962.

[12] Walter Gonzalez, Chief, Colonization Division of the Bolivian Government, in lecture at Pan American Union, Washington, D.C., Feb. 1963.

[13] *Alliance for Progress Weekly Newsletter* (Washington, D.C.: Pan American Union), Oct. 21, 1963.

[14] V. S. Naipaul, *The Middle Passage* (London: Andre Deutsch, 1962), p. 99.

[15] Preston James, "A New Look at Latin America—How Bright the Future: An Interview with Dr. Preston James," *U.S. News and World Report,* July 8, 1963, p. 75.

[16] Editorial, *Saturday Evening Post,* May 11, 1963, p. 84.

[17] *Ibid.*

CHAPTER 3

[1] Personnel Office, Agency for International Development, Washington, D.C.

[2] Herrell DeGraff, as quoted by Robert White-Stevens, in *Improving Agriculture through Agricultural Chemicals,* paper presented at the Agricultural Research Institute of the National Academy of Sciences, Washington, D.C., Oct. 14, 1963.

[3] *Time,* April 5, 1963, p. 23.

[4] Earl Coke, *The New Agriculture,* paper presented at the Agricultural Research Institute of the National Academy of Sciences, Washington, D.C., Oct. 14, 1963.

[5] Capitol Record No. ST1183.

CHAPTER 4

[1] John S. Benz and E. N. Holmgreen, *The Helmand Valley: An Overall Review,* a report to the U.S. Agency for International Development/Afghanistan, Nov. 22, 1962.

[2] John Crosby, *New York Herald Tribune,* Sep. 25, 1963.

[3] *New York Times,* Aug. 27, 1962.

[4] Hans Morgenthau, "A Political Theory of Foreign Aid," *American Political Science Review,* June 1962, p. 301.

[5] *U.S. News and World Report,* May 27, 1963, p. 52.

[6] Editorial, "The Somalis of Kenya," *New York Times* International Edition, Dec. 28, 1963.

[7] A. K. Cairncross, "The Contribution of Foreign and Indigenous Capital to Economic Development," *Journal of Agrarian Affairs,* Vol. III, No. 2 (1961), p. 79.

[8] *Ibid,* p. 101.

[9] V. S. Naipul, *The Middle Passage* (London: Andre Deutsch, 1962), p. 99.

[10] *The New Republic,* June 15, 1963, p. 16.

[11] William S. Stokes, "Honduras: Dilemma of Development," *Current History* (Feb. 1962), p. 85.

[12] *Ibid.*

[13] Betty Smith, *A Tree Grows in Brooklyn* (Philadelphia: Blakiston Co., 1943), p. 8.

[14] D. S. Greenberg, "Population Planning: 1963 Marked by Reduction of Controversy and Shift in Government Attitude," *Science,* Vol. CXLII (1963), p. 1556.

[15] *Ibid.*

[16] *Ibid.*

[17] Robert C. Cook, "Population Growth and Economic Development," *Population Bulletin* (Feb. 1963).

[18] *Ibid.*

[19] Anonymous, "Population of India," *Science,* Vol. CXXXIII (1961), p. 1063.

[20] *U.S. News and World Report,* Jan. 6, 1964, p. 28.
[21] William C. Paddock, *Guatemala's Agriculture* (Iowa State College—Guatemala Tropical Research Center Publication, 1954), pp. 1–29.
[22] Arturo Falla Confiño in letter to William Paddock, Feb. 22, 1963.
[23] Richard N. Gardner, statement in *Congressional Record,* Senate, Oct. 10, 1963, p. 18243.
[24] Anonymous, *United Nations Demographic Yearbook* (1962), p. 479.
[25] J. Mayone Stycos, unpublished data, 1963.
[26] Sylvia Plaza and Humberto Briones, *Revista Medica de Chile,* Vol. XCI (April 1963), p. 297.
[27] *New York Times,* Oct. 8, 1963.
[28] Jorgen Bisch, *Mongolia: Unknown Land* (New York: E. P. Dutton, 1963), p. 12.
[29] John D. Rockefeller, McDougall Memorial Lecture held at the Food and Agricultural Organization, Rome, Nov. 1961.

Chapter 5

[1] *U.S. News and World Report,* Sep. 9, 1963, p. 62.
[2] H. E. Thomas, *Cultural Control of Water Development,* Role of Science and Technology in African Development, National Academy of Sciences Panel meeting, San Francisco, Nov. 1963.
[3] John Balcomb, "Incaparina: A Support from UNICEF," *Journal of Home Economics,* Vol. LIV (January 1962), p. 36.
[4] Francis E. Dart, "The Rub of Cultures," *Foreign Affairs,* Jan. 1963, p. 365.

Chapter 6

[1] *New York Times,* Dec. 4, 1961.
[2] *New York Times,* Aug. 6, 1961.
[3] Anonymous, Housing Loans, Grants and Investment Guarantees, Office of International Housing, Housing and Home Finance Agency, Dec. 1963.
[4] *New York Times,* July 28, 1963.
[5] William Vogt, Report for the Conservation Foundation, New York, 1963.
[6] *New York Times,* April 25, 1961.
[7] Committee Print, Study of International Housing, Subcommittee on Housing, Committee on Banking and Currency, First Session, 88th Congress, p. 453.
[8] Kenneth F. Weaver, "Athens: Her Golden Light Still Lights the World," *National Geographic,* July 1963, p. 129.

Chapter 7

[1] Robert C. Cook, *Human Fertility: The Modern Dilemma* (New York: William Sloane, 1951).
[2] *Newsweek,* June 5, 1961, p. 92.
[3] *New York Times,* July 7, 1963.
[4] Walter Salant, unpublished "internal memorandum," Rockefeller Foundation, 1961. (Quoted by J. George Harrar, see next reference).

[5] J. George Harrar, "Making the Most of Human Resources," *American Journal of Public Health,* Vol. LIII (1963), p. 375.

[6] Howard A. Rusk, "The Price of Economy," *New York Times,* Sep. 15, 1963.

Chapter 8

[1] Obtained by telephone from U.S. Department of Agriculture.

[2] Harry LeBovit, Food for Peace (by telephone, Jan. 13, 1964).

[3] Asher Brynes, "LBJ and the Farmers," *New Republic,* Feb. 15, 1964, p. 16.

[4] Orville L. Freeman, in speech given at the World Food Congress, cited from *Development Research Digest* (Washington, D.C.: National Planning Association), Vol. II, No. 1 (July 1963), p. 3.

[5] *Time,* March 1, 1963, p. 23.

[6] Fairfield Osborn, *The Limits of the Earth* (Boston: Little, Brown, 1953).

[7] *Washington Post,* March 3, 1963.

[8] *Food for Peace: A Semi-Annual Report, January 1–June 30, 1963,* House Document, No. 149 (Washington, D.C.: Government Printing Office, 1963), p. 4.

Chapter 9

[1] *Time,* March 1, 1963, p. 64. (Quotation of John D. Black, Director of Stanford University Counseling Service and Associate Professor of Psychology.)

[2] Walsh McDermott, in seminar held at National Academy of Sciences, Washington, D.C., April 22, 1963.

[3] *World Survey of Education* (UNESCO, 1958), Vol. II, p. 838.

[4] Frederick H. Harbison, "Human Resources in Underdeveloped Countries," *Princeton Alumni Weekly,* Vol. 61, No. 27 (May 19, 1961), p. 20.

[5] *World Survey of Education,* pp. 156, 157.

[6] George Smathers, "Lack of Education in Nicaragua Blamed for Low National Income," *Miami Herald* (dateline: Managua, Nicaragua, Dec. 14, 1961).

[7] August Steinhilber, Department of Health, Education and Welfare, Washington, D.C., information by telephone.

[8] *U.S. Foreign Assistance and Assistance from International Organizations, Obligations and Loan Authorizations* (Washington, D.C.: Statistics and Reports Division, Agency for International Development), July 1, 1945–June 30, 1962, p. 32.

[9] *New Republic,* June 15, 1963, p. 16.

[10] *Ibid.*

[11] Frederick Harbison, "Education for Development," *Scientific American,* Sep. 1963, p. 144.

[12] Thomas Balogh, "What Schools for Africa?" *New Statesman,* March 23, 1962 (reprinted in *Current,* June 1962, p. 27).

[13] Document 3, Third Inter-American Meeting of Ministers of Education, Organization of American States (Bogotá, Colombia, 1963), p. 132.

[14] *Selected Economic Data for the Less Developed Countries,* Agency for International Development, Washington, D.C., March 1962.

[15] Robert B. MacVean, in correspondence with William C. Paddock, Feb. 3, 1964.

CHAPTER 10

[1] Salvador de Madariaga, *Latin America between the Eagle and the Bear* (London: Hollis and Carter, 1962), p. 6.
[2] Henry J. Taylor, *Miami Herald*, Nov. 28, 1962.
[3] Salvador de Madariaga, *Latin America, etc.*
[4] David Nott, *Fort Lauderdale News* (dateline: Caracas, Venezuela, Jan. 31, 1962).
[5] Eric Ashby, "Winds of Change in African Higher Education," *Africa Report*, March 1962 (reprinted in *Current*, June 1962, p. 30).
[6] John Rouleau, Department of State, 1964.
[7] Gordon Munson, in letter to William C. Paddock, Jan. 14, 1964.

CHAPTER 11

[1] Alberto Arca-Parró, president of the Economic Planning and Development Commission (Lima, Peru), Milbank Memorial Fund Conference on Demography and Public Health in Latin America, New York, Sep. 18, 1963.
[2] *New York Times*, March 15, 1959.

CHAPTER 12

[1] Jawaharlal Nehru, *Speeches, March 1953–August 1957* (New Delhi, 1958), p. 11.
[2] *Encyclopaedia Britannica* (1963), Vol. XII, p. 950.
[3] *The Way to a Prosperous Country*, by the Economic Planning Agency, Japanese Government, July 15, 1963.
[4] Paul R. Fossum, *Principles of Economic Development* (Tacoma: College Press, 1952), p. 24.
[5] Fairfield Osborn, *The Limits of the Earth* (Boston: Little, Brown, 1953), p. 63.
[6] Edward C. Burks, *New York Times*, Jan. 14, 1964.
[7] John J. Johnson, Professor of History, Stanford University, speech at Conference on Business Prospects in Latin America held by the School of Advanced International Studies, Johns Hopkins University, Washington, D.C., Dec. 18-19, 1962.
[8] United Arab Republic news release, *Arab Affairs* #4 (no date), p. 3.
[9] Harrison Brown, *The Challenge of Man's Future* (New York: Viking Press, 1954), p. 246.
[10] W. S. Woytinsky and E. S. Woytinsky, *World Population and Production: Trends and Outlook* (New York: Twentieth Century Fund, 1953), p. 391.
[11] Carroll Quigley, "The Brazzaville Twelve," *Current History*, Dec. 1962, p. 352.
[12] Henry C. Wallich, *Washington Post*, Sep. 20, 1962.
[13] H. B. Sharabi, "Libya's Pattern of Growth," *Current History*, Jan. 1963, p. 41.
[14] George B. Cressey, *Soviet Potentials* (Syracuse: Syracuse University Press, 1962), p. 47.

[15] Emil Truog and Emitri T. Pronin, "A Great Myth: The Russian Granary," *Land Economics,* Vol. XXIX (1953), p. 200.

[16] *Newsweek,* Jan. 20, 1964, p. 40.

[17] "Hunger Reshapes Pakistani Policy," *New York Times,* Jan. 3, 1957.

[18] *U.S. Foreign Assistance and Assistance from International Organizations, Obligations and Loan Authorizations* (Washington, D.C.: Statistics and Reports Division, Agency for International Development) July 1, 1945–June 30, 1962, p. 32.

[19] *Time,* Oct. 13, 1961.

[20] *U.S. Foreign Assistance and Assistance etc.,*

[21] *Time,* May 25, 1962.

[22] Harrison Brown, *The Challenge of Man's Future* (New York: Viking Press, 1954).

[23] *The Rockefeller Foundation: A Condensed Record of Activities from 1913 to 1963* (New York: Rockefeller Foundation, 1963), p. 15.

[24] J. B. Condliffe, "Foreign Aid Re-examined," *SRI Journal* (Menlo Park: Stanford Research Institute, Vol. VII, No. 1 (1963), p. 9.

Chapter 13

[1] *Time,* Jan. 26, 1962.

[2] Jasper Baker, Assistant Vice President, United Fruit Company, figures received by telephone.

[3] *Time,* Jan. 26, 1962.

[4] *Ibid.*

[5] *Ibid.*

[6] *Fort Lauderdale News,* Feb. 1, 1964.

Chapter 14

[1] Robert B. Keating, "Research for Transportation Development," *Development Research Digest* (Washington: National Planning Association, Agency for International Development), July 1963, p. 112.

[2] John Chamberlain, "A History of American Business," *Fortune,* August 1961.

[3] Dr. J. A. Rigney in conversation, Washington, winter, 1963.

[4] *Time,* Aug. 31, 1962.

[5] Samuel Shapiro, "Bolivia's Faltering Revolution," *Dissent,* Vol. IX, No. 4, (Autumn 1962), p. 398.

Chapter 15

[1] *Farmers in a Changing World,* U.S. Department of Agriculture Yearbook for 1940 (Washington: Government Printing Office, 1940), pp. 870–886.

[2] *Ibid.*

[3] *Ibid.*

[4] *Ibid.,* p. 877.

[5] Ross Pearson, "Land Reform Guatemalan Style," *American Journal of Economics and Sociology,* Vol. XXII, No. 2 (April 1963), p. 227.

[6] *Rural Development Program for Guatemala 1955,* report prepared by International Development Services, Inc.

[7] *Ibid.*
[8] *Ibid.*
[9] Oscar Delgado, "Revolution, Reform, Conservatism: Three Types of Agrarian Structure," *Dissent,* Vol. IX, No. 4 (Autumn 1962), p. 356.
[10] *Ibid.*
[11] *Ibid.*
[12] Rexford Guy Tugwell, "The Farmer and the Commissar," *Nation,* July 29, 1961.
[13] Delgado, p. 356.
[14] *Ibid.*
[15] Robert J. Alexander, *Prophets of the Revolution: Profiles of Latin American Leaders* (New York: Macmillan, 1962), p. 146.
[16] *Ibid.*, p. 395.
[17] *Ibid.*, p. 394.
[18] Edmundo Flores, *Land Reform and the Alliance for Progress,* Policy Memorandum No. 27 (Princeton University: Center of International Studies, Woodrow Wilson School of Public and International Affairs), May 1963, p. 1 and 7.
[19] James Reston, *Miami Herald* (*New York Times* Service), Dec. 14, 1962.
[20] David Weber, dispatch in *Newark News,* Jan. 17, 1963.
[21] Gerry Robichaud, *Newark Star-Ledger,* Jan. 12, 1963.
[22] John J. Johnson, Professor of History, Stanford University, speech at Conference on Business Prospects in Latin America held by the School of Advanced International Studies, Johns Hopkins University, Washington, D.C., Dec. 18–19, 1962.
[23] Frank Bonilla, "Rural Reform in Brazil," *Dissent,* Vol. IX, No. 4 (Autumn 1962), p. 377.
[24] William S. Stokes, "Honduras: Dilemma of Development," *Current History,* Feb. 1962. p. 87.
[25] William J. Hart, Park Planning Specialist, International Commission on National Parks, Washington, in conversation with William C. Paddock, 1963.
[26] Inscription, attributed to Thomas Jefferson, on the wall of the Jefferson Reading Room, Library of Congress, Washington, D.C.

Chapter 16

[1] Anonymous, *Proposed Mutual Defense and Assistance Programs FY1964,* summary presentation to Congress, Agency for International Development, 1963, p. 103.
[2] Frank M. Coffin, *Some Perspectives on the Current Debates on A.I.D.* Department of State Bulletin, Sep. 30, 1963, p. 515.
[3] Rowland Evans, Jr., *New York Herald Tribune,* Nov. 29, 1962.
[4] Hans Morgenthau, "A Political Theory of Foreign Aid," *American Political Science Review,* Vol. LVI (June 1962).
[5] *New York Times* International Edition, Dec. 18, 1963.
[6] D. C. Greenberg, "Birth Control: Swedish Government Has Ambitious Program to Offer Help to Underdeveloped Nations, *Science,* Sep. 28, 1962.
[7] AID Press Release #63-215, Oct. 9, 1963.

[8] Harry Ferguson, *Philadelphia Inquirer* (UP dispatch), Jan. 22, 1962.

[9] Anonymous, Point Four, Department of State Publications 3719, Economic Cooperation Series #24, 1950.

[10] *Ibid.*

[11] Anonymous, *Freedom from Hunger Campaign News* (U.N. Food and Agriculture Organization, Rome), Vol. 4, No. 25 (Sep. 1963), p. 2.

[12] Milton Esman, *Needed: An Education and Research Basis to Support America's Expanded Commitments Overseas* (Pittsburgh: University of Pittsburgh Press, 1961), p. 3.

[13] Frank M. Coffin (reference 2 above).

[14] Based on data appearing in *Minerals Yearbook* (Washington: Bureau of Mines, Department of Interior, 1962).

[15] Foreign Assistance Act of 1963 (Public Law 88-205), U.S. Congress.

[16] *Ibid.*

[17] *Ibid.*

[18] *Newsweek,* Jan. 20, 1964, p. 40.

Chapter 17

[1] *Freedom from Hunger Campaign News* (U.N. Food and Agriculture Organization, Rome), Vol. 4, No. 25 (Sep. 1963), p. 2.

[2] *New York Times,* Dec. 24, 1963.

[3] *Farmers in a Changing World,* U.S. Department of Agriculture Yearbook for 1940 (Washington, D.C.: Government Printing Office, 1940), pp. 1184–1196.

[4] U.S. Department of Agriculture Information Office.

[5] Herbert J. Muller, *Freedom in the Ancient World* (London: Secker & Warburg, 1961), p. 4.

[6] *Annual Report* (Ames, Iowa: Iowa State College, 1954–1955).

[7] Theodore W. Schultz, *An Efficient Approach for Modernizing Traditional Agriculture,* University of Chicago, Office of Agricultural Economics Research, Paper No. 6306:1–28, 1963.

[8] *Washington Post,* Oct. 1, 1963.

[9] Theodore W. Schultz, *An Efficient Approach, etc.*

[10] *Ibid.*

[11] Robert White-Stevens, *Improving Agriculture through Agricultural Chemicals,* paper presented at the Agricultural Research Institute of the National Academy of Sciences, Washington, Oct. 14, 1963.

[12] Robert K. Winters, U.S. Forest Service, information received by telephone.

[13] W. S. Woytinsky and E. S. Woytinsky, *World Population and Production: Trends and Outlook* (New York: Twentieth Century Fund, 1953), p. 324.

[14] Lucas A. Tortorelli, Forestry Specialist, Food and Agriculture Organization, at Escuela Agricola Panamericana, Honduras, 1962.

[15] R. H. Stover, in letter to William C. Paddock, La Lima, Honduras, March 6, 1962.

[16] A. R. Wallace, *Notes of a Botanist on the Amazon Andes* (London: 1908).

[17] Jay H. Hardee, in letter to William C. Paddock, Jan. 14, 1964.

[18] J. Roman Gonzalez and Jaime Morales C., *Nicaragua: Land of Lakes and Volcanoes* (Managua, Nicaragua: Instituto de Fomento Nacional, no date). Distributed at the U.N. Conference on the Application of Science and Technology for the Benefit of the Less Developed Areas, Geneva, Switzerland, Feb. 1963.

[19] Gilbert F. White, Editor, *The Future of Arid Lands,* Publication No. 43, American Association for the Advancement of Science, Washington, D.C., 1956.

[20] *New York Herald Tribune,* Aug. 18, 1963.

[21] *New York Times,* Nov. 3, 1963.

[22] *Ibid.*

[23] Conversation with Mrs. Cilley, U.S. Department of Agriculture, Personnel Office, September, 1963.

[24] Petra Duffett, "Mexico's M.I.T.," *Saturday Review,* Aug. 17, 1963, p. 42.

[25] Herbert W. Graham and Robert L. Edwards, "The World Biomass of Marine Fishes," in *Fish in Nutrition,* edited by Eirik Heen and Rudolf Kreuzer and published by Fishing News (London: Books, Ltd.), pp. 9-22.

[26] James Boyd, "The Pulse of Exploration," in *Science and Resources: Prospects and Implications of Technological Advance* (Baltimore: Johns Hopkins Press, 1959), p. 92.

[27] John S. Adams, "Exploring for Minerals," in *Science and Resources: Prospects and Implications of Technological Advance* (Baltimore: Johns Hopkins Press, 1959), p. 85.

[28] C. K. Leith, J. W. Furness and Cleona Lewis, *World Minerals and World Peace* (Washington, D.C.: The Brookings Institution, 1943).

[29] Bert Quint, *New York Herald Tribune* (dispatch datelined Mexico City, Aug. 18, 1963).

[30] W. D. Johnston, *The Role of National Geological Surveys in Mineral Resources Development,* United Nations Conference on the Application of Science and Technology for the Benefit of the Less-Developed Areas, Geneva, 1962.

[31] Adlai E. Stevenson, *An Emerging Consensus on Economic and Social Development,* State Department Bulletin 44: 265-272, 1963.

[32] Karl J. Pelzer, "Land Utilization in the Humid Tropics: Agriculture," Proceedings of the Ninth Pacific Science Association, Vol. XX (1958), p. 135.

[33] Ernest Imle, Director of Cacao Research Institute, Washington, D.C., in conversation, August, 1963.

[34] *Selected Economic Data for the Less Developed Countries,* Agency for International Development (Washington, D.C.), March 1962.

[35] "The Coffee Song."

[36] B. R. Sen, *Washington Post,* June 4, 1963.

[37] *Food for Peace, A Semi-Annual Report, January 1–June 30, 1963,* House Document No. 149 (Washington, D.C.: Government Printing Office, 1963), p. 4.

Conclusion

[1] Miguel Ydigoras Fuentes, in televised interview with Mark Evans, Washington, D.C., Channel 7, July 21, 1963.

Index